NEW LATINA
NARRATIVE

NEW LATINA

NARRATIVE

The Feminine Space of Postmodern Ethnicity

ELLEN McCRACKEN

The University of Arizona Press

Tucson

The University of Arizona Press
© 1999 Ellen McCracken
First Printing
All rights reserved
⊗ This book is printed on acid-free, archival-quality paper.
Manufactured in the United States of America

04 03 02 01 00 99   6 5 4 3 2 1

I am grateful to the following for allowing me to reproduce visual
images in the book: Visages, Los Angeles, photo of Sandra Cisneros;
Random House, front cover of *Woman Hollering Creek and Other
Stories*, by Sandra Cisneros; W. W. Norton and Company, front
cover of *So Far from God*, by Ana Castillo; Museum of American
Folk Art, "Mexican Backdrop Painter, Jacinto Rojas and Son";
Margarito Mondragón, "Santa Bárbara"; Gloria Fraser Giffords,
"Santa Lucía," "Santa Librata," and "Juan Diego with the Tilma of
the Virgin of Guadalupe"; Museum of New Mexico Press, Niño
Fidencio holy card and "San Antonio de Padua by José Benito
Ortega"; and Yolanda M. López, "Portrait of the Artist: Tableau
Vivant."

Library of Congress Cataloging-in-Publication Data
McCracken, Ellen (Ellen Marie)
New Latina narrative : the feminine space of postmodern ethnicity /
Ellen McCracken.
p. cm.
Includes bibliographical references and index.
ISBN 0-8165-1940-4 (acid-free paper)
ISBN 0-8165-1941-2 (pbk. : acid-free paper)
1. American fiction—Hispanic American authors—History and
criticism.   2. Feminism and literature—United States—History—
20th century.   3. American fiction—Women authors—History and
criticism.   4. American fiction—20th century—History and
criticism.   5. Hispanic American women—Intellectual life.
6. Postmodernism (Literature)—United States.   7. Hispanic
American women in literature.   8. Ethnicity in literature.
9. Narration (Rhetoric)   I. Title.
PS153.H56M43   1999   98-25528
813'.54099287'08968—ddc21   CIP
British Library Cataloguing-in-Publication Data
A catalogue record for this book is available from the British Library.

For Giuliana and Giancarlo,
masters themselves of language and narrative,
who one day may have much to learn from the
wisdom of these Latina storytellers.

CONTENTS

ILLUSTRATIONS

ACKNOWLEDGMENTS

I wish to thank the University of California, Santa Barbara, for a sabbatical leave and generous research grants from the Academic Senate and the Interdisciplinary Humanities Center under the directorship of Simon Williams, which aided the research and writing of this book.

Colleagues and friends such as Luis Leal, Daphne Patai, Marc Zimmerman, Elliott Butler-Evans, Francisco Lomelí, Nancy Sternbach, Alejandro Morales, María Herrera-Sobek, Víctor Fuentes, Richard Hecht, Alberto Sandoval-Sánchez, Silvia Bermúdez, Carl Gutiérrez-Jones, Sonia Saldívar-Hull, Ramón Saldívar, Geneviève Fabre, Catherine Lejeune, Jerry Carlson, Leonard Wallock, Santiago Vaquera-Vásquez, Alma Rosa Alvarez, Alberto Pulido, Luis León, and Gastón Espinosa offered helpful feedback on written or oral versions of the ideas presented here. I am particularly grateful for the incisive comments and suggestions of the readers who evaluated the manuscript for the University of Arizona Press. Almeida Jacqueline Toribio was especially generous in sharing her innovative research and analysis of bilingualism with me.

Mario García supported my work in numerous ways and offered important insights about Chicano/Latino history, culture, and politics. His kindness and ceaseless generosity in sharing the tasks of everyday life and his strong commitment to social justice make him a wonderful model for the new man of the twenty-first century. His exciting intellect and willingness to undertake joint research projects with me have made the porous and often quite disturbed border between the public and private spheres a dynamic space of partnership rather than the site of isolated individual work.

My dear friend and colleague Father Virgilio Elizondo generously shared many of his profound insights about Latino religiosity during his visiting professorships at UC Santa Barbara in winter 1997 and spring 1998. The generous invitation to participate in the Holy Week rituals in San Fernando Cathedral in San Antonio in April 1998 extended to me by Father Elizondo and Professor Timothy Matovina of Loyola Marymount University with the support of the Lilly endowment had a great impact on the discussion of Latino religion I present in chapter 4.

Several writers were kind enough to share information with me about their work and lives. Judith Ortiz Cofer and Rosario Morales answered questions during their visits to Amherst and Northampton, Massachusetts. Denise Chávez and Mary Helen Ponce took time from their busy schedules to give guest lectures in my classes at the University of Massachusetts, Amherst, and the University of California, Santa Barbara. Julia Alvarez and Cristina Garcia responded quickly to written queries and requests. Mickey Fernández shared information about her life along with the unpublished manuscript of her novel. Norma Cantú gave me valuable support and advice at conferences in Paris and Santa Barbara.

Pat Mora offered enthusiasm and dialogue at the opening of the Fray Angélico Chávez History Library in Santa Fe, New Mexico, and later through e-mail and the support of our wonderful mutual friends at the Pleasant Street Franciscan Friary in Cincinnati. Helena María Viramontes discussed her writing with me during her visit to Santa Barbara in May 1990. Roberta Fernández shared drafts of her work before publication and spent many hours in Amherst and Santa Barbara talking to me about Chicano culture. I am especially grateful to Sandra Cisneros, whose enthusiasm and support for my work (even my occasional criticism of her writing) is heartening. Her long conversation with me during a visit to Santa Barbara in 1990 and her sharing of the manuscript of "Little Miracles, Kept Promises" inaugurated the exciting new direction in my research into Latino material religious culture. Finally, Graciela Limón took time during the busiest part of the academic year to talk with me extensively and provide copious information and insight into her five novels, including the manuscript of the forthcoming *The Day of the Moon*.

I am grateful to students such as Patty Chan, Jennifer Strangfeld, Adrienne Pilon, Fatima Mujcinovic, Vivian Leal, Anne Phillips, Claudia Volpe-Konieczny, Antonio García, Stephen Dalton, Pamela Mishkin, and David Vásquez for insightful dialogue about the new Latina narrativists. Jessica Gray, Magdalena Torres, and Laura Weingarten provided valuable research assistance. Adán Griego's stellar command of Latin American and U.S. Latino bibliography is matched only by his friendship, humor, and generosity in sharing this knowledge.

My sincerest thanks to Joanne O'Hare, Christine Szuter, Julianne Blackwell, and the Editorial Board of the University of Arizona Press for their interest in the book and their strong support of it. I am grateful to Alexis Mills Noebels for her painstaking and thorough copyediting of the manuscript. The intelligent, demanding questions she posed have resulted in a much more readable book.

For their enthusiastic and timely assistance in giving or obtaining permission to reprint the photographs that are so integral to the book, I thank

Yolanda López, Margarito Mondragón, Gloria Fraser Giffords, Chris Muir of Visages, Laura Hanifen of Random House, Janey Fire of the Museum of American Folk Art, and Mary Wachs of the Museum of New Mexico Press. Doug Farrell of Photographic Services, UC Santa Barbara, produced many of the photographs that appear here.

Above all, I am grateful to my family for their loyalty and love and keeping me in touch with the real world during the long process of writing this book. They have all left their mark on the ideas presented here— from Giuliana and Carlo's welcome respites of daily cello and violin music to Sharon's comments on the Latina fiction she voraciously reads. And I will always be grateful to little Will McCracken, whose five short days in the world with us taught me a most important lesson about what is valuable in life and what is not.

NEW LATINA
NARRATIVE

Narrative and Social Change in the
Age of Multiculturalism

Some 120 years after the U.S. conquest and annexation of the north-
ern half of Mexico, the Chicano movement dramatically brought
to national attention the civil rights struggles of Mexican Americans underway in various forms since the early twentieth century. Emerging
from the sociopolitical space of the 1960s and 1970s in which blacks, students,
and antiwar groups agitated militantly for social change, Chicanos sought the
political rights and cultural recognition that eluded them under the traditional model of the U.S. "melting pot." Puerto Ricans—both on the island and
mainland—similarly engaged in militant struggle after the U.S. takeover of the
island in 1898, and a younger generation of Cuban Americans and other U.S.
Latinos also emerged from the period of the 1960s and 1970s as minorities
who refused the symbolic meltdown with other immigrants in the metaphorical pot. Indeed, the media and political commentators heralded the 1980s as
the "decade of the Hispanic," a moment of history in which this rapidly growing minority group would receive its long overdue rights and recognition.

Narrative played a central role in this social change from the start, for
indeed, such sociopolitical realignments are impossible without critical re-
deployments of narrative. A partial list of these narrative practices would
include the recuperation of oral traditions, popular religious rituals, fiestas,
and *canciones*; the utopian recovery of lost homelands in political narratives,
such as the reconquest of Aztlán, the mythical homeland of the Aztecs, which
Chicanos have superimposed on the American Southwest; political demonstrations and marches that deployed populist discourse and masses of human
bodies to construct narratives about social issues; public mural art in subway
stations and on the walls of freeway overpasses; the performances of Latino
theater groups in the alternative spaces of agricultural fields and urban streets
as well as in such mainstream venues as the Mark Taper Forum, Broadway,
and international stages; and the burgeoning of documentary and feature
films. Several forms of print narrative were equally central: alternative news-

papers, magazines, and journals; position papers and documents; the scholarly elaboration of each Latino group's history in the United States; and the immense flowering of Chicano/Latino literature. Throughout the 1960s and 1970s, alternative presses, magazines, and newspapers published hundreds of short stories, novels, narrative poems and plays by young Latinos. While some of these narrativists were women, the majority of the published fiction writers of this period were men.

This book focuses on the subsequent flowering in the 1980s and 1990s of Latina women's narrative, and its movement, after an initial marginalization, to the status of desirable and profitable postmodern ethnic commodity. It was to be expected that several dozen Latina women would recuperate narrative outside the private sphere, entering the public space of published fiction in the decades following the militant movements of the 1960s and 1970s.[1] While a number of Latinas had published poetry and political essays during the movement, the social and economic marginalization of these genres had led to difficulties in publication and an only minimal dissemination of this writing. The key issues of gender and sexuality around which large movements and national debates developed in the post-1960s decades required that alternate narrative focuses be taken up in the new writing by women. Despite their historical and literary importance, classic Chicano and Puerto Rican narratives such as Tomás Rivera's . . . Y no se lo tragó la tierra / . . . And the Earth Did Not Part (1971) and Pedro Juan Soto's Spiks (1973) viewed women's experiences from the outside,[2] leaving a number of political and cultural issues to be developed from the various perspectives of the new Latina narrativists. It was necessary, as Angie Chabram-Dernersesian and others have noted, to contest the preferred male subject of Chicano/Latino nationalism.

In separating Latina fiction writers as a group for the purposes of this study, I do not wish to suggest an arbitrary or stylish ghettoization or to imply that a cohesive literary movement has developed based on one form of gendered ethnicity. Indeed, as I discuss later, the commercial and ideological redeployment of some of these narrativists as postmodern ethnic commodities is a popular version of this stylish ghettoization and is fraught with contradictions. Most of the writers have not worked together, although several lend public support to each other's work. The label "Latina" to a certain extent reifies the wide cultural range of the authors included here, who are primarily of Mexican, Puerto Rican, Cuban, and Dominican descent and come from numerous locales across the United States. As I will show, the narrative concerns of this heterogeneous group extend beyond the important interfaces between gender, sexuality, and ethnicity.

It is important at the outset to reject the homogenizing view of Latinas that elides historical specificity, ethnic and racial differences, sexual preference, and varying class perspectives into a monolithic conception of the Latina narrativist. The national origin(s) of a Latina writer's parents, for example, cannot serve as an easy label for categorizing her fiction ethnically, as Ibis Gómez-Vega, a Cuban American who grew up on the U.S.-Mexican border shows in her 1991 novel, *Send My Roots Rain*. She blends elements of Cuban and Mexican culture just as Sandra Cisneros and Helena María Viramontes integrate in their texts the culture of Chicanos and other Latinos in Chicago, Texas, and Los Angeles, and as writers such as Viramontes, Demetria Martínez, and Graciela Limón include representations of Central American Latinos. The fluidity of identity and the difficulty of placing writers into discrete national categories is apparent in the description on the back cover of the 1993 novel *A Place Where the Sea Remembers*: "Sandra Benítez, who is of Puerto Rican and Midwestern descent, grew up in Mexico, El Salvador, and Missouri. . . . She lives in Minnesota." Where the mainstream press and hegemonic versions of multiculturalism conveniently group these writers beneath the label "Hispanic," distinct and complicated national elements of Latina ethnicity overcode these literary texts.

Latina narrativists are not only different from one another but are also different from mainstream cultural models. One of the striking ironies of multiculturalism is the notion of inclusion through the foregrounding of difference. As Ernesto Laclau has theorized, "the discourse of *integration* was founded on the articulation of an increasingly complex system of differences" ("Populist Rupture," 92). Writers such as Sandra Cisneros, Ana Castillo, Cristina Garcia, Julia Alvarez, Denise Chávez, and Mary Helen Ponce are valorized in the press and by publishers for their presentations of what many perceive to be the exotic Other. They are foregrounded as exotic and different from the mainstream precisely as they are being integrated into the mainstream, primarily because sameness is not as marketable in current conditions as is difference.[3] Conscious of their mainstream and non-Latino audience, these writers often include ethnographic passages in their fiction, explaining cultural practices for the benefit of various groups of "outsiders."

Indeed, a structure of reappropriation similar to that of Orientalism characterizes much of the mainstream incorporation of Latina writers. Some of the narrativists discussed here become, along with their texts, successful "minority commodities," versions of the Latino Other that mainstream publishing companies authorize, market, and even, to some degree, foment. These texts become "an accepted grid for filtering through [the minority] in Western consciousness," as Edward Said suggests is characteristic of the discourse of Orientalism (6). Although these Latina writers are ostensibly speaking for themselves, their discourse is framed, preceded by, and already shaped to a certain degree by the dominant discursive optic of multiculturalism. In some cases, the Latina writer succeeds in entering the mainstream by engaging in a modified Orientalism herself with respect to the minority culture she describes, relying on the agreed upon codes by which publishers have marketed successful minority commodities in the past. Nonetheless, as I argue in chapter 1, a discursive battle ensues between the dominant frame of multiculturalism and the many ruptural elements in the literary texts themselves that serve as disturbances in the larger text of multiculturalism. The Dominican American Julia Alvarez, for example, uses formal and thematic transgression to reveal identity to be an unstable category, undergirded by gender, ethnic, and class "trouble," to adapt Judith Butler's term. The Puerto Rican Carmen de Monteflores expands the practice of bilingualism into what some North African writers have termed "plurilingualism";[4] she combines the multiple perspectives of postmodernist narrative with the destabilizing voices of an interrupted American English, Castilian Spanish, and Puerto Rican *jíbaro* Spanish. While these linguistic codes may signify modes of self-representation for certain Latino/a readers, they are sometimes the disturbing mark of the Other for non-Latinos.

The diversity of contemporary Latina narrative is an outgrowth of the heterogeneity of the U.S. Latino population. Wide differences persist in preferred language; customs; cultural practices; economic levels; political attitudes; religious beliefs; sexual preferences; national, ethnic, and racial backgrounds; buying habits; and media consumption. Linguistic diversity, for example, includes not only the many varieties of spoken Spanish of the different regions and countries of Latin America but also the rich verbal adaptations that occur within the United States. The long history of immigration, along with the continued influx of Latin American immigrants into the United States,[5] has resulted in a wide range of linguistic practices among Latinos—from those who, after several generations here, now speak no Spanish, to those who speak no English, with numerous intermediary positions of varying bilingualism. Nonetheless, despite the claims of the Spanish-language media to advertisers,[6] many U.S. Latinos do not habitually consume mass-cultural products in Spanish—movies, television programs, newspapers, magazines, romance novels, and *fotonovelas*. Ana Celia Zentella notes that Spanish is being lost at a tremendous rate among U.S. Latinos, and that although there are seventeen million bilinguals in the United States, there are very few "ambilinguals" equally adept in both languages.[7] Even though the

Spanish-language media in the United States is prospering, and large publishing houses are now releasing Spanish-language editions of work by writers such as Sandra Cisneros, Cristina Garcia, and Mary Helen Ponce, the primary audience sought by the writers in this study is English dominant.

Although written primarily in English, many of the narratives analyzed here evidence linguistic diversity. While none of the texts is ambilingual, only one or two exhibit native English-dominant bilingual discourse patterns.[8] Instead, occasional bilingual gestures punctuate much of the writing, constituting one mode of self-presentation of ethnicity in this postmodern age that celebrates difference. As occurs in everyday speech situations, writers choose forms of address that coincide with the dominant language of the intended audience. The occasional Spanish markers that punctuate these narratives are sometimes immediately translated for those readers unfamiliar with Spanish, or, especially when they are taboo words or "crutching" words for which the English term is nonexistent or unknown, are left untranslated.

Also occurring in these narratives is a creative experimentation with what Frances Aparicio terms "tropicalized" English, "a transformation and rewriting of Anglo signifiers from the Latino cultural vantage point" (796). Ana Castillo, for example, deliberately uses the Spanish syntax of the double negative and calques of Spanish idiomatic expressions in the third-person narration of *So Far from God*. Using Aparicio's model, it might be argued that such techniques invite bilingual readers to recognize the Spanish subtexts beneath the English signifiers. Consequently, monolingual English readers are partially incompetent decoders of the text; for example, readers unfamiliar with Spanish will not understand Sandra Cisneros' linguistic humor in calques such as "Auntie Light-skin" and "Uncle Fat-face" in the story "Mericans" (*Woman*, 17). In effect, as Aparicio notes in her study of other writers, such a tropicalization of English privileges the bilingual reader but allows both non-Spanish-speaking and bilingual audiences to be reached.[9] I would add to Aparicio's argument that several of the bilingual experiments by the nonnative bilingual speakers among these writers might be productively read as innovative linguistic experiments that jar even native bilingual speakers, rather than as "ungrammatical bilingualism." Thus, when Sandra Cisneros uses unconventional code-switching such as "*la muy* powerful y miraculous literary *protectora*" (*Woman*, x), we might understand it as playful experimentation rather than a bilingual mistake. Crucial to such experimentation is the Spanish that Cisneros learned from her father, which, she notes, "links me to my other self . . . binds me to my ancestors . . . connects us to our center, to who we are and directs us to our life work" ("An Offering," M-1, M-6).

Although the narratives included in this study are diverse, they represent only part of a burgeoning area of new writing. I have focused on a selection of Chicana, Puerto Rican, Cuban American, and Dominican American narrativists who grew up in the United States. Beyond the two dozen writers I study here, another dozen are not included, and new writers and new works continue to appear each year.[10] Also beyond the scope of this study are several important narratives written in Spanish, including Erlinda González-Berry's *Paletitas de guayaba* (1991), Margarita Cota-Cárdenas' *Puppet* (1985), and the stories by Rosaura Sánchez and others in *Requisa treinta y dos* (1979). I have also not included the work of popular Latin American writers translated and widely read in the United States, such as the Mexican Laura Esquivel and the Chilean Isabel Allende, or "writers-in-exile" (Rivero, 197), or mass-marketed U.S. Latina fiction such as Soledad Santiago's *Streets of Fire* (1996).

Both large and small publishers have helped to carve out a space in the public sphere for writing by Latina women. Although I focus in the first chapter on the examples of four writers who have achieved mainstream commercial success, many Latina narrativists have been launched by Arte Público Press of Houston and the Bilingual Press of Tempe. The notion of the feminine space of postmodern ethnicity refers to the particular thematic and formal concerns of Latina writers published both by mainstream and regional presses in an age in which the code words "diversity" and "multiculturalism" both enhance and reify the lives of minorities in the United States. That is, the Latina writing published by both mainstream and regional presses embodies multiculturalism "from below," in which ethnic groups assert their presence outside of the metaphorical melting pot, and multiculturalism "from above," in which the mainstream exhibits an interest in diversity as a means of containing the ruptural elements of various social movements. The special issues addressed by the Latina writers considered here might be referred to as a "feminine space" that emerges within the social constraints of both aspects of postmodern ethnicity—hegemonic and populist multiculturalism.[11] Simultaneously, these narrative concerns constitute a liminal space on the eroded border between ethnicity and gender in which these ostensibly discrete categories are intertwined.

I argue in chapter 1, for example, that despite attempts by mainstream publishers to market Latina writers as ideal "minority commodities," these images do not succeed in containing Latina narrative; ruptural gender issues create a troubling feminine space in the texts themselves that coexists with and breaks through the idealist multiculturalist frame. Writers both employ and move beyond notions of ostensibly genderless ethnicity generated from above and below, infusing both varieties of ethnicity with contestatory gender issues.

Subsequent chapters study important elements of multiculturalism from below that narrativists textually elaborate. Writers such as Graciela Limón, Demetria Martínez, Mickey Fernández, and Nicholasa Mohr engage in the politics of signification, as I suggest in chapter 2, by decentering master texts such as the Bible and romance novels, reconfiguring received views of the Other, resignifying everyday life objects, and discursively reorganizing people and cultural symbols to revise historical memory. Writers also grapple with issues of individualism and collectivity as they engage with questions of identity; in autobiographical and semiautobiographical narratives, as I argue in chapter 3, Lucha Corpi, Judith Ortiz Cofer, Mary Helen Ponce, and Julia Alvarez develop a variety of strategies that only sometimes successfully integrate the personal and the political, linking fictions of the self to larger historical events.

Religion, another contested site for new Latina narrativists, is the focus of chapter 4. Rather than merely serving as markers of ethnic identity for consumers of multiculturalism from above, orthodox, popular, and syncretic religious images are narratively deployed as a means of reclaiming religion for social justice and a new moral vision. Lucha Corpi, Graciela Limón, and Demetria Martínez use modified confessional narratives to show the link between religion and politics. The syncretic religious practices of the Caribbean abound in the works of Julia Alvarez, Cristina Garcia, and Judith Ortiz Cofer, who embed both official and nonofficial religion in their narratives from the perspective of insiders who are at the same time outsiders. And emphasizing voice and vision, Chicanas such as Mary Helen Ponce, Denise Chávez, and Sandra Cisneros aesthetically recuperate the orthodox and non-orthodox religious practices of ordinary U.S. Latinos.

While numerous Latina narrativists deploy religious themes and imagery, some focus as well on transgressive motifs and ethnic subcultural expression as confrontational tactics directed from below to dominant sectors both within and outside their ethnic group. In chapter 5 I analyze examples of textual transgression that both explain and contest male subculture, break sexual taboos, and broach other interdicted topics. Mary Helen Ponce, for example, uses parody and the carnivalesque in a critical narrative about *pachuco* and *pachuca* subculture, its modes of disrupting mainstream culture, and the failure of these subgroups' strategies to symbolically recuperate community in the 1940s. Writers such as Alma Luz Villanueva, Ana Castillo, Nicholasa Mohr, and Cristina Garcia present female sexual transgression in both individualist and wider social terms. Pat Mora and Sandra Cisneros transgress dominant norms by relating religion to sexuality, while other Latina authors focus on lesbian sexuality and abortion. With both positive and negative portrayals of subcultural transgression, Latina writers interject elements of multiculturalism "from below" into the mainstream discourse.

Beginning with issues of identity politics, I focus in chapter 6 on the narrative harmony and dissonance that arise in various writers' treatments of questions of gender, ethnicity, politics, and the aesthetic. Writers such as Helena María Viramontes, Carmen de Monteflores, Cherríe Moraga, Julia Alvarez, Rosario Morales, and Aurora Levins Morales harmoniously integrate these questions as elements of a continuum, while others such as Sandra Cisneros, Roberta Fernández, Margarita Engle, and Himilce Novas sometimes foreground one or another of these issues in unidimensional terms.

The rich narrative production of U.S. Latinas in the 1980s and 1990s defies the limiting title "New Latina Narrative" by continually disrupting the convenient borders imposed by such a term. Although I have attempted in this study to delineate some of the principal preoccupations of Latina narrativists in the final decades of the twentieth century, my approach based on the competing tensions of multiculturalism from above and below is only one point of entry into this heterogeneous group of narratives. As Latina writers continue to create works that spill out of the critical categories that academic criticism proposes, we can expect a continued aesthetic vibrancy and cultural leadership that will achieve its well-deserved place in the American canon.

Postmodern Ethnicity as Commodity: Containment and Resistance in New Latina Narrative

I n the fall of 1989, the *Los Angeles Times* attempted to entice readers with large photos of five Asian American writers beneath the headline "Hot Properties: More Asian Americans Suddenly Are Winning Mainstream Literary Acclaim" (Iwata, 1). Highlighting seven recently published works of fiction, prestigious poetry prizes, plays performed in big-city theaters, and several new literary anthologies, the article briefly compares this so-called renaissance of Asian American culture to the mainstream interest in Jewish, black, and Native American writing.

Missing from the scenario delimited here was the parallel entrance of U.S. Latina writers into mainstream publishing. That fall, Sandra Cisneros had signed a contract with Random House and would shortly become the first Chicana writer engaging with Chicana themes to be published by a major New York press.[1] The previous summer, mainland-based Puerto Rican writer Judith Ortiz Cofer published a novel with the University of Georgia Press, highly praised in the *New York Times Book Review* and later in *Glamour* magazine. A first novel by the Dominican American Julia Alvarez, *How the García Girls Lost Their Accents*, appeared in spring 1991 and received dozens of laudatory reviews in major newspapers across the country and magazines such as *Cosmopolitan* and *Mirabella*. Cristina Garcia's *Dreaming in Cuban* was launched in early 1992 with a glowing review in the *New York Times* and became a finalist for the National Book Award. In spring 1993, Norton released Ana Castillo's *So Far From God*, Ballantine reissued Sylvia López-Medina's *Cantora* (originally published in 1992 by the University of New Mexico Press), and Simon and Schuster launched Sandra Benítez's *A Place Where the Sea Remembers*.

The trend continued with Alvarez's second novel, *In the Time of the Butterflies*, released in summer 1994, followed by Farrar, Straus and Giroux's publication of *Face of an Angel* by Denise Chávez, and Vintage's launch of Esmeralda Santiago's *When I Was Puerto Rican*. Dutton followed in spring

1995 with Helena María Viramontes' *Under the Feet of Jesus*. Anchor Books republished Mary Helen Ponce's *Hoyt Street* in English and Spanish editions in 1995[2] after having published a new edition of Alma Luz Villanueva's *The Ultraviolet Sky* in 1993. Ballantine bought the rights to Demetria Martínez's *Mother Tongue* and released an attractive hardcover edition in 1996. Meanwhile, Alvarez's *In the Time of the Butterflies* had secured a movie contract[3] and her second novel, *¡Yo!*, was published by Algonquin in early 1997. Castillo released a new volume of stories, *Loverboys*, in 1996, and Cristina Garcia published her second novel, *The Agüero Sisters*, in 1997.

This well-deserved notice marks the entrance of Latina writers into a different sector of the public sphere than was available to them in the previous decades. Despite the groundbreaking work of small presses such as Arte Público, Bilingual Press, Firebrand, and Spinsters/Aunt Lute, whose importance I do not wish to undervalue, the writing of most Latina narrativists did not receive wide critical attention in the 1970s and 1980s. Now, more and more U.S. Latina writers are receiving the national attention and exposure they deserve. This new recognition in the 1990s functions at the same time, however, as an attempt (albeit never completely successful) to secure the closure of commodification on both the literary production and the writers themselves.[4] The creation of "minority commodities" attempts to reabsorb writers and texts into mainstream ideology as desirable elements of postmodernity that can be purchased and, to some degree, possessed.

Nonetheless, as I will argue here, focusing on the work of four of these writers—Cisneros, Garcia, Alvarez, and Castillo—a system of competing discourses structures these texts and their reception, continuously working against the attempted closure of the mainstream publishing industry. Commodification is not the necessary site of a monolithic reification. Rather, the literary commodity is often a contested space wherein struggles for closure, and resistance to that closure, are frequently underway.[5] As Raymond Williams has argued, "no dominant culture ever in reality includes or exhausts all human practice, human energy, and human intention" (125). Various readers engage in different interpretive acts at successive moments of the reading process.

Rather than make reductionist arguments about the interpretive strategies of diverse groups of readers, I will focus here on the ruptural potential of certain textual strategies that these writers deploy. In contrast to Henry Louis Gates Jr., who argues that "commodified postmodern ethnicity" is like the "Benneton model: 'All the colors of the world,' none of the oppression" (186), I will show that crucial social antagonisms rupture through the commodified surface of these minority women's narratives. As Latin American cultural theorists García Canclini and Martín-Barbero have insisted, rather than romanticizing ethnic groups as either autonomous or co-opted, a middle ground is necessary in which ethnic groups can be understood as an integral part of capitalist structures while at the same time they are producing cultural truths not consumed by these structures.[6] In other words, these cultural forms enjoy "relative autonomy": they are doubly encoded and therefore neither completely controlled by nor completely autonomous from hegemonic institutions. And, as Juan Flores and George Yúdice have suggested, since "the presumed 'subcultural' tributaries feel emboldened to lay claim to the 'mainstream,'" the mainstream itself now faces redefinition (79).

Reabsorption through Difference and the Scriptural Economy

As I have noted earlier, one of the striking ironies of multiculturalism is the notion of inclusion through difference. As Ernesto Laclau has argued in his studies of the ideological containment of populist movements in the political sphere, the mainstream integrates antagonistic forces in society by establishing "an increasingly complex system of differences" ("Populist Rupture," 92). Primarily because difference is more marketable than sameness, contemporary mainstream publishers in the United States—along with critics, academics, and the press—valorize writers such as Cisneros and Garcia for their presentations of what is perceived to be the exotic Other. In this version of multiculturalism articulated from above rather than below, the language of difference, to use Laclau's terms, is substituted for that of social antagonism. In the attempt to contain ruptural popular movements by winning the struggle for ideological closure, dominant groups soothe over fundamental social contradictions beneath the celebration of diversity.

The Chilean cultural critic Nelly Richard has made a similar argument about the changing relations of the periphery to the center under postmodernity. Aiming to reappropriate the alterity of a periphery such as Latin America, the center writes a metanarrative about the crisis of centrality, foregrounding the rhetoric of difference and universalizing its own prestigious theoretical paradigms. Richard is skeptical about the ostensible new centrality of the margins, which she perceives to be the continued discursive monopoly of the First World over the periphery's right to speak.

I would argue, however, that the attempted commodification of minority texts and authors as one response of contemporary American society to the social antagonism of the preceding decades is an encoding marked by contradiction. Interactions between cultural production by minorities and other events in the everyday lives of readers, along with ruptural elements within the texts themselves, work against their smooth absorption into the discourse of multiculturalist difference and begin to reassert the discourse of social antagonism. The text's relation to its various audiences is never static, and it is impossible to predict the semiotic dynamics that may obtain at various sites of reading.

The work of de Certeau offers another optic through which to view the question of reabsorption, for indeed, mainstream appropriation of minority texts parallels his notion of the scriptural economy. Minorities and their texts function to a large degree as what de Certeau terms the smudge on the page of the written text of the canon; like Friday's footstep, they are the quotation of an ominous, unknown pre-text that constitutes a crack in Crusoe's scriptural empire. Even as they are being canonized, these texts continue to evoke "the presence of an absence" (de Certeau, 155), for the minorities they metonymically stand for have yet to achieve full equality in U.S. society. Contemporary multiculturalism might be understood as an example of heterology, the science of the different, whereby "primitive orality [is] written in the ethnological discourse" in an attempt to "*write the voice,*" to give it "a place in the text" (159). Canonization and commodification by the mainstream function as a kind of heterological system that works like ethnography in an attempt to contain differences within its system.

Importantly, however, de Certeau argues that heterological writing never entirely succeeds in its enterprise: "scriptural conquests . . . multiply products that substitute for an absent voice, without ever succeeding in capturing it, bringing it inside the frontiers of the text, in suppressing it as an alien element" (161). Reading Laclau through de Certeau's logic, we might argue that multiculturalism's attempted reconversion of social antagonisms is constantly plagued by what might be termed the return of the repressed or contained. While writers such as Cisneros, Garcia, Alvarez, and Castillo—along with their texts—are commodified and absorbed into the mainstream, the process at the same time fails to attain closure, as we shall see in the four texts studied here.

Sandra Cisneros: Feminist Rupture, Rearticulated Religion, and Politicized Postmodernism

The marketing of Sandra Cisneros exhibits some of the contradictions of the mainstream's efforts to script the voice of the Other. Advance advertising for her April 1991 *Woman Hollering Creek and Other Stories* included the July 1990 publication of the title story in the *Los Angeles Times* Sunday supplement, "Tales for a Summer Day." Sandwiched between a feature entitled "Wake Up a Tired Bedroom with Personal Style" and an ad for Suave skin lotion in the November 1990 *Glamour*, as if it were a parallel commodity, is her essay "Only Daughter," captioned by a large-print quotation from Cisneros: "Even though my father can't read English, everything I've written has been for him" (256). In the April 1991 *Mirabella*, Rachel Pulido termed Cisneros' new book "a particularly spicy brand of text mex." *Newsweek* included the book among its "Seven for Summer" (3 June 1991: 60), and *Elle* in August 1991 pictured her dressed in a folkloric costume that allows an exotic decoding of the "typically Mexican" for many non-Latino readers (fig. 1.1). In November 1991, *Elle* published an article by Cisneros on "Mexico's Day of the Dead" beneath the heading "Travel: A Chicana Finds her Roots in Ritual." In May 1992, a *New York Times Magazine* supplement, "The Sophisticated Traveler," featured a piece by Cisneros, "The *Tejano* Soul of San Antonio," which, as I will show, engages in the same strategy of double encoding that structures *Woman Hollering Creek*.

As noted earlier, one line of cultural criticism has argued that these modes of incorporating minority artists ultimately secure the closure of reification on minority texts. Elliott Butler-Evans, for example, insists that "ethnic discourses and artifacts in general are simply appropriated for the sensual gratification of bourgeois audiences." Further, he argues, ethnic artists often facilitate this process of reabsorption by attempting "to provide 'truths' about 'real' ethnic experiences through romanticized ethnographic narratives. Hence these artists play a significant role in the processes by which their own cultures are reified and commodified."[7]

Rather than decrying the incorporation of Cisneros and her work as "minority commodities," I would like to argue here that *Woman Hollering Creek* is doubly encoded as complicity and critique in what Linda Hutcheon terms postmodernism's political ambivalence (142). In Eagleton's version, "much postmodernist culture is both radical and conservative, iconoclastic and incorporated, in the same breath" (373). I will argue that the above advertising strategies work together with and against the book's transgressive elements, its re-elaboration of traditional notions of ethnicity, gender, and icons from both the religious and mass-cultural spheres. Both the hegemonic and the oppositional intersect in this text, not because Cisneros is politically ambivalent, but because in order to reach a wide audience, she is dependent on a mainstream publishing outlet bent on selling her as a minority commodity.

Hutcheon has argued that there is an underlying incompatibility be-

Figure 1.1. Portrait of Sandra Cisneros in Elle *magazine, August 1991 (photograph by Blake Little; courtesy of Visages, Los Angeles)*

tween the various feminisms and postmodernism because while the former have "distinct, unambiguous political agendas of resistance" (142), the latter is politically ambivalent; rejecting a privileged position to avoid totalization, postmodernism has failed to theorize agency. Although Hutcheon speaks of feminisms in the plural, she in effect portrays feminism monolithically, implying that all versions of feminism insist that "a real transformation of art . . . can only come with a transformation of patriarchal social practices" (168). While the political normativity she implies does not prevail in all feminisms, especially the more celebratory varieties, the central dichotomy she analyzes obtains on certain levels in *Woman Hollering Creek*.

Consider, for example, the cover art, a painting by the Chicana artist Nivia González (fig. 1.2). While serving as a positive source of identity for some Chicana readers, proud to see their art validated in this mainstream outlet, the cover is a polysemous text that simultaneously can work to confirm stereotypes of the Mexican woman as a folkloric figure for other readers who lack in-depth contact with Mexican Americans. Together with the picture of Cisneros wearing a rebozo on the back cover, it can constitute a palatable multiculturalist frame of commodified ethnicity.[8] (One reader remarked to me, for example, that Cisneros' covers assuaged her with nonthreatening images of Mexicans, in contrast to the more violent images common in the Southern California news media.) The elements of ruptural feminism in *Woman Hollering Creek*, however, move the ambivalent postmodern veneer of the covers to the critical pole; in effect, the text uses postmodernism's complicity with the dominant order to critique that very order. The text works against containment even as it is being contained.

Although the *Los Angeles Times* and *Newsweek* attempted to encode the title story "Woman Hollering Creek" as a tale for a summer day, the brutal, continued beatings of the protagonist Cleófilas by her husband destroy this veneer. So does the story's transformation of the figure of victimization, "La Llorona" (the wailing woman), into the symbol of action, "La Gritona" (the hollering woman).[9] While Cisneros shows the artificiality of the separation between mass culture and real life, she does not make this connection at the level of postmodernist celebration. The site of escape from brutal patriarchy is precisely the means of engendering that violence; Cleófilas' husband hits her with a Corín Tellado romance novel, and what hurts her more than the physical blow is that her primary pleasurable space within her oppressive marriage has been used against her. The postmodernist simulacrum is now a gender-coded nightmare: "Cleófilas thought her life would have to be like that, like a *telenovela*, only now the episodes got sadder and sadder. And there were no commercials in between for comic relief. And no happy ending in sight" (52–53). When the nurse who helps Cleófilas to escape remarks that life is "a regular soap opera sometimes" (55), it is from an empowering disaffection with this continuum between the real world and the media. Postmodernism's political ambivalence is harnessed to a feminist political stand in the story.

Figure 1.2. Cover of Sandra Cisneros' Woman Hollering Creek and Other Stories, *1991 (courtesy of Random House)*

Elsewhere in Cisneros' book, mainstream mass-cultural icons such as the Marlboro man and Barbie dolls take on a double voice as they are reconfigured within the ethnic, working-class experience of U.S. Chicanas. The two intertexts remain as unmerged voices, creating a new "C cell" in a modified version of Eisenstein's theory of montage, in which the A and B cells are linked but not fused. In the story "The Marlboro Man," the billboard and print campaign featuring this mass-cultural figure hovers as a larger-than-life intertextual icon;

it is in montage with the two interlocutors' renderings of received ideas about this figural representation of masculinity and the always already signified actor himself. In "Barbie-Q," the singed Barbie dolls that the girls buy at a fire sale continue to function in relations of intertextuality with the marketing jargon that even a fire cannot silence: "And if the prettiest doll, Barbie's MOD'ern cousin Francie with real eyelashes, eyelash brush included, has a left foot that's melted a little—so? If you dress her in her new "Prom Pinks" outfit, satin splendor with matching coat, gold belt, clutch, and hair bow included, so long as you don't lift her dress, right?—who's to know" (*Woman*, 16). The chinks in the veneer of the perfect mass-cultural commodity, clearly visible because of the intertextual structure, move the postmodernist recuperation of mass culture in the book away from the purely celebratory to the pole of the critical.

While the reconfigured mass culture of the burned Barbie dolls serves as a positive mode of asserting identity, Cisneros also highlights negative signifiers of the identity imposed by the dominant order. Reminiscent of the slum dwelling in "A Rice Sandwich" (*Mango*) through which a nun attempts to delimit Esperanza's identity as Other, the red sweater in the story "Eleven" (*Woman*) functions as a negative metonym for the contested identity of the protagonist Rachel. In both stories, teachers attempt to fix a young Chicana's identity as Other within a set of limited stereotypes. Rachel rejects the sweater discursively by terming it old, smelly, itchy, and "full of germs that aren't even mine" (8). It is not poverty per se that the two protagonists reject but rather the symbols of poverty that the dominant order (here represented by teachers) insists on reinforcing. In contrast, the "aqua flip-flops" bought for seventy-nine cents at Kmart are a positive source of identity in the opening story of *Woman Hollering Creek*. Although the sweater, the flip-flops, and the Barbie dolls are all commodities, they are reappropriated ones and contest the external efforts to contain the book as a postmodernist commodification of ethnic identity.

Cisneros works against this new, marketable version of ethnicity by foregrounding a series of unmerged polyphonic voices[10] that form a collective *testimonio* in "Little Miracles, Kept Promises." Here, as will be discussed in greater detail in subsequent chapters, ordinary Chicanos offer prayers, mementos, and "milagritos" (copper or brass ex-votos that are pinned on the clothes of statues of Christ, the Virgin, and various Catholic saints to petition for a favor or give thanks for a "miracle" received; see figure 4.16). A fictional man from San Antonio promises to walk to the Virgin of Guadalupe's shrine on his knees if she will help him to recover $253.72 in unpaid wages for sixty-seven and a half hours of work; a teenager prays to San Lázaro, who was raised from the dead, for help with his perceived impossible problem—acne;

and St. Jude, the patron of lost causes, is invoked for help in passing a course in "British Restoration Literature." As Anita Brenner has argued with respect to Mexican ex-voto paintings (the visual-verbal intertexts of Cisneros' story) (see figure 4.14), these brief *testimonios* about everyday life are an important source of history: "A collection of the ex-votos from all over the country would give the lives, the thoughts, the happenings and concerns of each place and of all its people, and would give them much more honestly than any narrative, and more accurately than the most careful statistical survey" (11).

One character in "Little Miracles" who signs herself "Ms. Barbara Ybañez" reconfigures the signifier "man" by asking a saint for a "man man. . . . someone who's not ashamed to be seen cooking, or cleaning, or looking after himself. . . . a man who acts like an adult" rather than "someone like my brothers who my mother ruined with too much chichi" (117–18).[11] Besides redefining in her prayer the received views of manhood, Ybañez assumes a strong, self-confident attitude by telling the saint: "I'll turn your statue upside down until you send him to me. I've put up with too much too long, and now I'm just too intelligent, too powerful, too beautiful, too sure of who I am finally to deserve anything else" (118).

The last segment of this collective testimonial presents a strong statement of feminist transgression that rearticulates the figure of the Virgen de Guadalupe, as occurs frequently throughout the book. In a postmodernist turning back, multiple layers of textual self-reflexivity link readers, writers, and characters; Cisneros the author is the implicit double of Chayo, the artist/protagonist who writes this last narrative and alludes to having read some of the texts others have left for the Virgin—texts that readers also have just read. Chayo's segment is a combination prayer and narrative *testimonio* that typographically matches the rest of the book's primary narrative segments, unlike the written prayers that have structured the story to this point. Thus, there is an implicit convergence between Cisneros, the author of the book, and Chayo, the protagonist and utterer of this prayer that distinguishes itself visually from the previous written notes in the story. This five-page segment simultaneously represents the unwritten and the unsaid, even as it appears on the pages of the book, for it is the detailed explanation of Chayo's offering to the Virgin, absent from the short note that she has pinned up in the church. It thereby foregrounds the narrative incompleteness of the preceding prayer-texts and, indeed, its own incompleteness as a text.

Chayo's narrative reveals that although, to her family's dismay, she has gone against traditional expectations of women, she now has embarked upon a new, respectful devotion to the Virgin of Guadalupe. As I argue further in chapters 4 and 5, Chayo now recuperates her people's historical devotion to the Virgin by offering her braid as a "milagrito" or "little miracle" at the Virgin's shrine in tribute to her own independence and the Virgin's strength.

Cisneros' 1992 travel feature on San Antonio in the *New York Times Magazine* relates intertextually to the story "Little Miracles" and to other cultural and historical motifs in *Woman Hollering Creek*. Indeed, the travel feature is another postmodern text that both employs and markets minority culture as a commodity while at the same time subverting the attempted closure of the commodity structure. Here, Sandra Cisneros as a minority commodity herself —in the magazine's semiotic configuration of idealized travel—offers recommendations that will help to establish other forms of Mexican popular culture in Texas as desirable minority commodities for tourists to consume. But as in "Little Miracles," Cisneros does not exoticize the elements of everyday culture of Mexicanos in San Antonio. Photos of the Black Christ of Esquipulas and ex-votos in San Fernando Cathedral and a neon altar at Ray's Drive Inn (*sic*), along with verbal and photographic descriptions of other Latino cultural traditions in the city, elaborate on some of the motifs in *Woman Hollering Creek*.

Cisneros employs the technique of defamiliarization to naturalize and de-exoticize Tex-Mex culture for the non-Mexican reader. Describing the tiny gold hoop earrings, and those with the image of the Virgen de Guadalupe, that are sold at Ortiz Jewelry "for when you pierce your baby's ears," she interjects: "What! You don't pierce your baby's ears? Buy them for your boyfriend" ("Tejano Soul," 38). The mainstream U.S. practice of not piercing baby girls' ears is made to appear strange. As a remedy for this cultural "shortcoming," Cisneros humorously suggests, mainstream readers can employ the minority cultural artifact in a postmodernist fashion practice with which they might be more comfortable. Similarly, after readers have tasted breakfast tacos with hot sauce at Torres Taco Haven, Cisneros advises, they will "never settle for coffee and doughnuts again" (40).

In a rhetorical strategy parallel to these understated defamiliarizations, Cisneros also de-exoticizes other cultural practices as a means of recuperating the residue of history in the everyday. Explaining her purchase of *copal* (incense) in an herb shop, Cisneros remarks: "And somehow I feel as if I am buying history each time I ask for the little bag of gold resin wrapped in wax paper. As if each time I am repeating a rite that belongs to something larger than me" (36). Readers can buy *copal*, Cisneros notes, at the often overlooked Botica Guadalajara, where the original floor tiles and fixtures from 1893 re-situate the purchaser within Mexican American history in Texas. The ostensibly exotic objects in such overlooked shops are, in fact, the constituents of long cultural traditions that Cisneros attempts to make familiar to mainstream readers rather than market as exotic commodities.

By reappropriating the sacred within postmodern texts such as "Little Miracles" and the travel feature on San Antonio, Cisneros demonstrates that culture is a site of battle for competing definitions and visions of reality. Powerful religious symbols need not necessarily be left to those who enjoy patriarchal privilege, nor do non-mainstream cultural traditions remain only exotic commodities in a travel feature in a mainstream magazine. In contrast to the representation of a Mexican woman on the front cover of *Woman Hollering Creek*, which some will decode as folkloric, the testimonial voices in "Little Miracles" and throughout the collection work against the multiculturalist celebration of difference that attempts to assuage social antagonism. Cisneros reasserts the reality of social antagonism through feminist ruptures, religious transgressions and reconfigurations, and politicized appropriations of postmodernism. Thus, even while it is incorporated, the book remains unincorporated by transforming postmodernist ambivalence into socially committed critique and rupture.

Critical Unfinalizability and Feminist Rupture in Dreaming in Cuban

Cristina Garcia's *Dreaming in Cuban*, published in February 1992 by the Knopf division of Random House, was praised in the *New York Times* as "fierce, visionary . . . completely original" and a "dazzling first novel" (Kakutani, C-17). Knopf ran an ad in the *New York Times Book Review* (5 Apr. 1992: 23) with excerpts from glowing reviews of the book in such publications as the *San Francisco Chronicle, Time*, and *Publishers Weekly*. Amelia Weiss, for example, whose review in *Time* is entitled "Fantasy Island," situates Garcia's novel as a minority commodity by praising the book's style (redeploying some of Garcia's own turns of phrase) as "warm and gentle as the 'sustaining aromas of vanilla and almond,' as rhythmic as the music of Benny Moré" (67). The common thread in several of the reviews is the implicit or explicit comparison of *Dreaming in Cuban* to the work of Gabriel García Márquez and Latin American magical realism, two of the most common reductive modes by which the U.S. cultural mainstream has appropriated Latin American fiction of recent decades as a palatable Third World commodity.[12]

Focusing on three generations of women in a Cuban family, some of whom live in the United States, *Dreaming in Cuban* highlights the diversity of the Cuban experience through an intercalation of unmerged polyphonic voices. The female characters that predominate in the novel are *"subjects of their own directly signifying discourse"* (Bakhtin, *Problems*, 7) in the form of letters, first-person narratives, third-person accounts in which the characters' voices predominate, and the oral *testimonio* that is an alternative history of a character's life. The resultant unfinalizability of the text parallels its refusal to invoke the closure of a single truth about the Cuban Revolution or the Cuban experience of exile in the United States. As Garcia told Alix Madrigal of the *San Francisco Chronicle*, Fidel Castro and her own staunchly anti-Castro mother have an element in common: "The same rigidity, the same zealotry. They just believe completely opposite things." She decries the radical split in her family between those who support Castro and those who don't: "And they didn't speak for years. It's all so black and white, and I'm gray. They are like both sides of the same coin" (4). Against the univocal positions of Castro and her mother, and the two sides of her family, Garcia emphasizes a postmodernist indeterminacy, "grayness," and multivocal presentation of reality.

Although the multiple narrative perspectives work against the monologizing control of a central narrative consciousness, the figure of Pilar floats in and out of a central location throughout the novel and becomes coterminous with the author in a moment of self-referentiality near the end of the novel.[13] Pilar's mother and grandmother offer the antithetical perspectives of the fanatical anti-Castro Cuban exile in the United States and the ardent supporter of Fidel who has remained in Cuba. The grandmother, Celia, is developed somewhat more fully because the desire that underlies the narrative structure moves the novel toward Pilar's ultimate reunion with her "lost" grandmother in Cuba against the antagonistic force of her anti-Communist mother, Lourdes.

The first-person sections of the novel are reserved for Pilar's own generation, and while they present no resolutions of the political antithesis embodied in the grandmother and mother, the characters in these sections select courses of action that are distinct from those the two women have chosen. Most importantly, in the crucial final scene, Pilar acts against the wishes of the grandmother whom she has long sought to be reunited with by refusing to stop her young cousin, Ivanito, from leaving with other Cubans who in 1980 had sought asylum in the Peruvian embassy in Cuba. It is not that she is following the wishes of her mother, who has engineered the escape, but that she has made an independent decision to allow her cousin his autonomy. Garcia suggests that the young generation of Cuban Americans is unavoidably connected to both sides of the debate about Castro, to the culture and everyday reality of the island as well as to the reality of Cuban communities in the United States.

Although the multivocity of *Dreaming in Cuban* functions as one of the novel's primary modes of resistance to easy stereotyping and assimilation as a commodity, it simultaneously facilitates a range of reading positions that, by pleasing many sides, helps to sell books. To a certain degree, the novel's un-finalizability makes it all the more marketable as a postmodern commodity, a novel in which truth is decentered and political correctness eschewed, a book in which people of diverse political persuasions can find perspectives with which they agree. Garcia gives an example of the polysemous nature of her text, noting that she was amazed that her mother and other conserva-tive relatives liked the book; in their reading, the archconservative figure of Lourdes was the hero (qtd. in Madrigal, 4). Nevertheless, as is the case with Cisneros, a number of ruptural elements work against the easy mainstream containment of this text.

In a manner parallel to Cisneros, Garcia pushes postmodernism's politi-cal ambivalence to the critical pole most importantly through the strong ruptural feminism that permeates the novel. Transcending the dilemma that Hutcheon posited, in which feminism's political stance is incompatible with postmodernism's political ambivalence, Garcia's text works against contain-ment even as it engages in strategies of narrative unfinalizability and post-modern decentering.

The strong figure of the grandmother, Celia, who has remained in Cuba is an unconventional model of feminist strength as she rededicates herself to the revolution at age sixty-three, volunteers for microbrigades to cut sugar-cane, renders astute decisions in her role as neighborhood judge, and enjoys a sense of empowerment as she guards the Cuban coast as a night sentry from her seaside house. Her political views reflect her independence from her hus-band's anti-Castro stance, and she also contests his power by small, everyday transgressions such as playing Debussy on the piano despite his having for-bidden her to do so. Celia's international perspective on gender oppression erupts on the page as she dreams of "massacres in distant countries, pregnant women dismembered in the squares," herself "walking among them mute and invisible" (218).

One of Celia's most important feminist interventions in the novel is the series of letters she writes to her lover in Spain who will never return. Inter-calated throughout the text, these letters reappropriate the conventions of romance for political and feminist ends much the way Cisneros resignifies the romantic Corín Tellado novel, Barbie dolls, and the Marlboro man. In the letters, Celia records the personal details of her life, structured by the political and historic events in Cuba. In March 1952, for example, she writes, "That bastard Batista stole the country from us just when it seemed things could finally change. The U.S. wants him in the palace. How else could he have pulled this off? I fear for my son, learning to be a man from such men" (162). Concerned about her daughter Felicia's safety in the streets of Havana in 1954, she writes, "I've heard too many stories of young girls destroyed by what passes as tourism in this country. Cuba has become the joke of the Caribbean, a place where everything and everyone is for sale. How did we allow this to happen?" (164). Garcia's reappropriation of the romantic love letter, written to the abandoning lover who will never respond, like the Mexican writer Elena Poniatowska's use of the device in her 1978 *Querido Diego te abraza Quiela* [*Dear Diego*], turns this stereotypical image of women's weakness against itself. In this redesigned epistolary narrative, the private and public spheres become inseparable, foregrounding the politics of romance, gender, and history within the form of the love letter that no longer functions simply as a pleasurable product of narrative experimentation.

Abuse, disfigurement, and violation of women's bodies appear throughout the novel—from eating disorders and the transmission of syphilis from husband to wife, to the scars inflicted by knives during sexual assaults, rapes, and mastectomies. Garcia critiques the excessive appropriation of U.S. economic and cultural models by the fanatical Cuban exiles in a series of parodical images that foreground the gender issue of the eating disorder. Lourdes, who dreams of expanding her Yankee Doodle Bakery into a nationwide chain, gains 118 pounds by eating the sticky buns she sells, and then fasts and drinks liquid food substitutes until she has lost this exact amount. She falls victim to bingeing again at the annual American celebration of gorging, Thanksgiving Day. Garcia encodes Lourdes' abuse of her body within a series of parodical signifiers of her hyper-Americanism, foregrounding the culture and economics of excess that sustain both.

Other disfigurements include those of Lourdes, who had been raped and scarred by government soldiers in the early years of the Cuban Revolution, and her sister, Felicia, who had been infected with syphilis by her philandering husband. One hot day in August while he slept and she cooked, Felicia, nauseated by another pregnancy, retaliates. Setting him on fire with an oil-soaked rag, she succeeds only in disfiguring his face and banishing him forever from the house, not murdering him as she intended. Years later in New York, Pilar, believing the herbs she has just purchased from a *botá-*

nica will protect her from harm, is sexually assaulted as she takes a dangerous shortcut home. The tallest of her eleven-year-old assailants "presses a blade to [her] throat. Its edge is a scar, another border to cross" (201). Reminiscent of her mother's rape in Cuba, *after* which one assailant cut Lourdes' stomach with his knife and the other beat her with his rifle, the scene evokes the continuum of violence stemming from patriarchal oppression. The gender issues of bodily disfigurement, scarring, and violence overcode the political debate about whether capitalism or socialism is the better social system. As they violently erupt in the text, they resist the novel's encoding as postmodern ethnic commodity.

Garcia's deployment of magical realism in the text and her depiction of the practice of Santería in Cuba (discussed further in chapter 4) are, in principle, more susceptible to mainstream exoticizing and containment. But again, the novel deploys these themes in modes that often work against such containment. The visitations Celia's husband makes after his death both to her in Cuba and to Lourdes in New York are discussed among the family and acquaintances as if completely commonplace and expected. Her father's visit becomes the site of a feminist recuperation when he admits to Lourdes his misogynistic treatment of Celia and attempts to heal the rift between mother and daughter that his actions instigated. He admits in an "even" tone to knowing about his daughter's rape by the government soldiers, suggesting at the very least that he engaged in the complicity of silence with this crime. The public admission of this complicity with violent patriarchy, both to his daughter on the diegetic level and to readers on the pages of the novel, constitutes a ruptural feminism that overcodes the magical elements of the novel and thereby resists their containment as the exotic.

Although the front and back covers of *Dreaming in Cuban* employ exotic images—a light-skinned Cuban woman of the 1930s and the seal from a box of exported Cuban cigars—the novel transcends the parallel signs of the minority commodity depicted on this frame. Celia's mouth may be blocked out in the cover image, but her powers of speech will be recuperated in the text through diverse narrative modes.[14] And the new generation that Pilar represents will carry on the work of remembering so central to the critical project to which Celia has dedicated her life, precisely, in this instance, by writing a postmodern ethnic narrative in the United States.

Beyond the "New Spice in the Melting Pot":
Julia Alvarez's Narratorial and Gender Trouble

As I have argued, one of the key mainstream strategies of attempted containment is the gesture of inclusion through the foregrounding of difference. Several reviews of Julia Alvarez's *How the García Girls Lost Their Accents* suggest in their titles that the book is a tale of assimilation.[15] One review, however, perhaps unwittingly delineates quite precisely the dialectic of inclusion through difference in its title and subtitle: "New Spice in the Melting Pot: Alvarez Shows in First Novel How Immigrant Sisters Learn to Assimilate."[16] While "new spice" may be added to the melting pot, the title implies, these new elements of difference must eventually be boiled in with the other ingredients. Other reviewers delimit Alvarez's Dominican "spice" more specifically with descriptions such as "From Caribbean with Love," "a combination mambo . . . [and] waltz of voodoo skeletons" (*Tampa Tribune-Times*, 21 July 1991), and "[the novel] already looks gift-wrapped with its festive Caribbean motif on the jacket" (*San Francisco Chronicle*, 19 Dec. 1991: E-5).

Discourse theorists have delineated the crucial role of titles in framing and organizing readers' perceptions of the subsequent text.[17] I would add to this the importance of the composite verbal-visual "imagetext" (Mitchell, 89 n. 9) on the covers of these novels. The childish block-letters in black on the cover of the clothbound edition of Alvarez's novel are changed into the playful multicolored "dancing" letters on the cover of the paperback edition. The bright colors of the urban scene painted on the "gift-wrapped" cover of the cloth edition become even brighter in the rescoped version on the paperback, imparting a sense of exotic tropicalism to the usually drab urban housefronts in large U.S. cities. Similarly, bright yellow, blue, and fuchsia predominate on the cover of Alvarez's 1997 *¡YO!*, while the title letters form a triangle above a reclining nude embellished with exotic signifiers—headdress, scarves, bracelets, cushion, and a tropical plant. The optic of the assimilated Other who still affords a pleasing narrative exoticism—advanced both in reviews and in the imagetexts on the front covers—frames and helps to shape the interpretation of many fictional works by Latinas even before they are read. Although Alvarez, Cisneros, Castillo, and Garcia may be invoked to form a convenient female quartet representing the "Hispanic" slice of the American pie, the Dominican American, Mexican American, and Cuban American experiences they represent are quite different and far from the mere pleasurably exotic.

Despite the mainstream's efforts to make economic and ideological use of certain "model minority" writers whose texts can be used to satisfy the happily pluralist view of America in vogue in the 1990s, Alvarez's deployment of narrativized "trouble" in *How the García Girls Lost Their Accents* belies the smooth integration of the Latina immigrant into the U.S. mainstream. As I will discuss further in chapter 6, Alvarez shows identity to be an unstable category undergirded by gender, ethnic, and class trouble. At both the levels of discourse and story, formal and diegetic transgressions mark this novel. In addition to the thematic transgressions that I will discuss in chapter 5, several modes of discursive "trouble" figure prominently in the novel.

While Alvarez's narrative appears on the surface to be a straightforward telling of events, chinks in the veneer of simplicity are quickly evident. The fifteen stories, through which the same characters move in and out, appear in reverse chronological order, paralleling, as Alvarez has noted, the way memory works.[18] This inversion allows readers to engage with questions of narrative power; for example, in one story, readers know the outcome of events that the characters in the current diegetic plane have not yet experienced. The stories are told from varying narrative perspectives and in the voices of the various characters, sometimes changing within a single story. The opening story in the third section of the book narrates the family's last day in the Dominican Republic before their forced exile to the United States. Alvarez interjects "trouble" into the trusted third-person narrative voice by shifting the narrative perspective from character to character as the plot proceeds, all the while conserving the third-person narrative voice.

Earlier in the collection, the story "The Four Girls" functions implicitly as a metanarrative of the storytelling process in the collection as a whole. Foregrounding the power of narrative omission—what a text at various levels attenuates or forbids itself to say—the story offers competing versions of events for readers to compile. The mother's overpowering presence as a narrator, useful on one level as a recuperation of historical memory and family testimonial, is both the site of pleasure and of critique. Even as the stories she tells about each of her four daughters are narrated with interruptions and delays to enhance pleasure, the shortcomings of her narrating power are highlighted. Her story about her third daughter, Yolanda, the implicit author of the larger book, emphasizes the problems of the teller and the interlocutor. Unknowingly told to her daughter's secret lover, the mother's narrative assumes a series of humorous double meanings and ironic twists because of her incomplete knowledge of her listener.

These elements of narratorial "trouble" parallel the mother's difficulties throughout the novel in adjusting to American speech patterns. Her frequent malaprops ("peaches and ice cream skin" [52]; "It's half of one or two dozen of another" [138]; and "Necessity is the daughter of invention" [142]) reveal that the common expressions she tries to adopt belong to the Other. As does parody, Alvarez's malapropisms employ a double-voiced discourse, presuming the reader's knowledge of the "correct" intertext and revealing much about the ideal addressees of the novel. In Bakhtinian terminology it might be argued that the mother is engaging in a mode of "hybridization"—here the "dialogized transmission of another's word" ("Discourse," 358, 355).[19]

"The Four Girls" stands as a narratological microcosm of the larger book. Directly preceding on the temporal plane the events of the previous story "The Kiss," the sisters (now between twenty-six and thirty-one years of age) uneasily converse with one another shortly before a family gathering. Yolanda, the implicit author of the larger narrative, knits Fifi's new baby a blanket, missing stitches and making mistakes parallel to the errors of the larger narrative process; the metaphor of unraveling the knitting and refashioning the narrative "thread" together in a joint compilation structures the sisters' retelling and mimicry of their mother's versions of their lives, metanarratively reflecting on the larger text. Despite the assured tone of the book's title, Alvarez's stories do not constitute the definitive narrative of the girls' lives. We are invited to be as distrusting of it as the daughters are of their mother's stories of their childhood, gleaning some information but not relying completely on any single text.

The story encourages a similar awareness of the multiple addressees of narrative utterances, including those of the larger book. Each of the mother's narratives about her four daughters' childhoods is addressed to strangers—wedding guests, a man in the adjacent seat at her daughter's poetry reading, a hospital psychiatrist, and another infant's father at the window of a hospital nursery. These diegetic narratees parallel Alvarez's diverse audience for the larger novel. This element of narrative "trouble" is emphasized in the story's representation of the mother's narrative to the staff psychiatrist as she commits her daughter Sandra to a private mental hospital. A poignant story of the daughter's anorexia and mental breakdown, the mother's utterances appear in montage with the father's observation of the hospital groundskeeper's methodical lawn mowing outside, and his eventually blurred vision as the story progresses. Although the father is ostensibly distracted, staring out the window and not listening to the story, the single mention of his view "blurring" (54) encapsulates the narrative's effect on this secondary narratee. Although ostensibly directed only to the doctor, the mother's words have several narratees, including her husband and the book's readers, all of whom decode her utterances distinctly, as the montage of this section emphasizes. The larger narration ultimately privileges its extradiegetic narratees, who are invited to decode the section's final image; here, an estrangement device simultaneously signifies the lawn mower and the daughter with the eating disorder: "a roaring animal on a leash, its baglike stomach swelling up as it devoured the grasses" (56).

Paralleling the narrative "trouble" at the level of discourse, on the level of story[20] Alvarez links the phenomenon of ethnic identity to "trouble" both on the mainland and on the island. The opening text, "Antojos," describes Yolanda's return to the Dominican Republic in the 1980s and the transgressions she unwittingly engages in as the cultures of her old and new worlds clash. Desiring to satisfy her craving for fresh guavas, she ventures alone into the lush hills of the interior. Her encounter with two unknown men in the countryside frightens her, revealing the difficulty the exiled woman has in conjoining the lifestyles of the two places she has known as home. Nonetheless, by having the two men "disappear into the darkness of the guava grove" (22), Alvarez co-inscribes the two pleasures of Yolanda's transgression—the level of sexual attraction to the forbidden men and the "antojos" (cravings) for the island fruit she has been denied. Yolanda's transgressions on the island are set against sharply delineated class divisions and a tripartite figuration of gender. She reminds herself of her upper-class connections in order to allay her fears in the unfamiliar situation involving the two men. Three distinct images of women punctuate her forbidden venture into the interior: the triviality exhibited in the appearance, gestures, and speech of her aunts and cousins who host her visit; the billboard image of the blonde Palmolive woman striking a sexualized pose in her ecstasy for the product; and the grandmotherly *cantinera*, who has "turned into the long arm of her family" (16), offering Yolanda a group of young boys to help her find and pick guavas.

In "The Blood of the Conquistadores," Alvarez intercodes Dominican history and family history, critically foregrounding the abuse of patriarchal power as the root of the trouble that forced her family to leave their country. She suggests that Dominican political history is characterized by the recurrent substitution of one set of *conquistadores* for another, with negative effects in the private sphere for both men and women. Yolanda's father is both a victim of, and helped by, the U.S. *conquistadores*, embodied by transient CIA policies and U.S. embassy personnel who change their minds about overthrowing the dictator, Trujillo, after engaging the father's help in the plot.[21] Yet, like the Dominican secret police who display the temporary power allowed them through the upward mobility of military enlistment, Yolanda's father engages in ostensibly playful yet cruel torture of his daughters in a game about the *conquistadores*. He holds his daughters upside down by their feet, until all the blood goes to their heads: "'Do you have the blood of the Conquistadores?' Yoyo always says no, until she can't stand it anymore because her head feels as if it's going to crack open and she says yes. Then he puts her right side up and laughs a big Conquistador laugh that comes all the way from the green, motherland hills of Spain" (197). As I will argue in chapters 5 and 6, the four girls will not escape the trouble of patriarchal power even after they leave the dangerous male-centered politics of the Dominican Republic.

In the multiple narrative perspectives of this story, however, Alvarez emphasizes the continuum of patriarchy, colonialism, dictatorship, and the secret police as the various representatives of these groups engage in sexual reification of girls and women. Trujillo's police express anti-gay sentiments and articulate gestural and verbal sexual innuendoes to the young daughters, or "doll-girls," as the men term them; in the youngest daughter's narrative of her remembrance of rebuffing the abuse, she terms Trujillo's henchman, "Some weirdo who was going to sit me on his hard-on and pretend we were playing Ride the Cock Horse to Banbury Cross" (217). The CIA agent, Uncle Vic, a contemporary version of the colonial patriarch, must be interrupted during his regular assignation with a young Dominican girl in a brothel to help the de la Torres in the dangerous situation with the secret police; he ignores Doña Tatica, the brothel manager who falls down in overwhelming pain from a serious illness as she delivers the urgent message to him, "leaving her to collapse in the arms of her own riffraff" (206). And the girls' father, although a victim of the military government in this story, nonetheless figures as part of the oppressive continuum as he insists on playing games that "nobody likes" to reaffirm his power over his daughters. Whether it's "the Blood of the Conquistadores" or "when he says, 'You want to hear God speak?' and you have to press his nose, and he farts. Or when he asks over and over even after you say *white*, 'What color was Napoleon's white horse?'" (197), the father crudely and authoritarianly reasserts his power over the young girls and their mother.

In this first novel by a Dominican American woman to receive widespread attention in the United States, ethnic identity is noticeably linked to "trouble" on several levels, undermining, to some extent, the happily pluralist view implicit in much contemporary multiculturalism. There is a parallel between the father's political transgressions against the dictator Trujillo, the daughters' sexual "revolution," Yolanda's transgressive actions on her return to the island, and the narratorial or formal "trouble" that Alvarez deploys in the book. By engaging in both narrational and thematic "trouble," Alvarez disrupts the celebratory aspects of multiculturalism, moving beyond the notion of "ethnic spice" and revealing immigrant identity to be the unstable site of ethnic, class, and, especially, gender battles. Transgressions with incestuous overtones, as occur in "The Kiss" (see chapter 5) may not be the usual fare of the mainstream's desirable multicultural commodity, but Alvarez's deployment of such narrative tactics foregrounds the centrality of the struggle against abuse of patriarchal power in this Dominican American's early contribution to the new Latina narrative of the 1990s.

Ana Castillo: Gender Trouble Forestalled in the Land of Enchantment

To promote the release of Ana Castillo's *So Far from God*, the cover of the *Los Angeles Times Book Review* (16 May 1993) paired it with a new novel by Bob Shacochis, *Swimming in the Volcano*. Beneath the headline "Lush Language" (in a red shade nearly matching the color of Castillo's book jacket title) and a picture of an open book in which exotic fabrics cover the pages instead of words, and coffee beans, chiles, and other exotic images float around it, the two reviews begin side-by-side, entitled respectively "Island Fever" and "Desert Heat." The cover of the book itself portrays doll-like figures in a stereotyped rural New Mexico, where the earth is bright fuchsia, the central adobe house has no roof, and a man raises a cross in the direction of the bright full moon (fig. 1.3). These images suggest that the marketing of the Latina writer as a postmodern ethnic literary commodity became predictably formulaic in the two years following the publication of Cisneros' book, and that Castillo's novel trades on several of these successful formulas. Her compelling storytelling and highly pleasurable representation of New Mexican ethnic culture are overcoded with the predominant tropes of the postmodern ethnic commodity.

Castillo marks the narrative voice with the accoutrements of one variety of Chicano English—a few calques, or transliterations from Spanish (for example, "the day her mother gave light to her" [224]) and frequent deployment of the double negative used in Spanish ("Tome never had no mayor" [137]). Yet the narrator is never anchored either as an intra- or extradiegetic figure, and therefore remains an amorphous, almost folkloric element of the novel's network of exotic postmodern ethnicity. (It might be argued that Castillo's introduction of the character Pastora from *Sapogonia* at the end of *So Far from God* is intended to suggest that this "alter-ego" figure of Castillo [Zimmerman, 80] is also the narrator of the 1993 novel. If this is the intention, however, the rhetorical device is very poorly developed, leaving readers immensely uncertain of the identity of the narrative voice.)

Figure 1.3. Cover of Ana Castillo's So Far from God, 1993 (courtesy of W. W. Norton and Company)

The ostensible narratee is non-Latino and primarily "gringo," evidenced in the constant explanation of Spanish expressions and Chicano customs. Castillo anchors the narratee as a mainstream reader who needs translation of Spanish in sentences such as, "Doña Severa was particularly proficient at curing 'suspension,' an ailment unknown to gringos and which has no translation" (234). And yet, the narrative voice betrays a love/hate relationship with the mainstream audience: while the multiple explanations of customs and linguistic practices reveal a desire to communicate with and gain the acceptance of the mainstream in a climate of profitable multiculturalism, the narrator also employs denigrating epithets such as "gringos" and "gabachas" (29) to refer to Anglos and their customs.[22] In the previous example, Castillo might have chosen to call those in need of translation "non-Latinos," which would have signalled nonpejoratively a wider intended audience comprised of both Anglos and other ethnic and racial groups.

In much of the narrative, an ethnographic voice painstakingly explains cultural traditions for the many non-Mexican readers who the publisher hopes will buy the book. Yet, the book's editing belies this desire for accurate communication of ethnic traditions. It appears that Norton did not employ an editor with expertise in Spanish, even though many Spanish phrases appear in the novel.[23] Misspellings of Spanish words and missing or misplaced written accents reveal that Norton is less concerned with accuracy than with the passable external appearance of multiculturalism. I refer to apparently unnoticed mistakes such as "salvages" for "salvajes" (55) "corage" for "coraje" (62), "vis-abuelo" for "bisabuelo" (217), "sinverguenzo" for "sinvergüenza" (105), "gias" for "guías" (232), "alabada" for "alabado" (197, 241), and frequent mistakes in written accents (e.g., "Esquipúlas" [73] for "Esquipulas"), as opposed to intentional, signalled variations in spelling as occurs in the phrase "'pantinghose' (as Doña Felicia called them)" (57), written imitations of diction such as "medio asustao" (45), and neologisms such as "traila," "trailita," and "Crismes" used throughout.

Where some might argue that Castillo is contesting dominant language patterns with such mistakes, the lack of spelling errors in English and their irregular appearance in Spanish suggests the absence of a knowledgeable editor rather than the intentional deployment of unorthodox spellings. Such editorial errors are distinct from what Frances Aparicio terms the deployment of a literary English as a "language tropicalized from within . . . the transformation and rewriting of Anglo signifiers from the Latino cultural vantage point" (796). On the contrary, in the examples of the ethnic writers cited here, the "minority commodity," like the deceptive packaging of many consumer goods, sometimes appears in inaccurate and misleading trappings.

The ethnographic description of non-mainstream cultural practices adds "spice" to the melting pot and at the same time educates readers about ethnic and interethnic differences. A conversation between two Latino soldiers becomes an ethnographic narrative explaining the distinctions of the term "Santería" in New Mexico and the Caribbean, and ethnography and narrative again merge in the description of Francisco el Penitente's work on his first wood carving of a saint.[24] Throughout the novel, many New Mexican Hispanic and Native American customs, rituals, and traditions are described for the outsider in an enticing manner attractive to insiders as well. Employing a technique used in the successful Mexican novel and movie *Like Water for Chocolate*, a subsection of chapter 10 presents "Three of La Loca's Favorite Recipes Just to Whet Your Appetite" (165); similarly, in "A Brief Sampling of Doña Felicia's Remedies" in chapter 3, the *curandera*, Felicia, herself recounts the procedures she employs to cure ailments in much the same narrative style as "Cartas a la bruja" [Letters to the Sorceress], an advice column in the popular magazine *Cosmopolitan en español*.

Numerous ethnic cultural traditions are central to the narrative, reflecting the variety of non-mainstream cultural practices in which U.S. Mexicans engage. Significantly, however, the variety includes only a few references to the participation of U.S. Latinos in mainstream culture. For instance, one of the four daughters is a television newscaster, yet this character is the least developed of the sisters, and most of her story focuses on her involvement with Rubén, who participates in Native American religious ceremonies at various pueblos while depending on her financially. Castillo focuses less on syncretic cultural motifs that join U.S. mainstream images to Latino ones (one Anglo character whose mother has named him "Sullivan" in honor of the "Ed Sullivan Show" is described as "Marlboro Man-ish" [196]), selecting instead clearly "ethnic" practices in which difference from the mainstream is decidedly marked. Very little attention is given to the important cultural force of Spanish-language mass media. Interestingly, one humorous scene in which this mass culture does appear foregrounds the more bizarre elements of the programming on the Spanish-language network Telemundo:

> [Domingo] was just sitting there all demoralized watching . . . telenovelas, and predictions by *Walter*, the Puerto Rican mystic, or talk shows like Cara a Cara, where they brought on experts on devil worship in East Los Angeles or discussed marital infidelity or one really weird time where they had the mother of a woman whose dead seventeen-year-old virgin daughter was exhumed and raped by the camposanto caretakers in Miami (Híjola!) and fifteen-minute programs sponsored by Goya Foods. . . . (217)

The programs Castillo highlights here emphasize the strangeness of U.S. Latino culture, portraying it as even more outrageous than mainstream U.S. talk-show fare; this characteristic also underlies many other cultural motifs in the novel's frequent ethnographic sections. Although Castillo presents a number of ethnic cultural practices, the selection is primarily limited to those customs, beliefs, and motifs that foreground the U.S. Latino as Other.[25]

The lengthy and numerous forays into ethnography that allow the Other to be profitably explained to a mainstream audience simultaneously function to overwhelm the novel's important forays into sexuality. Although the novel confidently and proudly explains many New Mexican, Chicano, and Native American cultural practices, it represses itself when narrating lesbian thematics; it is as if in the mainstream venue of commodified multiculturalism, desire may be tentatively expressed but not consummated. Thus, on one level lesbianism appears to be out of the closet, but on another it discretely remains inside.

This textual repression is especially significant given Castillo's transgressive narratives of autoeroticism and lesbian sexual desire in earlier works such as *The Invitation* and *Sapogonia*, which I will discuss further in chapter 5, and her extensive contributions to the anthology *Chicana Lesbians* (Trujillo). *So Far from God* sets up expectations early on that lesbianism will play an important, open role in the novel. Castillo introduces lesbian desire in a matter-of-fact narrative tone that startles those caught within the heterosexual optic:

> . . . Caridad, who had not been in love with anyone since Memo, fell in love that Holy Friday, and this took her by such surprise that every other marvel around her paled in comparison.
>
> So, the telling . . . of all the rest of that impressive spectacle will be forsaken because it was surpassed by the one of Caridad falling in love. . . .
>
> It was about then, however, that she stopped short at the sight of the most beautiful woman she had ever seen. . . . (74–75)

The estrangement of the heterosexual expectations of the usual romantic discourse is an important political rupture in this mainstream text. Similarly, Castillo shows the shared characteristics of lesbian and heterosexual desire later in the novel. As Caridad keeps vigil outside the house of the woman she desires, Francisco el Penitente keeps watch over her, filled with the same desire she feels but for a different object: "It just made her feel good to be close by, the way Francisco el Penitente felt good being close by to her. Yes, she had always known that he was there. How could she not feel his own nearby yearning for the impossible, which was so akin to her own?" (205). Later I will discuss the simultaneous imbrication of this passage with the novel's antipatriarchal optic, which condemns the violent practices of stalking, abduction, and rape that not only terrorize women but sometimes result in death. Here I wish to emphasize the important ruptures against heterosexual expectations that result from Castillo's narrative naturalizing of lesbian desire in these passages. In a similar fashion, Castillo parenthetically, and almost in passing, authoritatively states that "the first two humans . . . were also both female" (211), matter-of-factly countering the biblical narrative about human genesis.

Given these and other important naturalizations of lesbianism in the novel, how then does the text repress itself? While the novel announces early on the lesbian desire of one of its main characters as if it were a natural and expected component of the narrative, the story of this desire becomes increasingly muddled, hidden, and "closeted" as the book progresses. Chapters must be carefully read and re-read several times to secure even a minimal grasp on the events and people involved in this subnarrative of the book.

We see this ambiguity when Castillo introduces a cinematic high-speed "chase" scene in chapter 8 as an apparent deviation from the main narrative, along with the overt warning to readers that the chapter is vital to the larger narrative. Subtle clues here and elsewhere reveal that the woman whom Caridad desires is Esmeralda, later the lover of one of the lesbians involved in the chase scene. The slender, gun-firing man in a truck who terrorizes the women in chapter 8 (perhaps because they are lesbians, Castillo hints) might be Francisco el Penitente, a Vietnam veteran, who later stalks Caridad, abducts Esmeralda, and appears in the form of a coyote, motivating Esmeralda and Caridad to leap to their death after catching sight of him, in a literary quotation of the ending of the movie *Thelma and Louise*. Not only do the lesbian characters in the novel die before the relationship gets off the ground, but readers must search diligently to find the hidden pieces of the narrative of lesbian love, so attenuated is this aspect of the story. The discourse of ethnography, a much more palatable form of postmodern ethnicity, overwhelms the tentative lesbian thematics of the novel.

As occurs with Cisneros, Garcia, and Alvarez, however, a number of important gender and political issues rupture through the veneer of postmodern ethnicity in *So Far from God*. Castillo emphasizes the continuum that underlies patriarchal violence and exploitation, linking such ostensibly distinct acts as the stalking of a loved one, the abduction of a woman whom the loved one desires, the shooting at and terrorizing of lesbians who are visibly different from the mainstream, the rape and near murder by an amorphous coyote figure enacted as revenge for a woman's heterosexual promiscuity, the "social parasitism" of a husband who gambles away his wife's patrimony, and the sexual, religious, and economic exploitation of a woman by a man involved in Native American religious rituals. Castillo further elaborates the continuum in individual scenes, such as Sofi's loss of her family's home and small ranch to a judge involved in gambling with her husband. Patriarchy, the legacy of imperialism, the law, the judge, her husband, and even the Church are involved in the material loss she sustains, for she has remained in the destructive marriage partly in fear of the punishment of excommunication.

Throughout the novel, however, women transcend the role of victims, taking strong measures to control their lives with both large and small acts. Sofía becomes mayor of Tomé, socializes the ownership of her *carnicería*, and organizes a food co-op; Esperanza leaves the exploitative relationship with Rubén and pursues her career; La Loca performs an abortion on her sister and protests Farah jeans; Caridad leaves behind the alienated promiscuity that has exploited her, makes her own life choices, and pursues the woman she desires; and Fe finally stands up to the company that has forced her to work with toxic chemicals.

In an important reappropriation of a religious ritual, the people of Tomé modify the traditional Good Friday "Way of the Cross" procession at the end of the novel as a public protest of political injustice. In a syncretic montage, Castillo intersperses the scenes of the religious reenactment of the Passion of Christ with the participants' brief political testimonies against social evils such as poverty, toxic exposure in factories, contaminated canals, AIDS, nuclear power plants, pesticides, and the Gulf War. In another syncretic cultural motif designed to show women's power and autonomy, however, Castillo, in my view, slips into a pan-Latino multicultural image that detracts from the political gesture. The final chapter describes the growth under Sofi's leadership of the international organization MOMAS, Mothers of Martyrs and Saints, in which women exercise control over who will be canonized and hold annual international conventions in which their transparent and incarnated children reappear. Although the feminist utopian gesture of this chapter positively attempts to reverse the patriarchal power of the Catholic Church throughout history, the images Castillo employs lead to a confusing pan-Latino version of multiculturalism. As in her earlier novel *Sapogonia*— in which Castillo merges culture, politics, and history from throughout the Americas—in *So Far from God* she plays on intertextuality with the important political group in Argentina, the Mothers of the Plaza de Mayo, disparagingly denominated "Las locas," who campaigned courageously for years during and after the 1976–83 dictatorship for information about their "disappeared" children. Castillo's mixture of parodied religion, political organization, and feminist reappropriation of Church authority results in a confusing multicultural image likely to promote an inaccurate image of Latin American and U.S. Latino history and culture among mainstream readers in the United States.

Although Castillo's text plays more heavily on salable multiculturalist imagery than do the earlier works of Cisneros, Garcia, and Alvarez, feminist and political ruptures nonetheless mark the text, thereby presenting readers with contradictory constellations composed of representations of social antagonisms and the pleasing images of multiculturalism. The narrative voice foregrounds its own political stance on several occasions, and multiple issues of social injustice appear throughout the novel. Although it might be argued that gender trouble (especially the issue of lesbian sexuality) is muffled by the novel's multiculturalist motifs, it is important that Castillo at least begins to raise these issues in the mainstream venue. Although muted, they continue to function as ruptures within the desirable postmodern literary commodity.

The pessimistic view that contestatory culture is inevitably co-opted by the mainstream reduces these narratives to their status as commodities and underestimates the polysemous nature of the discursive signs they employ. Cisneros, Garcia, Alvarez, and, to a certain degree, Castillo foreground a ruptural feminism that escapes the attempted reabsorption of these texts as exotic, pleasant "minority commodities." To return to de Certeau's image, they create smudges on the page of the heterological text of multiculturalism, destabilizing the mainstream's efforts at "scriptural conquest" and containment. The attempted reconversion of social antagonisms in order to sell books, magazines, and other mass-cultural versions of the Latina Other is marked by contradiction, for these narratives give voice to unexpected and uncontainable social problematics that break through the pleasing veneer of the ideal Latina postmodern commodity.

CHAPTER TWO

The Politics of Signification

I n the postmodern moment of the late twentieth century, cultural theorists have argued for a decentering of the written forms of cultural production that have traditionally enjoyed privileged status. Diverse forms such as mass culture, popular art, and "the practices of everyday life" such as de Certeau's "*la perruque*" (*Practice*, 25) and popular religious rituals—although not ensconced as the new center—have now become the objects of important theorizing. Nonetheless, an increasingly large group of Latina writers has continued to engage in a lengthy form of written cultural production—the prose narrative—in the postmodern decades of the 1980s and 1990s. One important reason for this apparent anomaly is the heightened awareness of the politics of signification and the key role of discourse in movements of populist rupture. A number of contemporary Latina writers choose to develop in their cultural production "linguistic strategies for inverting their institutionalized negation," to employ Harryette Mullen's terms. And, as Demetria Martínez has argued, the new U.S. Latino fiction is one of the few venues in which poor people can convey messages in their own voices to a mass audience; unlike the mass media, in which Latinos are only impersonal statistics, fiction gives voice to the powerless and can be seen as a kind of "literary liberation theology" ("What a Moment," 16). Fiction writes the lives of ordinary Latinos into the larger historical narrative, and even helps those committed to social movements and causes to begin to understand minorities as people rather than as multicultural ideals.

As theorists moved away from the notion of ideology as simply false consciousness to the Gramscian view that ideology is an arena of struggle between competing definitions of reality, they began to understand culture as a site of contestation for meaning, a process rather than a fixed purveyor of misunderstanding or truth. Stuart Hall developed an integrative model that conjoined semiotic theory with the work of Voloshinov and Gramsci ("Rediscovery"). Because a "historical bloc" for Gramsci is not simply one formed by the ruling class but is often an alliance of diverse social groups, it is necessarily unstable and involves a constant struggle for power. Following Voloshinov,

Hall has argued that much of this battle takes place at the level of discourse. Various social groupings, both those with power and those without, attempt to reformulate discursive patterns, rearticulating signifiers in new meaning systems for different political ends than in the previous hegemonic instance. A political battle is waged for the power of signification. The alternative appropriation of the word "black" by the Black Power movement in the 1960s exemplifies one political movement's new anchoring of a multi-accentual sign that had been previously inflected as the negative and the despised.

As Ernesto Laclau has argued, the discursive is not an element of the separate superstructure but rather is coextensive with the social; it is "the very condition of all social practice" ("Populist Rupture," 87). Rather than history and society being discrete spheres, they constitute "an infinite text." To extend his argument, the reconfiguration of signifiers must also be understood as a practice coextensive with the social. The new discursive models that a number of contemporary Latina writers develop in their works are an essential constituent of the populist rupture in which some sectors of the Latino community in the United States engage. These narratives are not aesthetic experiments conducted in an ivory tower. As I will show, both on the diegetic plane and in their production and reception, these narratives are crucially connected to the notions of difference, equivalence, and antagonism, which in Laclau's schema are essential to populist rupture.

Several contemporary Latina writers engage pointedly in the important social struggle within language, disarticulating signifiers from dominant meaning systems and rearticulating them in new connotational chains. In the narratives considered here, the battle for the power of signification is waged not only by the authors' attempts to resignify individual words, expressions, and larger master narratives, but within the plot and on the interpretive plane as well; the redeployed signifiers will be subject to negotiated and oppositional readings (Hall, "Encoding/Decoding") in addition to the preferred encodings that the writers attempt to anchor. The primacy of other forms of mediated and popular culture notwithstanding, these Latina writers continue in this age of postmodernity to engage in the linguistic struggle over signification in narrative prose.

Decentering Master Texts

Postmodernist narrative experimentation has questioned the aura of epistemological certainty and authority of the traditional narrative voice of master texts. Even modernist experiments such as stream of consciousness and dischronology purported to present a more ample, comprehensive, and "realist" rendering of the workings of the human psyche. Several new Latina narrativists, in contrast, present alternatives to totalizing master texts, resignifying the ostensibly univocal nature of such claims to truth and at the same time foregrounding the limits of their own narrative enterprises. As I will discuss further in chapter 6, while a novelist such as the Cuban American Margarita Engle works to contest one master text—that of the unnamed figure of the "Commander" (Fidel Castro)—she simultaneously establishes another sort of univocal master text in which alternate political views to her own are demeaned or ignored. In contrast, Graciela Limón's 1994 *The Memories of Ana Calderón* uses first- and third-person narration to elaborate the protagonist's counter-memory as a resignification of several master narratives; the various re-semantizations that the novel undertakes are a useful solution for the protagonist but are not set up as a new universal master text that all must follow.

Among the ostensibly univocal texts that Limón's novel resignifies are the Bible, patriarchal authority, popular cultural beliefs, pervasive mass-cultural themes such as those of the *telenovela* or soap opera, and master historical narratives about the past. The counter-narrative is structured around alternative reappropriations of the body, transgression, feminist strength, resignified religious imagery, and experiments with narrative voice that, unlike many High Modernist texts, remain accessible to a wide variety of readers.

Limón's protagonist's journey from rags to riches—literally from being a child in a palm-leaf hut in southern Mexico to becoming the successful head of a huge corporation living in an ocean-front mansion in Los Angeles—inverts the traditional soap-operatic conventions even as it deploys them. For each time it appears that Ana Calderón can sink no lower or have no greater adversity strike her, she saves herself by her own wits rather than by those of a glamorous man who romantically comes to her rescue. While the narrative outline appears on the surface to invoke the themes of melodrama uncritically, Limón in fact offers a re-reading of this master discourse: seduced and abandoned, Ana is nearly beaten to death by her father for being pregnant, while her lover watches. He later leaves her standing at the altar and then marries her sister. Taken in by a man and wife who read the Bible to her every night, she falls even lower when she is imprisoned for trying to kill the ex-lover who deserted her after stealing their child; an even greater calamity befalls her when he gives the child up for adoption while she is in prison. And in the final, modified Oedipal element of the tragedy, Ana falls in love with her adult son and unknowingly has an incestuous sexual relationship with him.

But Limón resignifies these conventions by suggesting in postmodernist fashion that although culture and life in these respects are sometimes co-terminous, alternate solutions to those of the usual televisual text are more useful. Ana's intelligence, innovative ideas, and courage save her at each apparent nadir. She realizes in prison that if she follows through with the escape she has planned, she risks an even longer sentence and no chance of getting to the outside to find her son who has been adopted. Later she astutely organizes her fellow factory workers and then stands her own as she successfully presents their demands to the owner; through education and talent, she rises to the top of the corporation and eventually becomes the executive, building it into a huge transnational enterprise. And at the end, after her final fall from grace into incest and the death of her son, she engages in a crucial resignification of the biblical master text, a more successful penitential rite than that traditionally expected of sinful women in Mexican culture.

When the man and woman who took her in earlier in the novel first read to Ana the story from Genesis of the slave girl Hagar who was forced to sleep with Abraham and bear him a son, the young, pregnant Ana timidly offers an alternate, decentering interpretation of the master narrative. What if the center of the story is Hagar herself and not the son she is to bear, Ishmael? In Ana's resignification, the story of the son who would become the head of a tribe is less important than that of the suffering, mistreated slave woman who was important in her own right, the prerequisite to the founding of the tribe, and who would go on to do greater things than bear a son. Engaging in the politics of signification, the character Ana re-reads the biblical master text in light of Limón's contemporary feminist concerns.[1]

The novel does not, however, offer an immediate, magical reconfiguration of the biblical text; instead, Ana's suggested resignification simmers for more than twenty years within her and the couple who earlier took her in. After her final fall from grace, Ana receives the old copy of the Bible in the mail, with the relevant passage marked, much as Ishmael and his father Abraham are marked in the biblical narrative by circumcision as a sign of the covenant with God. But here, Ana, who has verbally "marked" the passage with her spoken rearticulation, will create, along with her friend who has now marked the passage with writing, a new kind of covenant; Ana will now survive because of a positive sense of self and her personal strength, in contrast to a penitential woman in Mexico walking on her knees to the image of the Virgin of Guadalupe to ask pardon for her sins.

Besides resignifying pervasive master texts of mass culture and religion, Ana contests popular beliefs and practices such as the patriarchal authority of fathers, boyfriends, and bosses and nontraditional religious practices that focus on guilt rather than liberation and strength. Ana's body is the locus of several of these contestatory battles; against the double standard of her father's dictum that she may not have sex before marriage even though her partner can and should, Ana not only enjoys sex but undergoes great bodily injury as a consequence. Later in the novel she reconfigures her father's terrible beating of her (while her lover looks on without attempting to stop the attack) when she defends herself against a second beating by striking her father's head with a stone. In both instances, he pronounces a curse on her and her offspring— the product of her bodily transgressions—using his verbal authority to extend the punishment after his physical attack on her body ends. But even though several characters in the novel give credence to the father's curse, the novel suggests that particular acts of individuals lead to Ana's problems, not the father's verbal attempt to punish her in perpetuity. And just as she must heal and move beyond the punishing beatings, she must move beyond the penance of female *penitentes* who travel on bleeding knees to the shrine of Guadalupe to atone for their sins. This self-imposed bodily degradation, although part of popular religious practice, functions as a kind of master text that must also be transcended and replaced by images of feminist strength. In contrast to the surge of penitential bodies at the shrine to which the worshippers' crawl on all fours, their hands smeared with the blood of those who proceed and follow them, Ana stands tall at the end, at peace because she has discovered her self-value through the rearticulation of Hagar's narrative.

Limón's novel also presents itself as a site of literary experimentation that can decenter and amplify the standard master texts of history, yet not with such esoteric and formalist devices that it becomes inaccessible to a wide variety of reading publics. The intercalation of complementary third- and first-person voices gives the protagonist herself a more substantive role in the narration. The first-person sections do not merely repeat or amplify events that have already been narrated in the third person; the plot advances with both kinds of narration. In one section Limón conflates the third-person voice with the consciousness of the child Ishmael when he is taken from his mother, correlating the character's perceptions to the childlike narrative style. Although the novel begins with the quotation from Genesis about Hagar, a second title page follows, signaling that the subsequent pages are "The Memories of Ana Calderón," her version of events and her resignification of the historical narrative of the period from the 1930s to the 1960s. Beginning and ending with her first-person voice, the memories also counter the curses and obscenities directed at her by patriarchal figures.

Significatory Reappropriations of the Everyday

The short story "Grace" by Mickey Fernández, a not yet widely known Chicana from Southern California, presents alternative signifying systems on several levels. The story's primary narrative strategy recodes for readers and, on the diegetic plane, for the two female characters entering adolescence the public view of their Aunt Grace as a "bad mother" and "deserting wife." Buttressing this larger project of significatory reappropriation is a series of everyday reconfigurations—of bodily and physical spaces, of relationships with men, and of pleasurable mass culture—that constitute Grace's strategies of resistance throughout the story.

Fernández's alternative encoding of the pejorative signifiers "bad mother" and "deserting wife" begins with a narrative doubling that pairs two temporally separate moments of young girls' entrance into patriarchally constrained puberty. Reunited with her young nieces, the wise-aunt figure Grace remembers her own sexual transgressions a generation earlier. Against a repressive father and misguided mother, she had styled her hair into a pompadour, worn lipstick, and climbed out of her bedroom window at night to meet her boyfriend, Joaquín. These efforts to control her own sexuality through a subcultural style and transgressive sexual encounters, although pleasurable, in fact represented a movement from one system of male power to another. What she perceived to be liberatory later reveals itself to be part of a continuum of misogynist patriarchal authority passed down from husband to son.

An early decoding of the dark side of patriarchal authority occurs in Grace's memory of her wedding day at age seventeen, three months pregnant. With her swelling body squeezed into the satin gown Joaquín has bought to ensure that she fit the dominant proprietary model of the virginal bride, Grace suffers an infantilizing slap on the rear from her father, who reminds the new property owner, Joaquín, "to do the same if she got out of hand" (123). The previously passionate kisses guarded intimately within the private sphere become quick kisses in the public setting of the reception, accompanied by the words "You're mine now, baby" and engaged in as a kind of punctuation to Joaquín's "boasting about his beautiful bride" to his drinking buddies. As Joaquín grabs her to dance a *corrida*, Grace "felt like a doll being dragged through the room" and ends up with a torn and stained gown that signifies the underside of romantic love.

As she moves into the more advanced system of male power that follows, Grace learns a debilitating self-hatred. Fernández exposes the increasing consolidation of patriarchal power within the household as Joaquín and their son

band together almost unconsciously to form what might be termed a hegemonic bloc in the domestic sphere. The two "seemed to merge in their mean-
ness and constant use of her energy" (129). And both exercise flattery and
charm to derail her efforts at resistance. In a pivotal scene, the patriarchal duo
together engage in verbal and physical violence against Grace; when the eight-
year-old son reinforces his verbal aggression toward his mother by throwing
his plate of breakfast at her, his father aborts Grace's attempt at retaliation,
assaulting her so severely that she must recuperate five weeks in the hospital.

This violent eruption of the patriarchal authority passed on from father
to son enables Grace to free herself by leaving the abusive situation, although
others code her actions as those of the deserting wife and mother. Fernández rearticulates Grace's moving away to live alone as empowerment. In the
present of the story of 1960, "Grace no longer carried herself in the timid
Mexican-American manner of her childhood days—a face tinged with fear,
two paces behind her man, and a sweet-wanting-to-please smile on her
mouth. . . . She stood straight and tall behind no one" (124).

Parallel to her newly strong physical appearance is Grace's reconfiguration of her living space. She has painted a mural on the walls of her small
rented house and arranged collected objects and souvenirs to cover "every
available" space. Her reappropriation of this rented domestic space "kept her
secure" and parallels the manner in which she arranges her own body. Like
the "bright, childlike mural" with which she refashions the walls of her house,
she arranges her hair "in the style of the teenagers twenty years younger than
she" (124); the youthful rebellion that Grace exhibited in adolescence perse-
veres in these semiotic reappropriations of physical and bodily spaces.

While the visiting young nieces view their Aunt Grace's current love relationship as routinized and old-fashioned, Fernández urges readers to see it
as a site of cultural resistance and autonomy. The nieces, as surrogates for the
son Grace has lost and the daughters to whom she never gave birth, represent
the youthful, uncritical acceptance of patriarchal authority. In counterposition to one niece's boyfriend and her own relationship with Joaquín during
adolescence and marriage, Grace and her current companion, Victor, preserve
one another's autonomy in their relationship. Fernández exposes the ways
in which Grace and Victor positively employ cultural traditions: the brightly
colored Mexican party dress that Grace wears for their night out, knowing
that it is "outdated and silly" but also that "it fit her need for fantasy" (127);
their courtship ritual in which Victor tells her that she is beautiful in the outrageous dress and she plays "hard-to-get"; and, as Fernández describes one
instance of this couple's reappropriation of received patriarchal cultural tra-

ditions, "They both knew the outcome of the dance they performed each Saturday night, but it was important that they play it out, that they give each other the flattery and courtesies they could get nowhere else" (128).

These modes of cultural resistance and autonomy allow readers to re-code an instance of Grace's apparently uncritical relation to mass culture as the story closes. Although, in the final paragraph, Grace might appear to en-gage in escape from the painful truth of her past by loudly playing a romantic Elvis Presley song as she and her nieces drive down the highway, the story urges readers, as it suggests Grace herself is doing, to begin to engage with such signifiers critically. It is probable that Grace's enjoyment here of Elvis' "Now or Never" is a critical reappropriation parallel to her reconfiguration of her bodily and domestic spaces and the inverted rituals of her relationship with Victor. In opposition to the dominant meaning—conveyed by the patri-archal voice of the song attempting to convince the implicitly reluctant young woman to be "his" tonight—the previous paragraph suggests that Grace will interpret the song in the context of her decision to try to contact her son one last time. Just as she must write to him "now or never," so too must he agree to resume their relationship because of its "now-or-never" urgency. Using the meager resources available to her, Grace recovers important elements of the agency that men have denied her from childhood through adolescence and into marriage; in reconfiguring physical and bodily spaces, relationships with men, and pleasurable mass culture such as the Elvis song, Grace establishes an agency and autonomy that might well inspire her nieces, these younger versions of herself who have come to visit her.

Like Fernández, the mainland-based Puerto Rican writers Aurora Levins Morales and Rosario Morales resignify the everyday in their coauthored book, *Getting Home Alive*. Among their many narrative recodings of the everyday are several images of food. Reversing the usual First World norm for women ("thin is beautiful"), their book positions the motifs of nourishment, kitchens, meals, fatness, and life at the positive pole in opposition to hunger, thinness, and death. Rosario contrasts one of her healthy pregnancies with a precarious one. Remembering the first, she voices pride in her large "belly": "I'm proud of it. It's mine, it's large, I'm large! I've gained a lot of weight, and for the first time in my life I'm fat, my face round as the moon. . . . I'm happy" (32). In the second, she was "thin all over except for my belly" (33), having miscarried once and nearly losing another child in this pregnancy. Aurora re-narrates her grandmother's oral tale about having tried to nurse her infant daughter while going without food for three days during the Depression. When her husband finally found work and brought food home, he had to spoon-feed her as she lay in bed, the child all the while trying to nurse. Aurora's narrative then resignifies from a materialist perspective the title of Richard Rodríguez's controversial text *Hunger of Memory*, as she notes, "There is a memory of hunger in me, a hunger from before birth that aches" (42).

The negative pole of denied food and unhealthy thinness sometimes includes death, the authors emphasize, and they transmute the meal into a revengeful weapon, a lesson to be taught to someone who has misunderstood its life-giving function. Narrating the details of her miscarriage and her mother-in-law's unsympathetic reaction, Rosario imagines in a poetic interlude a transgressive reversal of the usually life-giving meal preparation in which mothers engage: "I could serve a platter of placenta / Young, quite fresh and delicately braised / Garnished with parsley / Set it in front of the cold hard faces / that mock and sneer at the near mother's pain / and towering large and menacing / Invite: *Ess, ess mein kind.* / Eat!" (101). Rosario merges images of life and death here as a means of reversing what she considers to be the misuse or absence of the positive life-giving maternal functions. If her mother-in-law has criticized Rosario's choice to bear children and has failed to extend sympathetic support when Rosario miscarries at home, the author will imagine enshrining the now useless placenta within the trappings of an aesthetically presented meal; she will turn the ostensibly life-giving function of maternal meal preparation back upon itself to suggest that, in her mother-in-law's case, it in fact only minimally disguises its opposite.

Similarly, both Rosario and Aurora reinvest the sensually pleasurable images of ethnic food with the underside of women's hard work that often remains invisible in the final product. Rosario counterposes the traditional dinner party of the privileged classes with its linens and fine tableware to a dinner that poorer women prepare for their own enjoyment: in place of fine linens is "a cloth woven by one, dyed by another, embroidered by another still. It's too small for the table but is put there in the center every year in memory of our mothers" (51); the meal is communally prepared and serves to honor their female forebears "because they have kept it all going, all the civilizations erected on their backs, all the dinner parties given with their labor" (51–52). Similarly, Aurora links the Puerto Rican food she is preparing in her California kitchen to "the hands of women who came before me, washing rice, washing beans, picking through them so deftly, so swiftly" (37), encoding meal preparation as "a magic, a power, a ritual of love and work" (38). In both cases, the life-sustaining function of food is linked to the labor of the women who prepare it.

Helena María Viramontes also resignifies the everyday in her story "The

Moths" by highlighting the syncretic reconfiguration of everyday objects that the protagonist's grandmother has practiced. Joining the elements of both Mexican popular cultural practices and consumer mass culture, the grandmother raises herbs and flowering plants in red Hills Brothers coffee cans and prepares a curative balm from dried moth wings and Vicks Vapo-Rub. Utilizing toothpicks, mayonnaise jars, sweet potatoes, and avocado pits, Abuelita creatively alters her domestic space, enclosing her house in vines that produce flowers and food—beauty and utility.

In a parallel fashion, this matrilineal model of syncretic reappropriation of the everyday and nature will help the narrator to transcend the negative criticisms of her "masculine" traits in popular diction. She refuses to accede to interpellations that criticize her "male" traits from within the male optic, and using male terms: because her hands were too big to do stereotypical "girl things" such as crocheting or embroidering, her "sisters . . . called [her] bull hands with their cute waterlike voices" (23). Under her grandmother's tutelage, however, she engages in the equally precise work of planting and growing: holes are punctured in the coffee cans with the "precise" hit of a nail, and the allegedly "bull" hands make nests for the seeds in the soil that are exactly "four fingers round" (24). Thus, shared knowledge about cultural practices preserved and passed down through the narrator's matrilineal heritage serves as a defense against the negative interpellations lodged against her from within patriarchal discourse.

Far from serving as local color or creating ambience in these narratives, everyday objects are important material constituents of these women's struggles for control and autonomy. The painting and decoration of bodily and domestic space; the collection of objects; courtship rituals; rock songs on the radio; the enjoyment, preparation, and even subversion of meals; alternative body images; syncretic herbal and brand-name medicinal remedies; and elaborate gardens fashioned from the most common of everyday objects are strategies of cultural production that redeploy ordinary signifiers for important new ends.

The Repositioning of the Other

Crucial to the process of reclaiming the power of signification is the repositioning of the Other in discourse for both male and female, Latino and non-Latino U.S. audiences. Here, "the Other" represents anyone who has heretofore been understood only superficially, from the outside; it functions as a floating signifier in many Latina narratives, with diverse elements of the audience fixing its meanings differently, depending on the various relations of alterity in which they participate.

In "The Cariboo Cafe" (*Moths*), Helena María Viramontes reconfigures Others such as undocumented Latino immigrants and refugees, a mother who kidnaps, and an ostensibly upright cook in a café. By focusing on relations of power and strategies of survival, Viramontes establishes an alternative system of values within which various sectors of the audience can reposition Others. A political refugee who "kidnaps" two lost, undocumented children in Los Angeles is rearticulated as a heroic, loving mother whose victimization by a brutal political regime in Central America is at the root of her aberrant behavior in the United States. The positive surrogate mothering she gives the two lost children is her attempt to reconnect with her son, whom a Central American military regime has abducted.[2]

Viramontes establishes a new system of equivalences through direct renderings of the woman's troubled subjectivity, revealing that international political homologies structure the diverse U.S. Latino community. The police or "polie"—who are, according to popular wisdom, "La Migra in disguise" (61)—become in the woman's subjective vision the Central American soldiers who have abducted her son. Heroically, then, she clings to her surrogate Chicano son during the police raid of the café, symbolically attempting to return him to her womb "so that they will not castrate him and hang his small, blue penis on her door, not crush his face so that he is unrecognizable, not bury him among the heaps of bones, and ears, and teeth, and jaws" (74); she throws two pots of steaming coffee into the policemen's faces, reappropriating an everyday object as the only weapon available to her. Viramontes portrays the woman's struggle against the police in Los Angeles as structurally homologous to other struggles in Latin America against oppressive military regimes. She overcodes the woman's ostensibly criminal behavior (kidnapping, resisting arrest) as a kind of heroism—one of the small struggles against oppression that links Latinos in the United States to those in Latin America.

In contrast, the restaurant cook, ostensibly the upright citizen who betrays his undocumented customers by calling the police, is repositioned in the story as a misguided misogynist. Similarly troubled because he has lost his son in Vietnam, the cook sides with the repressive state apparatus instead of contesting it. Whereas the woman compensates for the loss of her son by lovingly mothering the lost children, the cook gives day-old donut holes to the thirty-five-year-old drug-addict Paulie, whom he begrudgingly adopts to replace his dead son. Whereas the woman contentedly views the lost boy "sucking milk from a carton" she has given him (72)—her replacement for maternal suckling—the cook, claiming to be too busy to be "nursing the kid" (Paulie), concentrates instead on a reifying image of one female customer's "unique titties" (65) in an entire paragraph of misogynist rambling. Whereas the Central American woman heroically gives her life to save her surrogate son from what she believes will be capture by a military regime, the cook works together with the repressive force, informing the police about his surrogate son Paulie just as he tells them about other undocumented restaurant customers.[3]

The "Nuyorican" writer Nicholasa Mohr also repositions the Other, especially in her short story collections *In Nueva York* and *Rituals of Survival*. Here she reinscribes such Others as a dwarf immigrant from Puerto Rico, a homeless former sailor blacklisted in the 1950s, the young wife of a restaurant owner, the apparently hysterical mother of a murdered young robber, a lesbian who is also a "deserting mother" figure, and a recent widow. An excellent manipulation of narrative suspense in "The Operation" (*Nueva York*), for example, positions us for most of the story, along with the parents of a missing girl, to fear that the homeless stranger whom the girl meets in an abandoned building is a child molester and murderer. For some readers, this Other is rearticulated as most likely harmless when he explains that he is out of work because of McCarthyist blacklisting; for others, the stranger's benevolence is secured shortly thereafter when he expresses concern that the girl's parents will be worried about her. Mohr has offered narrative positions for readers here that rearticulate this Other as a sympathetic speaking subject.

In "The Robbery" (*Nueva York*), Mohr introduces the figure of a "crazy woman," Roberta Rodríguez, who demands that a Puerto Rican restaurant owner pay for the burial of her son, whom the owner killed after the youth robbed the restaurant. By the end of the story, the woman has convinced many readers—along with several of the restaurant customers in the story— that her demand is justified, revealing that other social issues in the community are more important than the law-and-order discourse of the ethnic shopowner. Mohr narratively establishes a new system of oppositional equivalents, as Ernesto Laclau has theorized is essential to populist rupture. For Laclau, true disarticulation of hegemonic discourse must show antagonism between social forces, not mere difference. While all language involves a system of differences, populist discourse produces differences that are antagonistic; it does so by collapsing spurious differences, establishing new equivalences, and simplifying the social space into two opposed camps: "the same equivalences which in a genetic discourse present themselves as a *system of differences* are reorganized as a *system of equivalences* by the discourse of antagonism." Laclau is suggesting that beyond ordinary oppositions in language (the word "map" is

distinguishable visually and aurally from the word "mad," for example), political language must show equivalences in opposing groups; then "the discourse
of antagonism can become a discourse of rupture."[4] This process of forming
new equivalences allows groups in moments of populist rupture to see the
commonalities among separate discursive elements of an oppressive force; for
example, soldiers, their voices, their weapons, and their distinct skin colors.

By showing us that the young robbers are not the real enemy, Mohr's
story develops a new system of oppositional equivalences in which readers'
understanding of both the positive and negative poles is modified. The Latino
restaurant owner who has been robbed moves, by the end of the story, into
a relation of equivalence with the oppressive law-and-order forces of mainstream society, failing to understand the larger social issues that link him to
the Latino community. The character of "the Other," which Mohr's story originally positions us to view as a "crazy" woman overcome by grief for her dead
son, becomes by the end the articulator of a new and more accurate system of
oppositional equivalences that can begin to pave the way for populist rupture.

As does Mickey Fernández, Mohr also recodes the figure of a "deserting mother" in the story "Brief Miracle" (*Rituals*). Here the protagonist suffers
from a doubly transgressive alterity: a lesbian who is also a "bad" mother, Virginia is rearticulated in the story as a sympathetic woman who herself must
shatter the mystique of family and ideal motherhood. Just as the Virginia
known only as a lesbian in the popular rumors is resignified as a good mother
in the story, so too does she herself puncture the received myths of romantic
heterosexual love, family, and mothering by living them as realities. When at
the end she "deserts" her new lover and his children, whom she has admirably
mothered for several weeks, readers are left to choose a decoding of this transgression based on an inside view of the character no longer completely Other.

While at this level the story effectively repositions the figure of a doubly
transgressive Other, it simultaneously offers an ambivalent portrayal of a lesbian. The protagonist appears to shift easily between lesbian and heterosexual
love affairs and, in cowardly fashion, leaves her experiment with traditional
family life without an explanation or good-bye to those who have come to
depend on her emotionally in the preceding weeks. It may be argued as well
that Mohr in fact "de-lesbianizes" the figure of Virginia, portraying the character only during the period in which she re-enters the heterosexual order.
In effect, Mohr portrays as Other one of the very figures she on one level
seeks to de-Other, for some may leave the text mistakenly confident that they
have come to grips with a part of the lesbian experience. Instead, the story
confronts only one of the predominant received views of lesbians—certainly

an important political project—but refrains from significantly portraying the lesbian experiences in Virginia's life. Some readers might wish for a stronger, more positive image of a lesbian woman, although to its credit, the story honestly portrays one woman's human frailty.

In contrast to this ambivalent recoding is the strength exhibited by Carmela, a woman recently widowed in Mohr's "A Time with a Future" (*Rituals*). As her adult children reduplicate positions of patriarchal authority and power structures, attempting to arrange their mother's future in accordance with their own needs, Carmela engages in the speech and action she has been disallowed during her long marriage. The key phrase "a time with a future" brackets the story as its first and last words, in structural opposition to the children's inaccurate view of their parents' marriage expressed in the optimistic truism that one of them utters: "a whole lifetime together" (35). Just as Carmela's children enter a new system of equivalences in the story, aligning themselves with patronizing patriarchal positions rather than with their mother's real needs, so too does Mohr reconfigure the mistakenly perceived marital bliss of their parents' relationship.

In counterposition to the mode by which she survived married life, the story now reveals Carmela's own views: a festering resentment because her husband would not allow her to be at their son's bedside when he died, redoubled by the husband's insistence when his own death was imminent that she remain constantly nearby; the lengthy details of her nurturing care in the final year of her husband's illness; and finally, her secret mode of coping throughout her marital ordeal, her purchase of a "room of her own," a co-op into which she will move now that her husband has died. In this reversal of the intrafamilial Othering that her children and husband have consistently practiced, Carmela finally engages in the speech and actions forbidden to her throughout her marriage.

Some of Mohr's characters themselves struggle to rearticulate signifiers on the intradiegetic level, precisely the mode by which their apparent alterity is inverted for readers. Amy, a young mother left in dire poverty by her husband's death, scrapes together a few dollars to invent a substitute Thanksgiving dinner. Replacing the traditional turkey with a dozen hardboiled eggs that she colors bright orange, Amy deftly exerts cultural leadership, convincing her children that they are eating a delicacy. What the children initially decode as "Easter eggs," Amy rearticulates as "turkey eggs"; the cultural strategy she invents to cope with her poverty is so successful that reality is temporarily altered, its constant semiotic mediation highlighted for readers: the children comment, "Wonderful, Mommy. . . . It tastes real different" and

"Oh, yeah . . . you can taste it right away. Really good" ("A Thanksgiving Celebration," *Rituals*, 87).

Amy has engaged in a cultural version of *la perruque*, one of the everyday life practices that de Certeau studied (*Practice*, 24–28); instead of using company time or supplies for her own small projects, as occurs in de Certeau's *perruque*, Amy uses the meager commodities available to her in capitalist society for her inventive cultural production. Rather than using the workplace as a site of struggle for control of one's time and creative labor, she centers her *perruque* on ideology as the locus of a struggle for the control of signification. Narration is one of her crucial tactics as she uses stories about her grandmother to uphold the story she has invented about the eggs. And it is the story in which she is a character that constitutes Mohr's repositioning of her as Other.

Lucha Corpi performs a similar revisioning of the Other in one section of her 1992 mystery novel, *Eulogy for a Brown Angel*. In chapter 13 she depicts an alternative view of a Chicano gang member and the youth subculture he participates in, suggesting that not all gangs are bad: some are like a family, close-knit and united and positively focused. For the teenager Mando, some members of the Santos gang are surrogate fathers for him, replacing his biological father who deserted the family at Mando's birth. Not involved in drugs and violence, the Santos serve as protectors of the neighborhood community so that the older people can walk the streets without fear. Like an army, the gang members wear a subcultural "uniform" that allows them to recognize one another immediately, and they have secret "chantes," or hideaways, where members of the "familia" stay when there is trouble. The solution to the mystery in the novel turns on discovering the identity of an outsider who has disguised himself as a Santos member and murdered a four-year-old Chicano boy during the 1970 Chicano Moratorium in Los Angeles. In developing the themes of the recuperation of family, the protection of the members of a community, the strategic role of stylized clothing, the appropriation of that style by an outsider who is an enemy of the community, and the group's distrust of the police, Corpi not only advances and strategically delays the mystery narrative but presents an alternate view of the Chicano gang member Other.

The Semanticization of a Threatened Community

As discussed earlier, Laclau believes that populist rupture requires producing a discourse of antagonism. Relations of power and domination often remain occluded until reality is semanticized into the discourse of antagonisms; that is, an oppressed group must reorganize the outward differences in which the oppressor appears into a system of equivalences. At the same time, however, a discursive reorganization at the positive pole of the opposition must also take place; that is, a threatened group or community semanticizes itself, organizing itself around a group of positive equivalents.

Roberta Fernández, for example, suggests that several key cultural practices constitute a system of positive equivalents around which Chicanas can discursively organize themselves to reappropriate historical memory. Characters in *Intaglio* who engage in these important cultural practices include Amanda, a seamstress and embroiderer; Filomena, an *altarista*; Andrea, a dancer and actress; Nenita's mother, who compiles an album documenting Andrea's artistic career; and Nenita herself, the narrator of the stories in the collection, who sews *milagritos* on the satin lining of her Aunt Zulema's coffin and re-creates her family's cultural history in her journal—the prototype of *Intaglio* itself. As Fernández has noted, with the exception of Nenita, the characters engage exclusively in the creative outlets that were available to women in a preliterate society.[5] Fernández does not elaborate this series of "positive equivalents" as static symbols that invoke the past in a reactionary gesture. Rather, the cultural practices are transformative in these stories. The photo album that documents Andrea's career, for example, is delineated as both a positive and negative arena for cultural and historical remembering.

Andrea is both the subject and object of history in the blue album that her cousin (Nenita's mother) has assembled from the photos and news clippings sent by Andrea. While the creation of the album offers a positive cultural recuperation of the past through which Nenita can attain a partial understanding of her family's history and the broader immigrant history in which they participated, the story also critically contests the status of the scrapbook as representation. Nenita comes to terms with the partial truths that the photos signify. On the one hand, the album is "more than a record of Andrea's career. . . . it will always be the repository of our own dreams and aspirations, of the past as we would have liked for it to have been" (30). On the other hand, it is an inaccurate recording of the larger reality of immigration for it cannot reveal, as the story does, the conflict between Consuelo and Andrea; the narrative makes available the details about one sister who remained more Mexicanized, finding it difficult to assimilate into U.S. society, and the other who experienced acculturation more easily, becoming "Americanized" while still not losing her ties to Latino culture.

The ambiguous destruction of the album at the end (was it Consuelo or Andrea who in fact destroyed it?) points to its problematic status as a representation of the past. Andrea and Nenita have learned, as Barthes has noted, that "the [p]hotograph mechanically repeats what [can] never be repeated existentially"; and because the photograph is a "certificate of presence," its "power of authentication exceeds the power of representation" (4, 87, 89). Just as the photographs in the album authenticate Andrea's path of modernization —her assimilation into U.S. society—so does the story that Nenita narrates authenticate the existence of the now-destroyed testimony to Andrea's artistic career. "Andrea," the written text, functions as the story behind the story, the underside of the remembered past, the unphotographed narrative. Fernández shows that these photographic objects, which an endangered community sometimes employs to create unifying equivalences, are not straightforward, univocal representations of the past. Their destruction serves as important a role in ethnic unification, as did the earlier moments in which they began the painful process of remembering for the various members of the family.

Zulema's process of reappropriating historical memory involves both her own and the narrator Nenita's acts of re-semanticization. Denied access to her own life narrative at age six when her aunt hides her mother's death from her in 1914, Zulema begins and modifies her own oral storytelling in direct parallel to her chronological development. Early on, she gathers *testimonios* from participants in the Mexican Revolution that will later be integrated into her oral storytelling. At age nine, after realizing her mother will never return, she begins to tell her brothers alternative fairy tales in which, for example, the events of Sleeping Beauty are merged with contemporary events in the Mexican Revolution and her own personal trauma. When her audience dislikes her modifications of the traditional narratives, she decides to keep the stories to herself, but thirty-five years later her own niece, Nenita, becomes the appreciative audience. While Zulema weaves her stories, Nenita engages in a parallel metaphorical practice by braiding her Aunt Zulema's hair with a red ribbon. When Zulema dies in 1970, Nenita deploys first visual and then verbal signs to carry on Zulema's narration. As a visual artist she sews 180 *milagritos*—faces, hearts, and tongues of fire with red ribbons—inside Zulema's coffin, and she places marigolds tied in red ribbons to form a halo around her aunt. She also puts into the coffin some blank 45-RPM records for Zulema to record her favorite stories after her death. And she herself carries on Zulema's narrative by writing in her journal, which will become the book we are reading. Although the narratives woven by Zulema and Nenita are frequently imbricated with competing versions and counterclaims to "truth," Fernández insists that every narrative is a fiction. All narrative must both rely on and change the stories that precede; with respectful dependence on past oral tradition, the contemporary Chicana writer carries on that storytelling mediated by her own contemporary lens. This innovative yet historically based narrative is crucial to the re-semanticization of a threatened community.

Helena María Viramontes, as evidenced in "The Cariboo Cafe," encourages Latinos in the United States to see one another in terms of equivalence and solidarity rather than antagonism whether they have emigrated from Mexico, Central America, or another part of Latin America. A Central American woman whose child has been abducted by the military in her country of origin can nurture and heroically attempt to protect two lost Latino children in Los Angeles. Similarly, the story repositions as equivalents what appear to be separate repressive state apparatuses (Immigration and Naturalization [the INS], the Los Angeles Police Department, the military in Central America) and such figures as the cook who calls the police and collaborates in INS raids. Viramontes' double-narrative tactic of discursively repositioning both the oppressor and one's own subcultural group in terms of equivalences demonstrates an important mode through which a threatened community succeeds in semanticizing itself to begin the process of populist rupture.

Graciela Limón also re-semanticizes a threatened community. From 1986 to 1991 Limón participated in demonstrations at La Placita in downtown Los Angeles and at the nearby Federal Building against the United States' involvement in the civil war in El Salvador. At 6 A.M. on Wednesdays, concerned protesters, including celebrities such as Martin Sheen, would march with a large cross and sometimes lie down on the sidewalk to make chalk outlines representing the war dead in El Salvador. Limón worked as well with Salvadoran refugees who received asylum at the church at La Placita after its pastor, Father Luis Olivares, declared it a sanctuary. This involvement and conversations with the refugees inspired Limón to transcend geographic borders thematically in her 1993 novel, paralleling the lives of the refugees themselves. *In Search of Bernabé* suggests that the civil war in El Salvador and U.S. involvement in it are of central concern to Chicanos, other minorities, and the larger U.S. mainstream interested in the evolving multiculturalist discourse. The novel critically reconfigures the long civil war in El Salvador in the 1980s as an international conflict in which traditional categories of "good" or "bad" people must be reevaluated; several characters make questionable ethical decisions—not only a military general and a rich landowner but a U.S. priest, a Salvadoran seminarian, a dispossessed woman working as a maid, and a leftist guerrilla. Neither the left nor the right can be classified as entirely good or entirely evil. For example, a female "coyota" figure who transports undocumented refugees and workers into the United States for large sums of money is not entirely evil; she puts herself at risk by taking some of those with no place to stay to a Catholic sanctuary center in Los Angeles. As does Viramontes, Limón suggests that people in the United States must see the connection of their own struggles to those in El Salvador. In the reorganization of the positive and negative poles of social antagonism that Limón presents, a sense of ethics, morality, and social justice underlies the narrative development of people who play both good and bad roles in the war in El Salvador. By disrupting the easy categorization of people as "good" or "bad," Limón helps to re-semanticize the threatened community whose members are inextricably connected despite their separate geographical locations.

Three of the novel's characters, in particular, vividly reveal this moral complexity. Luz Delcano, for example is alternately characterized as a powerless victim of child abuse who later readily enters into a sexual relationship with her married employer, and as a courageous defender of the rights of other victims and a strong mother who tirelessly searches for her missing son. Viewed by some as a whore, she is also the polar opposite—a Blessed Mother figure constantly invoked by her son, Bernabé, in moments of trouble; as the search in the novel's title comes to a close, she finds her son murdered on "the mount" and embraces him in a pietà-like pose. Limón also connects Luz to the figure of Eve, who weeps "because her son murdered his brother" (155); but instead of placing the blame on the Eve figure in this resignified version of the biblical narrative about the legacy of original sin, Limón suggests that a Judas-like follower of Christ has misguidedly helped to foment the long years of fratricidal civil war in El Salvador.

Limón selects the figure of Father Hugh Joyce, a professor at a Catholic university, to represent the state of moral compromise in which many ordinary U.S. citizens are placed because their government has spent four billion dollars to underwrite and finance the slaughter in El Salvador.[6] During the intense fighting in San Salvador in November 1989, the worst in ten years of civil war, Luz narrates a confession-like *testimonio* to Father Joyce as they both huddle on the floor of a shelter. Reconfiguring the traditional rubrics of sacramental confession, Luz and Father Joyce alternately confess their sins to themselves, each other, a boyhood friend who appears in a vision and whose voice Father Hugh converses with, and, implicitly, the larger public reading the novel. In describing the physical destruction of churches in El Salvador during the war, Luz's narrative also implicitly points to Father Joyce's personal role in the death and destruction, and to the assassination a few days later on November 16, 1989, of six Jesuits, a female employee, and her daughter at the Universidad Centroamericana. As Father Joyce leaves the shelter and follows the crowds to the Jesuit residence where the murders were carried out, his connection to the destruction becomes explicit; near the bodies are the used shell casings of the arms that Father Joyce helped to sell to the Salvadoran military. In the words of his boyhood friend, "We might as well have loaded the weapons ourselves. . . . We're a part of it all, and we did a good job" (149). Limón suggests that just as the misguided Father Joyce involves his Catholic university in arms sales that contribute to death and destruction in El Salvador, so too have our misguided leaders involved us through investment, military training, and government aid in this bloody civil conflict.

Similarly, Limón casts Luz's son, Bernabé, as a fallible Christ figure who as the novel opens is a seminarian carrying a large cross in the procession to the cathedral in San Salvador for the funeral of the slain Archbishop Romero. When the Salvadoran military shoots guns and grenades into the crowd, Bernabé is forced to flee to the countryside and begins to fight with the guerrilla forces. By the end of the novel, after participating in brutal murders brought on by wartime tensions, Bernabé questions his role as a guerrilla soldier: "when he . . . realized that now he would never get to be a priest . . . he had persuaded himself that instead of peace, the gospel preached by Jesus was really one of murder and torture. . . . he had falsely convinced himself that as a guerrilla he could do more for his brothers and sisters than as a priest" (134).

Later he realizes that as he kills soldiers and tortures spies when fighting for the FMLN, he is ignoring that "the victims were his brothers, Salvadorans like him, and that each time he killed, he became less human" (134). Limón suggests subtly that it is perhaps these sins that the Bernabé-Christ figure must die for, and that all people must be wary of the extremes that they are sometimes called to engage in, even when fighting for social justice. By casting both the university priest and the Christ figure as fallible, Limón urges other readers with less official connections to morality and ethics to examine their voluntary and involuntary participation in the death and destruction in El Salvador.

Having traveled in 1990 with a Jesuit delegation to El Salvador to investigate the murders of the priests and laypeople at the UCA, Limón structures the novel on two key clerical assassinations that frame the beginning and end of the civil war: the murder and funeral of Archbishop Romero in 1980 and the killing of the Jesuits in 1989. The novel functions as a kind of liberation theology in which traditional religious motifs are resignified within the frame of these two watershed events in which politics invaded religious practice. Limón not only re-reads the Bible in terms of the contemporary political upheaval in Central America, but also extends this optic further by re-reading the social turmoil itself through ethical and moral values. Refusing to portray either the left or the right as entirely good or bad, she engages in a thoughtful version of liberation theology similar to that advanced by one of the slain Jesuits, Ignacio Ellacuría. Phillip Berryman has argued that Ellacuría was the "first liberation theologian martyred" (12) and has shown that his positions with respect to social justice did not always correspond to orthodox Marxist views. Limón shows that politics and religion are inextricably connected and that received moral values need constantly to be reevaluated and critiqued. She cannot accurately tell the story without reconfiguring a number of biblical motifs, thereby presenting a counter-narrative to the master text of organized religion.

Several re-semanticizations of the Bible structure Limón's novel. As the seminarian Bernabé carries a large cross in Archbishop Romero's funeral procession, he in effect begins his own version of the Passion and Death of Christ, which will end on El Playón, the mount where his mother recovers his body. His death is temporarily delayed by violent events in the civil war in which he assumes both Christ-like and non-Christ-like functions. In the aftermath of the attack on the funeral procession, he leads a crowd of Salvadorans across the river to escape a military aerial attack. He then descends into "the other world for three days" after blacking out and calls out "¿Mamá, mamá, dónde estás?" (36), reconfiguring Christ's invocation of his father as he dies on the cross. When Father Joyce sees Luz holding the dead Bernabé, he refuses three times to acknowledge his role in the death; the forty pieces of silver in the biblical narrative are reconfigured here as the priest's enjoyment of personal prestige at directing his university to a lucrative investment and endowment opportunity. The story of Cain and Abel is resignified as the literal and figurative fratricide of the Salvadoran civil war. Limón expands upon a quotation from the Book of Daniel in which the biblical master text condemns the elders' lustful behavior toward "the daughters of Israel [who] were too frightened to resist" (9). The novel's reconfiguration gives the Salvadoran daughter Luz a much greater narrative role, showing how despite child abuse, she develops into a strong woman who courageously defends the rights of a mistreated political refugee and persists in the difficult search for her missing son.

Limón's counter-narrative deploys both resignified biblical motifs and a new ethical system in which theories of social antagonism need to be reconfigured because issues are no longer clearly black and white. The novel speaks out against social injustice in a reasoned, believable fashion that will not please all sides. But as a historically rooted narrative, based on real events in El Salvador,[7] it functions as a kind of modified fictional *testimonio* and redeploys the strategies of liberation theology to encourage U.S. readers to engage productively in the politics of signification.

Resignification through Combination

Although I have separated the discussion of the politics of significa-tion into several subcategories in this chapter, there is often a conjoining of these levels in Latina narrative. Demetria Martínez's 1994 *Mother Tongue*, for example, engages harmoniously in a number of strategies of resignification. Among the Others she intends to reposition, for example, are Central Ameri-can political refugees who have entered the United States illegally and those involved in the U.S. Sanctuary movement who aid them. She attempts to discursively reorganize these two groups at the positive pole of oppositional social antagonisms in Laclau's model. One narrative strategy she employs to develop this reconfiguration is alternate significatory reappropriation of the everyday, following the political practices of the refugees and Sanctuary workers themselves. And drawing on events in her own life, she combines macro- and micro-narrative resignification throughout the novel.

When a federal grand jury indicted Martínez and Lutheran minister Glen Remer-Thamert in December 1987 on charges of conspiring to help two Salvadoran women enter the United States illegally, Martínez argued that her involvement was solely at the level of journalistic narrative—a story she was writing about the women for the *Albuquerque Journal*. A further narrative over-lay structured the two women's journey to the United States, which Martínez saw as an attempted resignification of the biblical Christmas narrative: preg-nant, the women had hoped to find shelter and asylum in the United States before giving birth in December but ended up having their babies without a new home.[8] Against the accusatory narrative of a federal grand jury, Martínez counterposes her professional involvement in journalistic narrative and the rearticulated version of the biblical narrative. Martínez elaborated various seg-ments of these narratives in published and unpublished poetry in the 1980s,[9] and later in the book *Mother Tongue*.

In the novel, the larger macro-narrative of U.S. and Central American history of the 1980s is resignified through numerous micro-narrative strate-gies that also engage in the politics of signification. Diary excerpts, letters, newspaper clippings, Central American poetry, a grocery list, recipes, and political bulletins are intercalated with self-referential narrative sections that encode the larger text of the novel as the written utterance of the protagonist Mary to her college-age son. Throughout, Martínez engages in further semantic reconfigurations at many levels. Besides recuperating the motif of the Holy Family by naming the protagonists Mary and José and giving them a central connection to El Salvador, the country named for Christ, Martínez rearticulates numerous religious motifs that I discuss in greater detail in chapter 4. The model of liberation theology, for example—which, as I noted earlier, Martínez associates with the fictional projects of many U.S. Latino writers— permeates several levels of this novel. As Father Virgilio Elizondo has pointed out, the figure of Father Gustavo in the novel invokes the seminal Peruvian liberation theologian Father Gustavo Gutiérrez (lecture, University of California, Santa Barbara, 19 May 1998). Just as practitioners of Latin American liberation theology rearticulated biblical narratives in terms of the contemporary social problems of common people, Martínez reads the survival strategies that the Sanctuary movement employs through the optic of everyday religious motifs. The group interprets the habits of border patrol officers (their lack of scrutiny of blond Anglo men, for example) as "a kind of liturgy" (37) on which Sanctuary workers and political refugees can count. Members of the Sanctuary group redeploy common semanticizations but add new signifieds to facilitate their clandestine transportation of refugees; a Reagan-Bush bumper sticker, a brown station wagon with a canoe on top (also described in Martínez's poetry), and a "fishing trip" that the Sanctuary workers simulate all rely on both common and extraordinary significations, just as the texts of liberation theology refer both to the ordinary and the sacred.

In another micro-strategy of resignification, the protagonist, Mary, will show readers modes of re-visioning the Latino Others in their midst in a city such as Albuquerque: "All over the city refugees were rendered invisible with each stroke of the sponge or rake they used to clean motel rooms and yards and porches" (35). As a counterstrategy to this myopia, Mary focuses on an indexical visual sign, the "white patch of fabric" visible in the plaza crowd that distinguishes José Luis in his T-shirt from the earth-toned Banana Republic clothing of the tourists. Here Mary resignifies vestimentary signs within a larger social structure as a means of repositioning the Other and re-semanticizing the threatened community of which José Luis is a part.

Realistically, however, Martínez also shows that the reconfiguration of the concepts of difference, equivalence, and antagonism for the characters themselves is a difficult process that sometimes violently erupts in the novel. The double meaning of certain signifiers such as "Ana," chalk drawings on the pavement, and the sound of church bells results in a breakdown in the relationship of Mary and José Luis. Here the signifiers participate simultaneously in contradictory codes: "Ana" designates both a Quaker Sanctuary worker and a murdered loved one in El Salvador; chalk drawings of human figures signify both life-renewing therapy and threats of murder by death squads. As José Luis notes in his journal, "The problem is we're not seeing or hearing the same things. Even church bells mean something different to us. [Mary] hears them and sets her watch. I hear them and remember the endless funerals in the villages outside the capital" (78). As the novel repositions these signifiers within two distinguishable semiotic chains in which readers can see both equivalence and difference, new definitions of social antagonism come to the fore.

The reconfigurations of the concepts of difference, equivalence, and antagonism in Martínez's narrative and the others discussed in this chapter enter into what Jean Franco terms the "struggles for interpretive power" in society at large (xi). The narratives of these Latinas represent a different mode of "plotting women" into the social text itself, contesting the dominant representations of their Otherness that flourish in a wide array of cultural forms. The social text into which these narratives intervene after publication is a parallel site in which the politics of signification are played out. The reconfiguration of spurious differences into systems of equivalences and ruptural antagonisms that these writers effect on the diegetic plane must begin to take place as well in the larger social text. As Henry Louis Gates Jr. and others have argued, real-world injustice is not automatically righted by critical semantic practices.[10] Nonetheless, those such as Voloshinov, Gramsci, and Hall who have focused on the great determining power of language in the construction of "the real" demonstrate that the work of rearticulating signifiers by linking them to new signifieds is not merely playful experimentation. Indeed, the initial efforts of these Latina writers to work at the level of discursive politics is a vital critical enterprise.

Beyond Individualism: Collective Narration, History, and the Autobiographical Simulacrum

I n the cultural battle waged for the power of signification, a necessary constituent of the struggle for full civil rights and social change, Latina women in the United States engage with the question of identity in diverse modes. All of the writers discussed in this book view identity multidimensionally; to varying degrees, issues of gender, ethnicity, race, class, and sexual orientation—the primary socio-analytic categories of opposition in the late twentieth century—structure their narratives. But the narrative strategies employed exhibit divergent configurations of these variables. As I will show in chapter 6, several of these texts posit feminist and ethnic autonomy as the necessary constituents of identity. Invoking other strategies, some writers foreground individualism, while others attempt to disrupt it formally and diegetically; some emphasize the crucial relation of the Latina subject to history, while others occlude this nexus; and some engage in post-modern autobiographical gestures to assert identity.

As Ramón Saldívar has shown, a writer such as Ernesto Galarza, in contrast to Richard Rodríguez, exemplifies Adorno's thesis in *Negative Dialectics* that the realm of the personal is already public; efforts to separate the two are doomed to failure. Galarza's autobiography implicitly critiques the "myth of innocently separable 'private' and 'public' roles of the self" (Saldívar, 169). In defining their specific politics of identity, some Latina writers foreground a conflict between the public and the private. While certain writers narratively delineate the politics of the personal, others ultimately substitute the personal for the political. The texts that are most successful, however, integrate the personal and the political, the individual and the community, and link personal empowerment to social empowerment rather than exaggerating subjectivity to focus on the first terms of these dichotomies.

The forging of a gendered ethnic identity, a vital strategy for combating a subgroup's invisibility both to the dominant culture and to its own class culture, always hovers on the edge of a lapse into individualism. The politics of difference, initially a positive movement against the totalizing discourse of Western humanism that sought to institutionalize one experience as the universal human experience, runs the danger of occluding the notion of community. Some argue, for example, that the masculinist bias of the Chicano movement or the blindspots of middle-class feminism irremediably contaminate these movements for Chicana/Latina women.[1] In the move to assert agency and to delineate the specificities of their own identity, some contemporary Latina fiction writers engage in isolationist recuperations of the individual. Rosa, for example, the protagonist of Alma Luz Villanueva's *The Ultraviolet Sky*, enacts a withdrawal into individualism by geographically distancing herself from two coterminous spheres—an urban setting and an oppressive domestic environment structured by patriarchal authority. Important moments of personal rebellion move the novel forward, with gender, ethnicity, and the aesthetic functioning as the key narrative themes around which this personal struggle is waged. Although the protagonist interacts with others in the novel from time to time, her personal struggle is the central organizing motif. In contrast, a writer such as Graciela Limón in *Bernabé*, as discussed in chapter 2, moves beyond a primary concern with the individual, suggesting that the problems of war-torn El Salvador are of necessity the concerns of those in the United States as well.

The Disruption of Narrative Individualism

Several experimental works among the new Latina narratives of the 1980s and 1990s stand out for their anti-individualist strategies. While they are not autobiographies in the strict sense of the word, they might be read as collective oral *testimonios*. Similar to Sandra Cisneros' story "Little Miracles, Kept Promises," which presents thirty-four intimate yet public prayers of U.S. Latinos that collectively narrativize representative elements of everyday life, Denise Chávez's "Novena Narrativas y Ofrendas Nuevomexianas" presents nine fictional women who tell their stories in their own words to the Virgin.[2] Another work, *Getting Home Alive*, the jointly written text of the mother and daughter Rosario Morales and Aurora Levins Morales, disrupts traditional narrative individualism in several ways. In a different vein, Sylvia López-Medina's 1992 novel, *Cantora*, straddles the boundary between fiction, autobiography, and oral *testimonio* as a novelistic adaptation of the oral histories of the women in López-Medina's family.

Although on one level a series of monologues scripted for a single actress,

Chávez's "Novena Narrativas" is consistently dialogic, and the sole actress is always simultaneously herself and another. An implied interlocutor, either an intradiegetic character or the audience itself, underlies and structures each monologue, while the representation of the Virgin on the home altar on the stage is the overarching addressee of each speaker in this variation of the nine-day religious ritual. The narrator, Isabel, becomes each of the other eight characters by metonymic repositioning, donning one or two accessories that signify the character. Narrative stage directions such as "Becoming Jesusita, she puts on the collar Jesusita wears" (88) and "Isabel sheds Jesusita and becomes Esperanza" (90) emphasize the dialectic of unity and difference among the nine women.

Chávez counters the individualist mystique of the great writer by coding the piece in the introduction as a collaborative effort of five women artists. Against the usual authorial aura, the dramatic narrative reveals itself being written and revised immediately in the first scene as the author-narrator-character figure Isabel corrects the script that we are reading, the same artifact that she is rehearsing and at the same time ordering and writing.

Like "Novena Narrativas," Morales and Levins Morales' *Getting Home Alive* works against narrative individualism as a joint artistic production by a mother and daughter team. Even as it presents autobiographical accounts of the two women's lives, it communizes the technique of first-person narration through the project of joint authorship. The absence of the authors' names from the intercalated narrative segments allows the text to be read as a continuum in which two women's experiences are intermixed. Although each writer's work is distinguished visually by only slightly different typefaces, readers who wish to attribute personal authorship to individual segments must repeatedly refer to the table of contents. By doing so, readers obtain important information about the enunciators of the individual narrative segments, although the text continues to function as part of a jointly authored collection. Thus, the individual and the collective coexist in this autobiographical narrative.

Intradiegetically, as well, the text decenters individualism on numerous occasions. Aurora's grandmother, for example, recounts a story of early Puerto Rican solidarity in New York in 1930; upon hearing of a job opening for a janitor, a group of Puerto Ricans, all needing work themselves, help Aurora's grandfather to obtain the job because his wife is nursing their new baby, and mother and child are near starvation: "There was a group of Puerto Ricans, tú sabes, people who all knew each other and looked out for each other, not familia, but parecido, because you know there weren't so many of us in New

York then" (42). Against the traditional American individualism of "each man for himself," ethnic solidarity here reasserts the notion of community even in one of capitalism's extreme moments of crisis.

The book's only jointly written narrative segment, "Ending Poem," merges the two authorial voices to move against the fragmentation and atomism of contemporary social space. The women emphasize the multiple but not limitless permutations of their identities. Together they identify as light-skinned Caribbeans, immigrants to both the United States and Puerto Rico, "*Boricuas . . . from the isle of Manhattan*" (212), children of many diaspora, but *not* African, Taino, or European; while African, Taino, and European cultures have helped to shape their roots, they cannot return to these cultures. It is their solidarity with other women, however, that most effectively unites them: "I am a child of many mothers. *They have kept it all going* / All the civilizations erected on their backs. *All the dinner parties given with their labor.* We are new. *They gave us life and kept us going,* . . . And we are whole" (213). The two women's multiple ethnic, racial, and national identities are celebrated and at the same time overcoded with a feminist recuperation of women's everyday life and labor — the principal basis of unity between mother and daughter.

The politics of identity for Aurora and Rosario Morales is a complicated configuration of inversions that illustrates the heterogeneity of the Latino population in the United States. Rosario, born in New York to Puerto Rican parents, also feels linked to Jewish immigrant culture through childhood friends and her marriage to Dick Levins, the son of Russian Jewish immigrants. Aurora, who spends her formative years in Puerto Rico, is connected to both Puerto Rican and Jewish immigration to the United States through her two sets of grandparents. She herself will retrace a version of her maternal grandparents' journey to the mainland from Puerto Rico when her family moves to Chicago. While for her mother the nostalgic homeland is the island of Puerto Rico, for Aurora, "New York is the Old Country" (89). For each of these U.S. women of Puerto Rican descent, ethnic identity, while pivoting on similar structures, represents a very different cultural configuration.

Bilingualism and biculturalism function differently in the two women's lives. Aurora, for example, displays resistance by refusing to speak Spanish in her nursery school in Puerto Rico; after moving to Chicago at age thirteen, her bilingualism "masquerades as dyslexia, stuttering, halting" as she is "unable to speak the word which will surely come out in the wrong language" (84). Rosario's goal, in contrast, is to integrate the nuances of Puerto Rican Spanish into her use of English in writing and speech with the celebratory tropicalization that Frances Aparicio discusses. Rosario criticizes other minorities who have brilliantly mastered English but purged the mother language from their texts:

> But I'm sad, too. For the English language robbed of the beat your home talk could give it, the words you could lend, the accent, the music, the word-order reordering, the grammatical twist. I'm sad for you, too, for the shame with which you store away — hide — a whole treasure box of other, mother, language. It's too rough-mannered, you say, too strange, too exotic, too untutored, too low class.
>
> You're robbing us, robbing the young one saying her first sentence, reading her first book, writing her first poem. You're confirming her scorn of her cradle tongue. You're robbing her of a fine brew of language, a stew of words and ways that could inspire her to self-loving invention. (145)

For Rosario, however, the mother languages are many — "a linguist's treat" — including Yiddish, Spanish, "college educated english and irish which I mainly keep in my prayers" (138). While some might prefer Latina writers for whom Latino culture plays a more exclusive role, Rosario Morales delineates here a complicated cultural formation, one that is proud rather than ashamed of its diverse cultural roots. She reveals one important mode of identity formation among the many and varied conceptions of self in the heterogeneous Latino population in the United States.

Biculturalism for the two women is similarly a configuration of several cultures. Rosario makes knishes with "(forgive me!) pork," raisins, garbanzos, and green olives, and prepares "Morales blintzes in the mountains of Maricao . . . Jewish chicken soup with cilantro and oregano" (116). For Aurora, the lone rooster crowing in the Chicano barrio on Fifty-ninth Street in Oakland symbolizes "Puerto Rico waking up inside her, uncurling and shoving open the door she had kept neatly shut for years and years" (84). At the same time, she identifies with her paternal grandparents, immigrants from Russia.

Although written by a single author, Sylvia López-Medina's *Cantora* also disrupts narrative individualism on several levels. Merging autobiography and fiction, López-Medina aesthetically amplifies the oral *testimonios* of her family to reconstruct the narrative of four generations of women, creating a "human bridge of voices" to the past (vii). The protagonist Amparo's search for her own identity and origins moves beyond individualism to involve the identity of other members of her family. Following the implications of her given name, Amparo will aid and give refuge to her family members by renaming them and rewriting their history. As her uncle tells her at the end of the novel, "Today, Amparo, you have set us all free" (300). Having been "kissed to consciousness by the Women's Movement" (viii), López-Medina presents her narrative as an oppositional rewriting of the history that patriarchy has attempted to repress; the names that patriarchal authority has changed and silenced will be resurrected and uttered publicly in *Cantora*.

Parallel to human memory, the novel weaves in and out of the past, with flashback scenes intercalated to substitute for indirect narrative retelling by the characters in the present. Thus, López-Medina cinematically amplifies the conventions of oral *testimonio* to bring key scenes before the reader in more immediate dramatic form. In many of these scenes, patriarchal authority rears its ugly head in violent repression of women—a father's unsuccessful attempt to arrange a marriage for his daughter Rosario, his banishment of her from the hacienda when she is in dire need, her daughter Pilar's rape outside a convent where she has been interned, and, finally, years later, her brother Victorio's abduction of Pilar's newborn baby from Mexico to the United States because the Church will not baptize the infant or give her her father's name.

The preoccupation with names and their transformation structures the novel. Although the prologue opens with the words "My Aunt Pilar," in the epilogue the name is officially changed to "My Grandmother Pilar"; the narrative voice has repressed itself, only revealing at the end the secret identity it has hinted at throughout. Amparo's search for Pilar's real identity—and therefore her own—is the narrative desire that impels the plot forward. The power of naming is a battle waged within and against patriarchy and deployed on the pages of the novel as López-Medina intentionally misnames Pilar to parallel Amparo's state of knowledge. When Pilar's baby is abducted moments after her birth, the patriarchal figures of the uncle and father battle one another over who will possess the newborn and therefore name her; the baby's father, Gabriel, desperately prays: "Her name is Veronique. Her name is Veronique. Please God, her name is Veronique" (297). This elderly patriarch who has left his wife and grown children for Pilar, and who has literally purchased the right to live with her, is now himself the victim of another branch of patriarchal authority as his child is taken away.

Although some characters know the secret family history, they refuse to reveal it, while the task of the novel as a whole is to do precisely the opposite—to unmask the evils of patriarchy along with the true matrilineal heritage. Irony overcodes various characters' utterances in the novel as readers begin to suspect Pilar's true identity. And part of the finally revealed truth is the implication that Pilar herself knew about the abduction of her daughter when she buried Veronique's birth certificate with the baby's clothes in a trunk but chose to remain silent about it. *Cantora* deploys naming and fictionally amplified oral history to tease out the repressed truth of the family's collective autobiography. Personal identity is linked to the larger collective identity of the family, to women's struggle for autonomy, and to the control of naming.

The individual and the collectivity are also linked in Sandra Benítez's *A Place Where the Sea Remembers* (1993), which like Cisneros' *The House on Mango Street* and Fernández's *Intaglio*, is a hybrid narrative genre that merges the short story and the novel. Reminiscent of works such as Sherwood Anderson's *Winesburg, Ohio* (1919), Tomás Rivera's *. . . Y no se lo tragó la tierra/ . . . And the Earth Did Not Part*, and Nicholasa Mohr's *Rituals of Survival*, the text presents a mosaic of interconnected lives in a small seaside town in Mexico. The individual and community are intertwined through separate short stories that present narrative close-ups of eight characters who also weave in and out of one another's sections. The moral issues around which each story pivots connect the individual to the larger community, and the form of Benítez's novel echoes this imbrication.

Although not given a close-up narrative herself, the *curandera* Remedios provides an enclosing narrative frame at the beginning and end, as well as connective links in four vignettes intercalated with the other stories. Narrative is central to the *curandera's* practice because the townspeople are revived through telling her their stories, and she in turn transmits the tales implicitly to us. Working together with the sea, the unceasing witness of the townspeople's narratives, Remedios touches sea water to her tongue in a ritual gesture so that "the stories come" and "the sea retells" (2). The identity of the mysterious body that the sea hides, briefly alluded to in the introductory narrative frame, can only be revealed through the collective narrative in the ensuing chapters—a social rather than individual moral problem.

A central trope of the narrative on both the formal and diegetic level is that of prolepsis, fortune telling, and the gradual revelation that occurs throughout the novel and in individual stories. While the reader is only minimally discomfited at the beginning by the brief mention of a body in the sea, a more jarring readerly prolepsis occurs in chapter 10 when the previously pregnant sixteen-year-old Marta is casually referred to as living with her young son, although readers have not been advised that the birth has occurred. This passing allusion to the birth, as if it were in fact an analepsis, or flashback, parallels two other key images of the story—the telegram that arrives with a message about the past but concerns events still in the future for the character Justo, who will read it, and the fortunes that Justo sells to people on the beach to earn his living. Like the novel itself, whose plot is already written yet lies ahead in the future for the reader, the telegram, read to the illiterate Justo after much delay, will tell him about tragic events connected to his own past unethical behavior. The interchange of proleptic narratives whereby the person he has just sold a fortune to reads him his own "future" in the telegram parallels the interdependence of author and reader in the larger novel.

A related diegetic and rhetorical device is the image of the curse, through which the young, misguided Marta hopes to secure a home for her unborn baby. Perceiving that the community has failed her when her sister reneges on her promise to raise the child as her own, Marta hires the local *brujo* to relieve her of her burden by causing her sister's baby harm. Soon contrite, she approaches the *curandera* Rosario for a counter-remedy to undo the *brujo's* spell. Narratively, the magical curse on the unborn child functions like the motif of the fortune, or Justo's telegram, in which one's fate is already written. But because the characters and readers improperly decipher the meaning of the *brujo's* proclaimed spell, they experience unexpected reversals at the end. The novel both deliberately misleads us and tells us part of the truth when it says "Tonito was gone" (160), just as the *brujo* misleads through the double signification of his promise to Marta that through his spell her son would "no longer be a burden" (60).

Several of the moral errors in the novel involve the misreading of signs — the incorrect closure of univocity on polysemous signifiers, and a privileging of the self over the community. Marta, for example, interprets the *brujo's* words to signify "wresting the baby from her sister's womb" and "her own child taking its place in Chayo's arms" (61). Benítez signals the misguided moral justification people give themselves for such individualist solutions to their problems, noting that Marta was surprised at how correct her assent to the *brujo's* spell seemed to her. In another chapter, the photographer Fulgencio Llanos misreads the visual material signifiers that overlay the stranger who gives him a ride; the merchandise in the back of the gringo's "woody" station wagon and his physical appearance as a hippie do not in fact signify that the gringo is a thief about to steal Fulgencio's camera. Fulgencio's morally compromised attempt to escape with the gringo's car and leave him stranded on the beach comes full circle to be Fulgencio's own fate, although the gringo offers a higher moral ground by returning the valued camera as he departs.

In contrast, the ritualistic deployment of signs in certain forms of popular religiosity can have a much more salubrious effect. Remedios, for example, combines indigenous and Christian symbols on her "mesa santa," a home altar at which she performs alternative religious rituals that empower her as a person with knowledge and the powers of speech. Beto, the son of the fisherman César Burgos, in contrast, has lost the power of speech after the death of his mother and brothers in a highway accident.

If the form and diegesis of the novel are characterized by prolepsis and the telling of the future, the young boy Beto functions as a kind of anti-novel in which a future is precluded because no telling can take place. He is reintegrated into the larger community, and into the power of telling that the novel as a whole represents, by the deployment of signs in a roadside shrine to memorialize the site where his mother and brothers died. The double referents of the verbal signifier "concha" enable him to deploy one visual sign on the shrine to signify the other referent: the sea shells stand in for his mother, Concha. As the boy holds one of the decorations from the sea on the shrine with his fingertip, he is reminiscent of the *curandera* Remedios, who puts the sea water on her fingertip and into her mouth to symbolically begin the telling of the stories. Beto, too, will soon begin to tell his story as he places his mother's prized rebozo over the cross on the shrine "as if [the rebozo] were an offering" (100). The confessional narrative that then spills out of him functions as a talking cure and enables the father to assuage Beto's misdirected self-guilt for not having prevented the deaths of his loved ones. Benítez shows that the boy's individual recuperation through deploying the signs of popular religiosity can take place only with the material support and encouragement of several members of the local community.

History and the Autobiographical Simulacrum

In his study of Stendhal's autobiography, Louis Marin discusses the related effects of simulacrum that operate in both narrative fiction and autobiography. Narrative, which of course has been written by someone, often tries to appear to have been written by no one; a simulacrum functions because the narration's own power does not usually declare itself as such in the narration. In autobiography, this effect is reversed: simulacrum is at work, but now as a presence, not an absence. The autobiographical narrator openly declares the power of simulation, that she or he is creating a representation of real life.

Even though the autobiographic simulation is more open about its narrational power, it often functions as well to occlude its own simulation; that is, it establishes itself as testimonial representation: an accurate, firsthand account of the events in a person's life. Readers often forget the fictionality of the autobiographic mode, temporarily believing that they are experiencing life as it was at the time of the narrated events. In fact, it is even more important to evaluate the mediated history of the autobiographic mode because, although on one level it openly declares itself to be a simulation, on another it claims more truth value than does fictional representation. As Paul John Eakin has argued, the referential dimension of autobiographical texts is "vexingly un-verifiable"; autobiographical "truth" is an evolving content in which fact and fiction are "slippery variables." The self at the center of all autobiographical narrative is necessarily a fictive structure.[3]

Among the large number of narratives recently published by Latina women in the United States are several that introduce the autobiographical simulacrum to varying degrees, thereby invoking questions about the individual and the subject's link to history. There are openly autobiographical texts such as Judith Ortiz Cofer's *Silent Dancing: A Partial Remembrance of a Puerto Rican Childhood* and Mary Helen Ponce's *Hoyt Street: An Autobiography*, implicitly testimonial narratives such as the first half of Lucha Corpi's *Delia's Song*, and autobiographical innuendoes established by postmodernist meta-narrative devices in the fiction of Cristina Garcia, Carmen de Monteflores, Sandra Cisneros, and Julia Alvarez. And writers such as Cofer and Alvarez have published companion texts in which fiction and autobiography offer competing versions of real events, challenging the expectations that readers bring to both modes of narration. How do these writers variously reveal and occlude their powers of simulation? As they move between fictive and auto-biographical narrative strategies, they interweave personal and public history, "sitting on the borderline," as Linda Hutcheon has argued, between the public and private spheres and showing the two to be inseparable (161). De Monteflores, Garcia, and Alvarez, for example, crucially link their personal narratives to Puerto Rican, Cuban, and Dominican history, respectively, as they engage in postmodern metanarrative strategies.

Sandra Cisneros foregrounds the constructedness of her fictionalized autobiographical narrative in the last section of *The House on Mango Street*.

> I make a story for my life, for each step my brown shoe takes.
> I say, "And so she trudged up the wooden stairs, her sad brown shoes taking her to the house she never liked."
>
> I like to tell stories. I am going to tell you a story about a girl who didn't want to belong.
>
> We didn't always live on Mango Street. Before that we lived on Loomis on the third floor. . . . (101)

Reproducing the first paragraph of the book in this last section, Cisneros turns the text back on itself, allowing the narrative to declare its own power of simulation, estranging the text as an elaboration of the real. In *Woman Hollering Creek and Other Stories* she encodes the name "Anguiano," that of her maternal grandmother subtly mentioned in the dedication, into the fictional diegesis as the last name of the childhood friend Lucy in the first story, and later as the unfriendly owner of the religious goods store. Subtly, then, with a hint of utopia, Cisneros inserts into the narrative her real childhood desire to have a sister through the use of the documentary name. And through other accurate autobiographical references in the book, such as the real address of her paternal grandfather in Mexico City, Cisneros forces the text to inhabit the increasingly porous border space in postmodernism between fiction and autobiography.

Norma Cantú delights in the mutual imbrication of the fictional and the autobiographical in *Canícula* (1995). Inspired by the death of Roland Barthes in 1980 and the publication shortly thereafter of his book on photography, Cantú departs from a series of historical family photographs to create poetic remembrances of her family's narrative that are simultaneously veridical and fictional. She notes that "the story is told through the photographs, and so what may appear to be autobiographical is not always so. On the other hand, many of the events are completely fictional, although they may be true in a historical context" (xi). Sitting on the border between the two genres, as Hutcheon has argued, a writer can have it both ways as Cantú does here: "although it may appear that these stories are my family's, they are not precisely, and yet they are" (xi). Readers are to be wary of the easy trap of autobiographical truth, as Cantú celebrates the emphasis of postmodernism on the continuum between fiction and reality.

Judith Ortiz Cofer's *The Line of the Sun* (1989) employs a transformative postmodernist technique as its ending that reconfigures the reading experience of the entire text. A postmodernist mixture of fiction and autobiography, the novel uses first-person narration and recounts many of the same events foregrounded openly as autobiographical in Cofer's subsequent book, *Silent Dancing*. Throughout *The Line of the Sun*, then, the veridical aura of autobiography overpowers the elements of simulacrum implicit in the text's generic self-positioning as fiction. The narrative events appear to be truthful events from Cofer's life.

The last paragraph of the novel explodes this documentary level of the text as Cofer foregrounds the representationality of the entire narrative. In this coda she refutes the closed ending she has given the novel in the previous paragraph, in which the transgressive Uncle Genaro falls blindly in love with a religious zealot and marries her, in effect surrendering to the modes of behavior prescribed by the ideological state apparatuses. Instead, through the alternative postmodernist ending, both the veridical trappings of the novel and the triumph of the ISAs are called into question:

> Guzmán's story did not end happily at the altar as all good fairy tales and love stories should. It continued through my mother's letters and in my imagination until one day I started writing it for him. And when I reached the part where he arrives with his beautiful new wife at La Cabra's valley . . . when she makes him kneel down right there in the mud and swear to her that he will never sin again . . . and when he actually kneels and swears for the hunger he feels in his heart—right at that point, when he and I tell our best lie, I say, this is the end. (290–91)

The text subverts itself here, openly declaring its own simulation. Now the entire novel is foregrounded as a representation, an arbitrary, selective, and imagined rendering of the past that lies because it only partially reveals the truth. Just as Cofer retrieves Genaro from recapitulation to the dominant moral order by revealing as a lie his promise to his new wife, so too does the text save itself from being read only as autobiography by foregrounding here the modes in which it has mediated reality throughout. Neither the narratorial "I" nor the figure of "Genaro" are to be trusted entirely. Although Cofer employs a documentary level in the text, at the same time she subverts it, never intending that the contradiction be resolved.

The Romance of Politics and the Politics of Romance

I turn now to two contrasting versions of the autobiographical simulacrum to study the problem of truth value, personal history, and the political. Lucha Corpi begins her novel *Delia's Song* (1989) with an implicit testimonial subtext, a narrative rendering of the violent struggle on the University of California, Berkeley campus in 1969 to establish a Department of Third World Studies. Judith Ortiz Cofer openly positions her 1990 *Silent Dancing* within the autobiographical mode, recounting her youth and adolescence in Puerto Rico and New Jersey. Corpi's fictional simulacrum, encased within a third-person narrative, engages much more problematically with history than does

Cofer's text, even though the latter positions itself as a subjective narrative focused on the individual.

Corpi's narrative simulacrum, with its implicit autobiographical subtext, sets up expectations in its opening pages that it will offer a counterhegemonic rewriting of history. Importantly, the novel counters the oblivion of the 1980s and 1990s concerning the political activism of the 1960s that enabled departments and programs of ethnic studies to be established on university campuses. Not only does the narrative begin to close these gaps of mainstream history, but it remedies the omissions of historians of countercultural periods such as Todd Gittlin, who in *The Sixties: Years of Hope, Days of Rage* (1987) does not mention the Third World Strike at Berkeley. Further, Corpi's text adds this important level of subjective, everyday life to the usual work of Chicano historians on the period.

Already in the initial narrative segment of *Delia's Song* a counterpoint is established between the political and the personal: the student strike at Berkeley and the protagonist's romantic interests. Interspersed with important details of the Third World Liberation Front coalition (including courageous supporters such as secretaries who passed on information, and the spontaneous use of everyday objects as weapons against police force) are details of the cat-and-mouse romance games of Jeff and Delia. A paragraph that begins with ruptural images of police intervention in a demonstration, for example, ends with Delia's romantic worries.

> Dark glasses Helmets at hand Clubs Gas canisters. . . . Twisted faces of people in pain The pungent smell of blood and gas The sound of clubs against skulls arms legs Glass shattering Screams then cold silence Paralysis. . . . February 19 The inevitable Police attack in full force Mace is used for the first time on campus I was writing the words I felt nothing Nothing Thinking of Jeff We never went riding Never another kiss. . . . Don't go Please don't go I wanted to say that to Jeff. . . . (32)

Progressively throughout the novel, history becomes a backdrop to the protagonist's romantic interests. What begins as a counterpoint moves to an ultimate privileging of the individual over the social so that romantic discourse undercuts political discourse in the text. The key means by which the narrative moves toward closure is the pivotal question, "which man will Delia choose?" The student-activist Jeff whom Delia has desired but not had a love affair with in the first section of the novel almost magically appears on her

doorstep years later ready to begin a relationship with her. Even his romantic language relegates history to a backdrop: "I wonder what it would be like
to make love to you among the [library] stacks. Good fucking in the middle
of all that knowledge, with the ghosts of the Californios bearing witness . . .
Vallejo, Moraga, Martínez, Cabrillo. . . ." (125).

Might this intercalation of history and romance be understood as a useful
representation of reality's overdetermination? Carl Gutiérrez-Jones has cor-
rectly foregrounded the competing modes of reading built into texts such as
Alejandro Morales' *The Brick People*; the presentation of "a collision of world
views" in the work of such writers as Morales, Ralph Ellison, Gabriel García
Márquez, and Oscar Zeta Acosta is a fitting representation of the overdetermination of reality. It is true that reality is often inflected with various "embattled ontologies," as Gutiérrez-Jones notes, and one might argue that Corpi
in *Delia's Song* is merely delineating the conflicting constituents of Delia's
overdetermined reality. However, Corpi weights one element of this complex
structure, privileging the romantic as the primary optic through which reality
is presented.

The movement from the political to the personal in this novel culminates
in Delia's self-discovery at the end, her decision to stop living the nightmares
that have plagued her: ". . . I want my life. I'm tired of being what someone
else wants me to be . . . being afraid of myself, always asking for forgiveness"
(190). She has "found" herself by escaping from the turmoil of the struggle
for social change and writing an implicitly autobiographical novel with the
requisite doses of postmodernist self-referentiality. She will test her new self-
confidence by engaging in the risk of allowing the people whom she writes
about as fictional characters (such as Jeff) to see the novel she has written —
the text we are reading. The fictional simulacrum appears to foreground itself
here, hinting at its autobiographical basis in real life, but in fact disguises the
narrative escape from politics beneath the guise of personal self-discovery.
Rather than delineating the politics of the personal here, Corpi has substituted the personal for the political.

Where Corpi develops the romance of politics, Ortiz Cofer in *Silent
Dancing* emphasizes the politics of romance. In both the principal narrative
and its tributaries, Cofer recurrently includes political details when recounting episodes of romance. For example, when as a young girl her Aunt Felicita
fell in love with a black boy, Cofer's grandfather threatened to cut the suitor in
half with a machete; he then beat both his daughter and wife, keeping them
imprisoned in the house. "There was talk at the time that the [suitor] may have
been fathered by the old man, who kept mistresses but did not acknowledge

their children. For his pleasure he nearly always chose black women" (40–41). Here a narrative satellite, exterior to the principal plot, parallels the racial and gender antagonisms of romance that Cofer will develop in the main story.

Cofer's observations about her "invisibility" to a boy with whom she wanted a romantic involvement early in high school are reminiscent of the theories of Sartre and Fanon: "In my mind there was no doubt that he would never notice me (and that is why I felt free to stare at him—I was invisible)." She adds, "He could not see me because I was a skinny Puerto Rican girl, a freshman who did not belong to any group he associated with" (125). Although "invisible" on one level in part because of the racial/ethnic politics of her New Jersey school, the young Cofer will transgress by appropriating the look of the Other, engaging in the techniques of erotic pleasure of the surveyor as she stares at her love object as often as possible.[4]

In recounting another of her youthful romantic adventures, Cofer again introduces the issue of race but this time seems to elide quickly over it: "I had two admirers: one black, one white, both handsome" (138). Although she at first attributes her mother's objections to the black boy to racial prejudice, Cofer states categorically, "soon I realized that race had nothing to do with her concern; she had just heard that Wilson was rapidly developing a reputation as a womanizer, and she was afraid that he would violate the limits of propriety if I gave him the chance" (138–39). Here, the autobiographical narrative voice that has appeared so openly to declare its presence throughout the text might indeed mask issues of race precisely as it appears to take them into account. For how, one wonders, might this suitor's race be separated in the mother's consciousness from the potential threat he poses to the young Judith's virginity?

Cofer's individual story is strongly rooted in the community and history. Autobiographical details of her first experience of schooling in Puerto Rico recount the effects of the U.S. conquest on everyday life in the classroom. Cofer relates her father's various lengthy absences from home as a member of the U.S. Navy to the specific historical interventions in which the United States was engaged during her childhood, including the Bay of Pigs and the Cuban missile crisis. She also alludes to the past immigrant history of the now Latino barrio in New Jersey where she spent some of her early years.

The community in which the partial autobiography is rooted involves strong family figures such as Cofer's maternal grandmother, who insisted on a room of her own as she raised eight children, and as chapter 5 demonstrates, a series of transgressive community figures whose stories become essential elements of Cofer's personal tale. Cofer links, for example, the story of a gay man who was her family's neighbor in New Jersey to the isolation and loneliness often experienced even in traditional nuclear families. She draws a parallel between her family's inability to communicate with one another after her father's return from "six months isolated on a ship circling Cuba" (114) and the solitude of her gay neighbor: "Sal, we are as alone as you: locked inside the bodies of strangers, unable to touch the ones we love the most" (115). Several transgressive Others like Sal are essential constituents of Cofer's personal autobiography rather than functioning as local color or historical backdrop.

Latin American History from the U.S. Side of Immigration

Julia Alvarez, like Cofer, integrates important community and social issues into the partially autobiographical *How the García Girls Lost Their Accents*. Alvarez's narrative is necessarily imbricated with history given the exacerbated pressures of the nearly defunct thirty-year dictatorship of Rafael Trujillo in the Dominican Republic, which forced her family into exile in the United States in 1960. Importantly, Alvarez's literary account of her family's final day on the island in the 1991 novel and a companion text, a 1987 autobiographical essay "An American Childhood in the Dominican Republic," present a firsthand insider's testimony about the U.S. role in the attempted overthrow of Trujillo, providing historians with a perhaps unexpected source of information about the events after unsatisfactory official reports left the issue of U.S. involvement delineated only ambiguously.[5] For here, in fictional and autobiographical narratives intended for other purposes, readers can glean everyday details of the involvement and rapidly changing policies of the U.S. State Department and CIA etched in the childhood memories of a U.S. Latina writer some thirty years after the events.

Nonetheless, the many Americans unfamiliar with twentieth-century Latin American history must do further reading beyond Alvarez's novel and essay to fully understand the novel's autobiographical elements. Although set in both the old country and the new one, the novel is more generous with information about the United States. Specific details about the history and politics of the Dominican Republic during her childhood seem to recede to a certain degree, as does human memory. It is as if the adult Alvarez recounts the tumultuous events in the Dominican Republic that resulted in her family's exile with the same level of historical detail that she would have known as a child. Where Alvarez consults scholarly books to augment her knowledge of Dominican history for the subsequent novel *In the Time of the Butterflies*, set entirely on the island, *García Girls* prioritizes the U.S. setting with Dominican history only as a backdrop. Thus, readers must turn to other sources outside the text if they wish more historical detail than the novel provides.[6]

Many U.S. readers, for example, are not likely to understand the historical significance of Alvarez's passing references in the novel and essay to the phrase "God and Trujillo," the "Era of Prosperity," and the Dominican World's Fair. Such narrative subtleties point readers only minimally to the larger social phenomenon of the time in which a neon sign with the phrase "God and Trujillo" was raised over the harbor of the capital, the slogan pervaded media discourse, and the press, professional organizations, and government edicts proclaimed the dictator the country's first lawyer, first engineer, and first intellectual; village water spiggots bore the sign "Trujillo Gives Us Drink," and hospitals displayed the slogan "Trujillo Cures Us." Trujillo's economic control of the country involved an estimated three-quarters of the employed population working for him, and it was argued that one could not eat, drink, smoke, or dress in the Dominican Republic without to some degree benefiting the dictator or his family.[7] The so-called "Peace Fair" (Feria Internacional de la Paz) in 1955, designed to celebrate the twenty-fifth anniversary of the dictatorship's alleged "Era of Prosperity," was economically disastrous for the country.

Alvarez makes only passing reference in the essay to her father's exile for nine years to Canada after his involvement in the "student underground." It appears this exile occurred from 1941 to 1950, but it is difficult to ground his participation in the Trujillo opposition in specific historical detail. Alvarez alludes to "two invasions" of the island, a term that many U.S. readers will not understand as referring to the landing of exiled leftist rebels on June 14 and 20, 1959, in a failed attempt to overthrow Trujillo. Readers might also be confused about the time frame in Alvarez's allusion to Trujillo's massacre of fifteen to twenty thousand Haitians on the Dominican side of the island, from which the family's long-time maid, Chucha, escaped, seeking refuge in the grandparents' home. "There's a river the bodies were finally thrown into that supposedly still runs red to this day, fifty years later" (218), Alvarez notes, confusingly suggesting that the massacre occurred in 1910, fifty years prior to the diegetic "day" (1960), rather than in 1937, fifty years before the writing of the novel.

American readers may be struck by Alvarez's description of the first modern grocery store, opened on the island by an ex-marine from Illinois who had participated in the earlier U.S. invasion. Only those unfamiliar with U.S. colloquial connotations could decode, as the child Alvarez remembers herself doing, the store's name as the epitome of the elegant and upper class. "Wimpy's" was an "elegant-looking" storefront, Alvarez notes, "No garish sign announced that this was Wimpy's. Instead, on the glass itself in dashing script was his signature—*Wimpy's*, the tail of the *y* underlining the whole word" ("American Childhood," 75). While readers may enjoy the irony of the cultural clash here, an important political detail remains unresolved. Was this American businessman the "Wimpy" involved in the overthrow of Trujillo in May 1961?[8]

An important positive deployment of history in *Garcia Girls* is the detailed, subjective side of one day of history represented in the story "The Blood of the Conquistadores" through a series of distinct narrative perspectives. Several sections outwardly deploy third-person narration while presenting the point of view of the character first named in the segment (for example, "As Laura nears her driveway, she honks the horn twice to alert the guard to open the gate, but surprisingly, it is already open" [200]). The perspectives include those of the adults and children of the de la Torre family, Trujillo's henchmen who come for the father, Mr. Vic Hubbard—the U.S. CIA agent who befriends the family, the family's black Haitian servant, and the Dominican woman who runs the El Paraiso brothel from which Mr. Vic has to be called for the emergency. Remedying some of the shortcomings of traditional linear historical narration, Alvarez engages in postmodern narrative shifts to enact a fuller representation of a moment of crisis in Dominican and personal familial history. And, as I argued in chapter 1, she makes crucial connections in this narrative between the legacy of Spanish and U.S. colonialism in the Dominican Republic, military dictatorship, and the patriarchal oppression of women.

Alvarez's 1989 story "The Summer of the Future" similarly joins personal and larger historical moments of crisis in a re-elaboration of the autobiographical simulacrum. An adolescent girl's rite of passage is narratively juxtaposed to the tumultuous political events in the Dominican Republic in 1963.[9] Public and private history converge both chronologically and thematically; Alvarez builds upon a chronological coincidence to elaborate the homologous structures of power that obtain in the public and private spheres. Although history is only briefly alluded to in the manner of a backdrop to the main events of personal history in the story, the implicit homology between the gender politics of the protagonist's rite of passage into womanhood and the political turmoil at the time in the Dominican Republic foregrounds the important issues of gender politics and patriarchal power.

The movement from childhood to adult female sexuality, for which menstruation functions as a metonymic sign, is as turbulent an event in the private sphere as is the political turmoil in the Dominican Republic in the years following Trujillo's assassination, Alvarez suggests. The euphemism "down there" is the common semanticization of the troublesome spaces of public and private history: the masculine space of political unrest on the island is signified in the father's discourse as "down there," just as the women of the family refer to the troubled space of their reproductive organs, the site of menstruation and incipient sexual activity, as "down there." The blood of the uncle's war wounds in the Dominican Republic is analogous to the two sisters' menstrual blood; one blood reminds the narrator of the other because both involve the exercise of power to control property—a national territory and a father's daughters. As men fight for political control of the island, girls are guarded more closely after menstruation in patriarchal attempts to control their sexuality. Like the men who carefully guard the secret of their rebel activities against the dictator Trujillo, the narrator's sister, fearing an increase in restrictions, refuses to tell her parents she has begun to menstruate. The entrance of girls into the realm of adult sexuality parallels the subversive activities of the father and his Dominican comrades, where metaphorical and literal prison bars attempt to discourage and control the troublesome activity. The older sister, who has already menstruated, attempts to alert the younger sister to the repressive control that she will soon also be subject to: "[Lydia] rolled her eyes as if all around there were prison bars. And to top that, she had to share her cell with me, who didn't even see them" (54).

Alvarez's narrative emphasizes the parallel violence that accompanies change in the private and public spheres. The execution of the girls' uncle in a Dominican prison during the 1963 turmoil produces a bloody wound in his side parallel to the narrator's first menstrual blood stain. The violence enacted against the uncle by the political power controlling the island parallels the imitative violence the teenage girls at the camp enact against the older sister, in which her movement into the sphere of adult sexuality is forcibly displayed semiotically in the public sphere. Just as their parents attempt to control them as they move into womanhood, they attempt to control one of their peers who has already entered puberty; they "imprison" and strip the older sister in the transgressive site of the camp bathroom so that the overt signs of her entrance into adulthood—developed breasts and blood-stained underwear— are publicly displayed. The episode reveals to the narrator that a parallel violence links the "strange, new country" (62) to the one they have left.

Although details of life in the United States predominate in *García Girls* and "The Summer of the Future," Dominican history and politics take center stage in Alvarez's 1994 novel, *In the Time of the Butterflies*. Now American readers must remedy the myopic narratives of history taught in many U.S. schools and become interested in the important history of a small Latin

American country many can scarcely locate on a map. Alvarez fictionally elaborates upon the true story of the Mirabal sisters, known as "Las Mariposas," who fought in the underground opposition to Trujillo and were brutally assassinated in 1960 by his forces. The book might be viewed as a kind of collective autobiography or *testimonio* of the women, both fictionally and historically reconstructed by another because the subjects themselves are not able to do so. Thus, a contemporary feminist U.S. Latina writer re-reads her first country's political history through important female political icons, insisting that the U.S. mainstream come to terms not only with recent Dominican history but with non-official versions of that history. Alvarez thereby refocuses the thematics of U.S. Latina narrative on a more hemispheric understanding of Latino identity, as have others such as Alejandro Morales, Cristina Garcia, Helena María Viramontes, Demetria Martínez, Graciela Limón, Arturo Arias, and Rubén Martínez.[10] With the increasing erosion of geographic and metaphorical borders in the current age of postmodernity and transnationalism, Alvarez narratively recuperates Dominican history as if it were a normal and necessary part of the narrative of U.S. history. And the history lesson is not such a bitter pill to swallow after all; her compelling book received important attention in national publications and by 1996 had a movie contract.[11]

Narrative disclosure is central to the text, both in the overall fictive re-elaboration of the Mirabal sisters' story and in the installment episodes of various moments of their lives intercalated throughout the book. The paratextual material with which readers begin includes a memorial "wall of names" of some of those killed under the Trujillo regime printed on the front and back inside covers; a dedication "For Dedé," the surviving sister; and an "In Memoriam" page listing the names and life dates of the four people killed in the Mirabal assassination by Trujillo forces in the last months of his dictatorship, names that were emphasized in boldface on the inside cover. The text of the novel will amplify these minimal texts, which are not yet narratives, moving primarily in chronological order from the girls' late childhood and early adolescence to their murder in 1960. Alvarez focuses on each of the four sisters in turn, in three periods of the assassinated girls' lives: the first disillusion with the deified icon of Trujillo in late childhood and early adolescence, the politicization of the girls in their twenties and early thirties and their participation in the armed struggle to overthrow the dictatorship, and the last months of their lives, January to November 1960, when they were killed at ages 25, 34, and 36.

Alvarez conflates physical and psychological rites of passage by narratively situating Minerva Mirabal's early disillusion with the deified Trujillo at the precise moment of her passage from childhood to adolescence. The diegetic disclosure of forbidden speech, the so-called "secret of Trujillo," occurs simultaneously with the onset of menstruation; Alvarez thus recuperates the homology developed in the story "Summer of the Future" between the public and private spheres, the personal and the political. Minerva's friend Sinita forbids herself to speak about the political for fear she will be killed, but narrative disclosure ultimately prevails. As Sinita finally tells Minerva the secret of Trujillo—narrating the dictator's assassinations of Sinita's uncles, father, and brother—Minerva's "tummy ache" begins again and Sinita's story "spill[s] out like blood from a cut" (18). The menstrual cramps that Minerva reads as a "tummy ache" correlate to Sinita's difficulty in narrating the dangerous story and to Minerva's reluctance to see the underside of the defied Trujillo, whose picture "hung on the wall by the picture of Our Lord Jesus" (17) in hers as in most Dominicans' homes. When Minerva realizes at the end of the segment that her female "complications had started," her political disillusionment with Trujillo is associated forebodingly with the motif of blood— the symbolic blood of the narrative that will not stop flowing, the blood of Sinita's brother, her own menstrual blood, and the ultimate blood of her and her sisters' future assassination.

In the case of María Teresa (called "Mate"), who is nine or ten in the first narrative segment, narrative disclosure occurs semi-secretly beneath the cover of a private diary. Because the name of a political activist who fools the regime by disguising herself as a nun appears in the diary, it becomes a forbidden text that Mate's older sister insists be buried in the yard, as will secret papers and arms later in the girls' lives. The novel as a whole fights against the interdiction of utterances as simple as a girl's first name by advancing the narrative even as it describes the silencing of narrative.

Whereas Mate's early disillusionment with Trujillo involves the prohibition of expression in her diary, the moment of truth for the third sister, Patria, occurs in a conflation of the personal, the political, and the religious. After suffering a miscarriage, the extremely religious Patria finds the truism "It's the Lord's will" to be a string of empty signifiers. Seeing the parallel between her loss and the deaths of Dominicans and Haitians at Trujillo's hands, Patria looks up to challenge the picture of the Good Shepherd next to Trujillo's in the Mirabal home and finds that the two faces have merged. Shortly thereafter, she realizes that she has been facing the wrong way at church, that the miraculous Virgin will appear across the weary, upturned faces of the congregation behind her, not at the shrine. These two early instances of merged visual images during a rite of passage foreshadow later moments in the novel when the Catholic Church will make political pronouncements against the dictatorship from the pulpit, and when a religious retreat is shelled by the military in retaliation for the "the invasion" or landing of exiled leftist rebels on the island in June 1959. The Fourteenth of June movement is then born in subsequent political organizing in the church setting. Like that of her sister Minerva, for whom political consciousness and menstruation occurred together, Patria's political coming of age is associated with difficulties in childbearing and later with the fatal wounding of her figurative "son" in the shelling of the retreat house.

In contrast to the larger narrative flow of profuse fictive detail about the lives prematurely terminated by the dictatorship, the text censors itself at two moments. In one form of self-censorship, pages are deleted from Mate's prison diary, and in the description of a torture scene she submits to a human rights commission, the names of the prisoners are blacked out as if the text were a subversive copy of a government intelligence agency document. In the second mode of self-censorship, the narrative stops itself at the moment the girls begin to drive toward the site of their imminent ambush. Although narrative details of the actual assassination will be reconstructed posthumously, as it were, in the novel's epilogue, the text's self-silencing here creates an enormous feeling of loss, lack of proper closure, and disruption. Although abundant narrative disclosure is central to the text throughout, Alvarez halts the flow at this strategic moment to parallel the diegetic moment of closure when Trujillo halts the girls' and their driver's lives.

Although Roberto González Echevarría contends that history in the novel is very blurry because the text does not correlate fictive events to larger social movements and pivotal historical events, I disagree; Alvarez does, in fact, achieve this correlation, and more pointedly here than in any of her previous texts. U.S. readers learn specific and thorough lessons about several key aspects of the Trujillo period, the U.S. role, and the everyday life of those important, ordinary people in the Dominican Republic who struggled for social change and justice.[12] U.S. Latina narrativists such as Alvarez are compelling the American public to understand this ostensibly unimportant history and enabling them to go beyond the multiculturalist or tropicalized views of Latin American history so abundant in the mainstream.

Earlier I argued that Demetria Martínez, Graciela Limón, and Helena María Viramontes similarly involve U.S. readers in the contemporary history of El Salvador. Limón carries readers farther back into Latin American history, to the colonial period in the 1996 novel *Song of the Hummingbird*. Previously, in the 1990 novel *María de Belén: The Autobiography of an Indian Woman*, Limón deployed a multiply overlain autobiographical simulacrum to narrate the life story of a fictional *mexica* woman who witnessed the conquest of Tenochtitlán. In the 1996 novel, Limón adapts the multivocity of the first historiographic text into a confessional *testimonio* primarily rendered as dialogue. Now an embattled conversation is narratively re-enacted between the same fictional woman, the eighty-two-year-old Huitzitzilin, and a young Franciscan friar, Benito Lara, who has come at her request to hear her last confession. In fact, however, wishing to tell her story as *testimonio* rather than follow the rubrics of the Catholic sacrament of confession, Huitzitzilin becomes the more powerful of the duo both because of her superior narrational position in knowing the story, and her interlocutor's desire for narrative information.

The rhetorical battle waged in the text between the rubrics of confession and those of the *testimonio* is a microcosm of the larger struggle between the master narrative articulated by the official Catholic Church about the Conquest and the counter-narrative of a marginalized firsthand witness to the cataclysmic events. In both the confessional and testimonial sections of her narrative (a unified whole in her consciousness), Huitzitzilin's utterances threaten and destabilize the established order of the official Church. Father Benito tells his superior that the way in which the woman tells her story "makes me begin to wonder if what she has done is sinful or not" (57). These words in turn provoke attempted censorship and silencing from the religious superior: "Never, never repeat that to anyone. . . . You did not utter those words!" (58). In an effort to maintain safe, classificatory divisions, Father Benito frequently switches from writing to listening as Huitzitzilin speaks, putting down the quill to pick up the sacramental stole when the narrative enters the arena of what he views as personal sin. Because there is no separation between personal and public sin in Huitzitzilin's alternative worldview, the narrative flow constantly transgresses these artificial borders, disrupting the discursive control that the priest would like to exert.

Huitzitzilin's oppositional narrative gradually begins to transform Father Benito's consciousness. While the indigenous religious practices she recounts do not triumph over the Christian beliefs of the conquerors in this alternative view of history, her narrative enables him to see that the conquerors' religious rituals were only "mutterings" to the native peoples and that in the name of proper Christian education, thousands of young children were taken from their mothers and sent to Spain. Huitzitzilin's rich narrative enables the young priest to understand her transgressions in the context of the everyday violence of the Conquest over decades; he ultimately substitutes mercy and forgiveness for his first impulse to bring her to justice for her sins.

Huitzitzilin transforms the conqueror's sacrament of confession into a means of obtaining another human being's forgiveness for the wrongs she has done rather than the forgiveness of the official Catholic deity as the sacrament prescribes. Her richly rendered counter-narrative transforms her interlocutor as it draws him in, as the unconventional chronicle he writes from her words is expected to do for future generations of readers. As have Alvarez, Martínez, and Viramontes, Limón draws U.S. readers into important events in Latin American history rendered through counter-narratives.

Interior and Exterior Views of the Self

Rather than setting her novel in a key historical period centuries ago as Limón does, Lucha Corpi in her 1992 mystery novel *Eulogy for a Brown Angel* employs history and the autobiographical simulacrum in an experimental fictionalized narrative rooted in the present moment. In *Eulogy* the protagonist, Gloria Damaceno, engages in first-person autobiographical narration in the first two-thirds of the novel; in the final third, Gloria's story continues eighteen years later, now narrated in the third person. This change in narrative voice parallels supernatural and psychic occurrences in the novel; the narrative moves from an inside, first-person view of the self to an exterior perspective on the action, parallel to the protagonist's description of her "out of body" experience on the second page of the novel: "For an instant, I felt that I was looking down at the child, at Luisa and at myself from a place up above while the action below me rushed, like an old film" (18).

The novel's "Prelude" encodes the first-person narrative voice with desire —not only for the solution to the mystery, but more specifically for Justin Escobar, the named narratee of the book's long first section. Gloria's autobiographical account of her discovery of a dead child during the Chicano Moratorium of August 29, 1970, and her efforts to find the perpetrator of the crime in this long first-person section are designated in the prelude as a lengthy elocution to Justin, whose energy made her "shiver . . . in excitement" as she extrasensorally experienced him as a blue light years before she would meet him. This "excitement" becomes progressively eroticized as the narrative proceeds, culminating in a kiss at the end of the novel. The process parallels what Dennis Porter terms the "erotics of narrative" (100), whereby the reader experiences pleasure through the two conflicting axes of detective fiction— that of progress toward the crime's solution and the impediments deliberately structured into the narrative to enhance the pleasure of the text through delay. The narrative by and about Gloria is not only overcoded with her desire for Justin but also with her and the readers' desire to solve the mystery.

Thus, the autobiographical simulacrum in this work is a narrative device both imbued with desire and linked to history. Although the story Gloria tells and participates in begins with the Chicano Moratorium, its roots and solution to the enigma lie in nineteenth- and twentieth-century Mexican and California history. Cecilia Castro-Biddle, whose mother was an adopted daughter of Vicente Peralta, the nineteenth-century owner of the land that is now the city of Oakland, leaves her studies at Mills College to give birth to a child out of wedlock in 1937. The baby is baptized Michael Cisneros Jr., and adopted by Mr. and Mrs. Cisneros of Oakland. Four years later, before the birth of their second son, Paul, Cecilia kidnaps Michael from Peralta Park in Oakland at the urging of Mrs. Cisneros' father, who resents his daughter's marriage. The child is quickly returned and the parents, fearing a scandal, say nothing to the police or press. The subtle suggestion is that Cisneros Sr. is the child's biological father, having "adopted" the baby from the young Cecilia after she had given birth to his child at a safe distance from Oakland in Mexico City.

The Cisneros' second child, Paul—whom the novel's resolution reveals to be the villain and perpetrator of the murder of the child at the Chicano Moratorium—has had a long history of sibling rivalry and resentment of his brother, Michael. As his grandfather had done years before, in 1970 he convinces the psychologically unstable Cecilia to kidnap his brother's four-year-old son during the Chicano Moratorium; Paul kills the child and then stuffs the corpse's mouth with excrement, re-enacting a childhood prank his brother had played on him years earlier. Unknown to Paul, he has killed his own son, for several years before he had raped his brother's wife, Lillian.

The issues of secret, contested, and unknown paternity and male sibling rivalry link the novel's events to Spanish, Mexican, and U.S. colonial history in the Southwest; contemporary Chicano history; protofascist international brotherhoods; and hostile transnational corporate takeovers. Cecilia aims to assert that she is both a direct descendent of Vicente Peralta and, in the strange kidnapping of 1941, that she is the mother of Michael Cisneros Jr. Although her mother was said to be the adopted daughter of the Peraltas, might not her mother also have been another biological daughter of Vicente Peralta, but not his wife's? In this way, the novel subtly foregrounds the repetitions of patriarchal power in the history of the Southwest, continuing through to the contemporary Chicano movement. The figures of Vicente Peralta, Michael Cisneros Sr., and Paul Cisneros carry through the tradition of secret or unknown paternity, "adoption" of the illegitimate child, and at the end, even filicide. Female figures in the novel such as Gloria Damaceno,

Cecilia Castro-Biddle, and Lillian Cisneros function as the conscience of history, revealing and asserting the occluded paternal lines.

Corpi links this female knowledge to the supernatural and extrasensory. A mysterious newspaper clipping found near the dead child causes Gloria great fear, nausea, and the repeated vision of a house near a park where an older man calls out for Michael. In addition to several "flying" or "out of body" experiences, Gloria recounts quite naturally the process of "[calling] on my newly-discovered powers to get more details about the killer" (75). She has visions of the future in which Lillian Cisneros painfully repeats the lyrics of "Un bel di" from Puccini's *Madame Butterfly* while a hand wearing a lion's-head ring wraps around Lillian's neck, which then becomes her own. Almost involuntarily, Gloria drives to a deserted lot where she witnesses Paul digging up an important metal box whose contents will help to restore the narrative equilibrium: "Paul's unearthing of his box was part of a plan that had been put into motion long ago. . . . Gloria had this knowledge buried in her psyche and it had driven her daily to the empty lot" (168–69).

Like the recurrent blue light, these supernatural experiences are linked to narrative desire and progress toward solving the mystery. This emphasis on the supernatural makes the novel unpalatable for some, and even Gloria remarks that she feels "touchy" about topics "that might put into question a woman's intellectual ability" (48). But as Porter has noted, the nineteenth-century detective story emphasizes "the powers of the mind beyond what is normally thought possible. Dupin's super-rationality borders on the supernatural" (25). While Corpi links several of the male figures in *Eulogy* to crime and death, female knowledge is encoded as a mode of super-ratiocination that deploys the psychic along with strong mental acuity.

Importantly, both the narrative device of the autobiographical simulacrum and the text's roots in history rely centrally on the racial problematics that underlie the history of the U.S. Southwest. The "brown angel" whose corpse is discovered when the novel opens is arguably a descendant of the early Peraltas and the family's various intermarriages with other Mexicans. Corpi links the sibling rivalry of Paul and Michael Cisneros for their mother's attention to racism in the larger society. Both Michael and his father are "brown," whereas Paul, whose mother was Swedish, did not look Mexican. Nonetheless, his private school friends taunt him that under his white skin he is brown like his brother and father. One day after school he scrubs his face with a hard-bristle brush until it bleeds, crying uncontrollably as he tries to put his schoolmates' charge to the test. His resentment of Michael is not merely because the brother gets more attention from their mother, but because Michael's brown skin serves to bring racial hatred upon him as well, reminding classmates of the family's Mexican heritage. Corpi carefully points out that racism transcends class lines; the filial hatred that results in the death of the "brown angel" child during the Chicano Moratorium is simultaneously a racial self-hatred fueled by the larger social practice of racism.

Unlike her first novel, Corpi employs the autobiographical simulacrum in *Eulogy* both as an enunciation overcoded with desire directed to the narratee Justin and as a contrasting discourse to the third-person narration that parallels the protagonist's out of body view of events. At the same time the text is importantly imbricated with the nineteenth- and twentieth-century history of Mexicans, Mexican Americans, and Chicanos in the Southwest and the accompanying legacy of racism. The novel both teaches and refreshes readers' memories about this history because the historical facts are crucial to the solving of the mystery.

In contrast to Corpi's explicit enunciation of the presence of an exterior view of the self in separate third-person sections of the narrative, Mary Helen Ponce outwardly appears to present only an interior view of the self. The central narrative voice of Ponce's *Hoyt Street* is the traditional autobiographical "I," and while it appears to be only an inside view of the author's life, we must remember that it is mediated by the temporally and socially "exterior" consciousness of the adult Ponce who now writes the narrative. Additionally, Ponce's interior view of the self is deeply rooted in history and the exterior world. In contrast to Judith Ortiz Cofer's acknowledgment that *Silent Dancing* is a partial remembrance of childhood, emphasizing the temporal and factual limitations of the text, Ponce employs the more totalizing subtitle "An Autobiography" to describe her narrative reconstruction of a limited period of her life ending with the onset of menstruation. So compelling and richly detailed is Ponce's lengthy narrative that one can easily fall under the mystique of the autobiographical simulacrum—the notion that one is experiencing an unmediated version of the past. Although Ponce reminds readers in the initial "Note from the Author" that she writes solely from memory uncorrected by corroborative historical research, she simultaneously claims a truth value for her narrative as a "communal history" (x). She is far from the postmodernist doubling of Cisneros' *The House on Mango Street* or Ortiz Cofer's *The Line of the Sun*, and at the opposite extreme from a Barthesian dissolution of the autobiographical self-construct into a kind of pure sign without a referent.

While Ponce does not explicitly engage with the autobiographical construction of the self as a fiction, or with Eakin's notion of the "slippery" nature of fact and fiction in autobiography, she quite successfully interweaves personal and public history, rooting the narrativized self in community and history. If we remind ourselves that the material she presents is highly mediated and constitutes only one point of entry into an understanding of the life of Mexican Americans in Pacoima in the 1940s, the text is a valuable and compellingly organized archive that gives us access to an important part of the past. Even the obviously fictionalized dialogue offers a clear, albeit mediated, sense of this period. We learn about the ordinary concerns of a young Mexican American girl (not one of the usual subjects of mainstream historical writing), popular traditions, everyday work and life in the Pacoima neighborhood in which she lived, the effects of World War II, special times such as *jamaicas* (Church fairs) and the circus coming to town, the integration of Mexican Americans into U.S. society, and the role of religion in her community.

Ponce notes that the autobiography began through religious remembrance and an oral history project in which she compared the Holy Week and Easter observances of three generations of her family. Indeed, an ethnographic tone imbues several sections of the text, pointing not only to an implicit documentary element in the narrative, but also to various implicit narratees who might need explanation of certain traditions, customs, and historical events outside of their own personal memories. With respect to the extensive description of religious practices in the text, which I discuss in greater detail in chapter 4, Ponce includes explanations to aid various "outsiders" who range from the non-Chicano or non-Catholic readers to Chicanos and other Catholics who themselves might be unfamiliar with certain popular religious practices.

Because Ponce roots the narrativized self in community and history, the book allows an important, if partial, point of entry into the rich experience of Mexican American immigrants and their children in Southern California in the 1940s. Proceeding from the feminist valorization of alternative forms of historical narrative such as personal life stories, Ponce includes important subjects such as menstruation and her relationship to her body and to food that are not usually the accepted subjects of historical narrative. And, as Sandra Cisneros has written for the back cover of the 1993 edition of the book, Ponce's project helps other Chicanos to know their history:

> For those citizens, like me, who have no history, who have stumbled among the rubble scavenging one's past, inventing, searching in between the lines of text, here is a cause for celebration. I am overjoyed to be invited into *la casita* on Hoyt Street . . . with its voices in English and Spanish and its Catholic rites and rituals. . . . Thank

you, Mary Helen, for placing your house on the map. . . . In naming your own life history on Hoyt Street you are also naming mine.

Cisneros' point is that the referent of Ponce's narrative is beyond the self; because the narrative is rooted in the life of the community, it merges the self
and history without foregrounding one or the other and provides valuable information about the history of a people that is only beginning to be written.

The balance between the individual and the social, the personal and the
political has been a recurrent literary problem. One solution developed by
the Cuban writer Alejo Carpenter in "Semajante a la noche" [Like the Night]
(1958) was to elaborate both synchronic and diachronic temporal planes in
which a single protagonist moves through a twenty-four-hour day while he
simultaneously recurs as a structural element in several centuries of human
history. In the new Latina narrative, both individualist and collective strategies
appear, sometimes in combination. The autobiographical and semiautobiographical narratives of writers such as Corpi, Ortiz Cofer, Ponce, and Alvarez
attempt to join synchrony to diachrony to present an accurate representation
of lived history.

To a large degree, Corpi, although she positions readers to expect an historical account because of the orientation of the first half of *Delia's Song*, fails
in this project of historical recuperation by allowing the discourse of romance
to predominate. Cofer, in contrast, whose text on the surface appears to contain less historical information, in fact manages often to integrate the personal
and the political, the individual and the community, and personal and social
empowerment. Similarly, Ponce offers a subjective narrative rooted in rich
historical detail that adds greatly to our understanding of Mexican American
life in Pacoima in the 1940s.

Alvarez, in the narrative of the García girls, succeeds in an important
synchronic elaboration of various cross-sections of daily life history in the
Dominican Republic at an important historical juncture. Although readers
must do more research themselves outside the text to learn important basic
facts about the Trujillo dictatorship and its aftermath, these historical attenua-
tions perhaps reflect the writer's own hazy memory of the past now that she is
so fully ensconced in U.S. society. The range of Alvarez's work includes, then,
a first novel in which history peeks a bit from the closet but remains primarily part of the background, and only marginally alluded to in the text; a
shorter narrative, "The Summer of the Future," in which the brutal Dominican military regime is read through gender politics; and the 1994 *The Time of
the Butterflies*, which is entirely imbricated with Dominican history.

The narrative simulacrum in the work of all of these writers, whether it is of the autobiographical or fictional variety or a combination of the two, must be deconstructed as a strategy of representation and evaluatively tested against other modes of understanding identity and history. By offering the beginning narrative details about the everyday lives and history of Latinos in the Americas, the new Latina narrativists point readers beyond the literary frames of these texts to other representations of lived experience. These narratives serve as invitations to the larger U.S. public to move beyond the myopia and shortcomings of the predominant First World views of the Latino Other, remaining all the while critical, demanding observers and readers.

CHAPTER FOUR

Remapping Religious Space: Orthodox and Non-Orthodox Religious Culture

As U.S. Latino writers work to reverse the melting-pot model of integration into U.S. society, they frequently foreground ethnic cultural markers that distinguish them from mainstream culture. Religious motifs are such markers, both facilitating narrative memory and serving as totemic signifiers of membership in a group. More importantly, however, these motifs are frequently part of a larger network of popular Latino religious practice with much broader functions than the mnemonic or totemic. In much contemporary Latina narrative the religious also emerges as a sense of social ethics and a new moral vision sometimes quite different from those of orthodox religion. Issues of social justice and the concerns of immigrants, feminists, gays, the landless, and other marginalized groups are articulated to the alternative religious practices narrativized in this new writing.

So pervasive is the religious imagery in new Latina narrative that I can focus here only on representative examples of Chicana, Puerto Rican, Dominican American, and Cuban American texts, omitting discussion of the deployment of religion in the writing of Graciela Limón, Ana Castillo, Pat Mora, Sylvia López-Medina, Carmen de Monteflores, Himilce Novas, Rosario Morales, and Aurora Levins-Morales, among others. The writers I discuss give testimony to the wide variety of spiritual practices among Latinos, including popular, syncretic, and official belief systems and rituals. An ethnographic dimension often underlies the description of religious practices in Latina narrative, for the writers embed explanations in the text to aid a variety of "outsiders," who range from non-Chicano or non-Catholic readers to Chicanos and other Catholics who themselves might be unfamiliar with certain popular religious practices. There are no privileged readers of these narratives who can be counted on to have "insider" knowledge of every aspect of religious culture in the accounts.

As have many theorists of subculture and popular expression, Orlando Espín has argued that popular religious practice re-reads official doctrines and rites, disregarding certain elements and giving a central role to other be-

Figure 4.1. Plaster statue of Santo Niño de Atocha, Chimayó, New Mexico

liefs, rituals, and behaviors that the official religious hierarchy de-emphasizes. Rather than completely abandoning official symbols, popular religion shares motifs, an ethos, and foundational figures and events with orthodox religion.[1] Latina narrativists engage in a similar rearticulation of Catholicism, emphasizing popular practices and alternatively interpreting mainstream symbols and doctrine. In some cases, writers carry this further, refashioning even the popular practices in light of contemporary social concerns. Denise Chávez and Sandra Cisneros, for example, reconfigure the both popular and official figure of the Virgin of Guadalupe, an official form of worship such as the novena, and popular religious practices such as those centered around *ofrendas, milagritos,* and ex-votos.

Figure 4.2. Tree-of-life candleholder, Mexico

The *altarista* Filomena in Roberta Fernández's *Intaglio* both preserves and adapts the rubrics of popular religiosity in the transborder sites of south Texas and Michoacán. Centered around Day of the Dead rituals and the assembling of *ofrendas* in honor of the dead on November 2, the story "Filomena" functions itself as an *ofrenda* for previous generations of Mexicans and Mexican Americans who, like Filomena, preserved and carried on important cultural traditions with dedication and love.[2] Rich in visual, olfactory, and auditory imagery, this verbal *ofrenda* arranges a variety of artifacts of popular religiosity: a quotation from Saint Francis as its epigraph, a tin *retablo* of the Holy Trinity, inexpensive statues of the Virgen de Guadalupe and Santo Niño de Atocha (fig. 4.1), tree-of-life candleholders (fig. 4.2), white sugar skulls

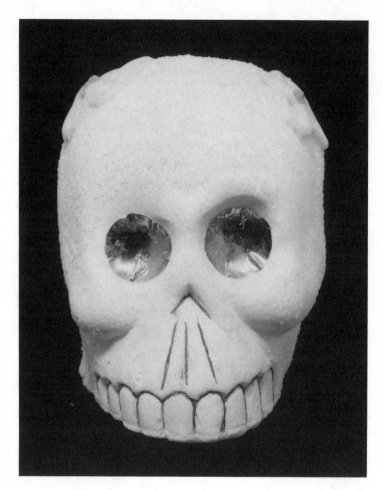

Figure 4.3. Sugar skull, Mexico

(fig. 4.3), miniature skeleton musician figures (fig. 4.4), crosses covered with yellow chrysanthemums, incense, and the melodious music of dozens of birds. For the narrator, the sensory richness of these Mexican forms of popular religiosity stands in contrast to the "strangely austere altar" (82) of official religion in the chapel at the university she later attends.

Filomena enlarges and redesigns her home altar in response to three moments of tragedy in her life—the deaths of her father, her husband, and finally her son.[3] Initially dedicated to La Virgen de San Juan de los Lagos (fig. 4.5), the altar begins to grow while her husband serves in World War II as she adds an offering for each month he is away. This prefiguring expansion of the altar is a preparatory ritual for its further enlargement after his death, when

Figure 4.4. Skeleton musicians, Mexico

she adds a picture of the sacred heart of Mary, a statue of Guadalupe, and a *retablo* of the Trinity. When her son, Alejandro, dies in the Korean War, she re-designs and reassembles the altar to include the birds and cages he had given her to remember him by before he left: "There she had hung her bird cages, seemingly to include the birds' warbles and the parrot's noisy voice as part of her offering. Moved by the beatific spirit of Filomena's simple heart, I took off my gold chain with the tiny medallion of the *Virgen de Guadalupe*, then placed it on the altar in front of Alejandro's picture" (71). The narrator, along with many of Filomena's visitors, will add symbolic ritual objects to the altar as they engage in the alternative spiritual rubrics of their popular religiosity.

Indeed, Filomena takes on the role of priest in the communal religious rituals she and her neighbors practice around her altar. After a pilgrimage to Michoacán for beautiful Day of the Dead rituals with other family members, Filomena returns to Texas from a sense of duty to continue the tradition for her loved ones buried there. The narrator, who accompanies her to Michoacán and has an epiphanic vision of the beloved Alejandro, learns that Filomena's apparent passive acceptance of the tragedies in her life in fact represents Filomena's taking charge of ritual and responsibility for her own spirituality. As

Figure 4.5. La Virgen de San Juan de los Lagos, popular holy card

an alternative priest and leader, Filomena, with her parrot Kika on her shoulder, leads neighborhood children (several of whom are characters in other stories in the collection) in Day of the Dead prayers around her expanded home altar. After the epiphanic vision of Alejandro is repeated, the parrot ensconces itself at the center of the altar as a reconfigured version of the Holy Spirit. Fernández invokes Flaubert's "Un coeur simple" with this image of the parrot, for Filomena's "simple heart" (71) is a Mexican American version of the Felicité figure in the nineteenth-century story.

"Filomena" examines the practice of representation in cultural and spiritual popular expression. The central motif of representation is echoed on several levels of the story. Just as Filomena and her real and surrogate families enact elaborate Day of the Dead rituals in Michoacán and Texas for Alejandro, who himself deeply loved ritual, so will Nenita, the narrator, enact a parallel "modern" version of the ritual by burying a drawing of Kiko along with Virgin of Guadalupe earrings as an *ofrenda*. Just as Filomena (and Felicité) substitute a parrot for the official image of the Holy Spirit, Nenita integrates into her modern *ofrenda* an icon of her own time—the Guadalupe earrings worn by Chicanas and others in the United States. Similarly, the story itself, as an *ofrenda* to Filomena and other ancestors, reminds readers about the strategies of representation in popular ritual practice that they may have forgotten about in assimilating to life in the United States. Rather than signifying a passive submission to one's fate, these material religious strategies allow people to take control of their spirituality and healing and must be carried on with new adaptations by each generation.

In *Woman Hollering Creek and Other Stories* Sandra Cisneros also employs religious motifs of a predominantly unofficial variety. Her greatest fascination is with material religious culture and alternative practices that mark a specifically Mexican variety of Catholicism.[4] As Luis Leal has noted, Cisneros completes a figurative pilgrimage from Mango Street to Tepeyac with the publication of the 1991 book (134). In attempting to recover an autobiographical past in stories such as "Mericans" and "Tepeyac," Cisneros employs public material symbols and practices peculiar to Mexican Catholicism rather than standard church ceremonies shared by Catholics around the world; the markers she chooses to represent these moments of her childhood are those religious symbols readily visible to the outsider as different from his or her own. Cisneros, the "Merican" child who visits her father's parents in Mexico City during the summer, views her grandparents' culture partially as Other, focusing on the particularly Mexican aspects of religious practice.

Autobiographical with fictional trappings,[5] these narratives centered on her grandparents foreground religion as one element of cultural identity in the unstable border space of Mexico City marked by migration, tourism, and cultural hybridity. The narrative remembrance begins as if it were a postcard scene at nightfall of the old Basilica of Our Lady of Guadalupe, which the young Cisneros sees at the end of each day when she meets her grandfather at his hardware shop. She twice remembers the commercialized religious symbols visible on the street—the photographers' canvas backdrops with the image of the Virgen de Guadalupe and the words "Recuerdo de Tepeyac," in front of which believers and tourists materially document their visit to the shrine (fig. 4.6). Although the basilica is a similar visual backdrop to her

Figure 4.6. "Mexican Backdrop Painter, Jacinto Rojas and Son," ca. 1989, Mexico City (from the permanent collection of the Museum of American Folk Art, New York, N.Y.; courtesy of the Museum of American Folk Art)

memory of her grandfather, she appends a verbal narrative to the image, moving beyond the touristic postcard and the souvenir photograph: "we walk past the basilica, where each Sunday the Abuela lights the candles for the soul of Abuelito. Past the very same spot where long ago Juan Diego brought down from the *cerro* the miracle that has drawn everyone, except my Abuelito" (22). The massive religious symbol is narrativized as personal family history and as part of the larger national context of Mexico's history as the adult Cisneros attempts to retrieve the irretrievable after her grandfather's death.

"Mericans," the story that memorializes Cisneros' grandmother, employs much more religious imagery because religion played a much more central role for her than for her husband. The grandmother's great religious devotion struggles for survival in the hybrid border space of Mexico City, where her Americanized grandchildren come to visit during the summer. For the young protagonist—"Micaela" to her grandmother but "Michele" to her brothers—Mexican religious symbols and practices exist in an unstable hybridity with contrasting cultural motifs. The American tourists who wish to photograph Michele and her brothers outside the cathedral are disturbed to learn that the children are not "authentic" Mexicans but rather "Mericans," border subjects who embody a wide range of cultural influences. For Cisneros' fictional persona Michele, the inside of the church in which the grandmother prays is like a movie, with statues of saints that appear to move and wink at her if she stares at them long enough; outside the cathedral, Flash Gordon, the Lone Ranger, and Tonto are the children's playtime identities. Even in emphasizing this hybridity, the story conveys a rich sense of the traditional religious culture that the grandmother strives to preserve to counteract not only her own family's indifference to religion but also the "barbaric" ways of her grandchildren's country.

As the grandmother drops pesos in the offering box, lights votive candles and genuflects, kisses her thumb after making the sign of the cross, and mumbles a litany of prayers for her unfaithful family outside, the devoted walk to church on their knees, some with rags and pillows to shield their legs. The young granddaughter, forced to kneel with her grandmother inside, feels her knees "grow fat as a mattress of pins" (19), an image that links her to the devoted worshippers outside, painfully making their way to the church on their knees with rags and pillows. The object of their devotion is the image of the Virgin of Guadalupe, preserved behind glass on the main altar "because she's a big miracle," in contrast to the bent crucifix relegated to a side altar "because that's a little miracle" (18). As Cisneros delineates the markers of Otherness that distinguish Mexican religious practice from traditional Catholicism, she lays the groundwork here for her feminist recuperation of the Virgin of Guadalupe figure later in the book in "Little Miracles, Kept Promises." Although she arrives at this alternate interpretation of the religious figure from her position as a border traveler between "barbaric" America and the Mexican homeland, it is precisely this position as an outsider that enables her to compellingly narrate these aspects of Mexican religious practice.

Religion, Politics, and the Confessional Narrative

Although Lucha Corpi's "Los Cristos del Alma" (1984) was published in Spanish and therefore not strictly within the purview of this book, it offers an important comparison to Demetria Martínez's *Mother Tongue* (1994) as a re-elaboration of the religious rite of confession, a device that Graciela Limón also employs in *In Search of Bernabé* and *The Song of the Hummingbird*. Corpi's and Martínez's narratives demonstrate the imbrication of religion and politics and the efforts of ordinary people to attain social justice. The protagonist-narrators of both stories move beyond the orthodox sacrament of Penance or Reconciliation by telling key elements of their troubled past to a nephew or son—narratives that at the same time enter the more public space of the printed page. Both confessions are also testimonies that inscribe the narratives of ordinary people into the larger historical master text; religious motifs, personal struggles, and larger political issues are equally important elements of these revisionist narratives.

In "Los Cristos del Alma," Corpi frames the protagonist-narrator's account of political turmoil in Mexico with traditional religious imagery. Paula, a sixty-year-old Mexicana who has lived in the United States for thirty-five years, narrates the story of her perceived egregious sin in a confessional monologue to her nephew as she nears death. The "Christs of her soul" are the figures of her father and brother, whom she killed with their acquiescence thirty-five years earlier in Mexico when, after the official party stole a local mayoral election, national troops were dispatched to quell the protests. When Paula's brother and father are imprisoned and sentenced to death, the local caudillo—whom she terms "la maldad hecha carne" [evil made flesh] (5)—insists that she decide which one of the two should be spared execution. Instead, she herself kills both prisoners, who tell her, "Que sea el dedo de quien en verdad nos quiere el que apriete el gatillo y no el del enemigo. Devuélvenos la dignidad" [Let the finger that pulls the trigger belong to someone who truly loves us and not the enemy. Give us back our dignity] (10). As in the case of Abraham with Isaac, she recounts, God tested her, "pero no me detuvo el brazo" [but he did not hold back my arm] (4). Her guilt is compounded a few days later by an earthquake that creates havoc and enables her and others to escape. "Si tan sólo hubiera temblado antes . . . Pero no. La tierra tiembla sólo cuando los cristos del alma yacen inertes en la cruz, atentos al segundo advenimiento del hijo del hombre" [If only the earthquake had happened earlier . . . But no. The earth shakes only when the Christs of the soul lie inert on the cross, alert to the second coming of the son of man] (12).

Convinced that she is condemned to hell, Paula has suffered for thirty-five years with this enormous guilt and looks forward to her own death as a kind of relief. The traditional Catholic practice of confession and penance has not been adequate to assuage her guilt; she cannot engage in the standard ritual of sin, confession, and prayer and become "limpiecita y olorosa a santidad como esta mañana" [as completely clean and smelling of sanctity as the morning] (4). Instead, she confesses finally to her nephew, whose father and grandfather she killed, as the church bells toll at the beginning and end of the narrative—this time for her.

Demetria Martínez's 1994 novel *Mother Tongue* is similarly framed as a testimonial and confessional narrative addressed to the narrator's son, who will come of age in the twenty-first century. As does Corpi's story, it deploys politically imbricated religious practices, but for Mary, the contemporary Chicana in New Mexico who is protagonist and narrator, religious imagery is rearticulated in predominantly non-orthodox modes. An activist in the Sanctuary movement in the United States, helping refugees from the civil war in El Salvador in the 1980s, she gives shelter to and falls in love with José Luis, a former seminary student persecuted by death squads after they assassinate his village priest during Mass. Religion and politics are mutually imbricated both in El Salvador and Albuquerque; in speeches to church activists in the United States, José Luis describes conditions in El Salvador: "People are hiding their Bibles. If you are caught with one, the authorities assume not only that you are literate but that you might press for change. The government wants us to go back to the days when the Kingdom of God referred to heaven only and not to what is possible on earth" (22).

Mary wears an Our Lady of Guadalupe T-shirt, acts out her emotional suffering by burning her finger above the flame of her Guadalupe candle, and frequently alludes to the anchoring image and bells of the San Rafael Church (San Felipe de Neri) in Old Town Albuquerque. The altar she arranges in her bedroom in 1982 contains the figures of Santo Niño de Atocha and the Virgin of Guadalupe, a film canister filled with holy earth from the sanctuary at Chimayó, a mouthwash bottle with holy water blessed by a priest, an African fertility doll, and a Taos Pueblo incense burner. In Mary's view, these eclectic religious objects are more hospitable than the traditional Catholic deity: "I liked it that José Luis and I made love in the presence of my santos. I knew they had blessed my love for him, however imperfect it was, however mad. They were not like the white God I'd had to kill, that women like me must kill if we are to have any hope of ever finding God" (59). Just as a number of Salvadoran Catholics adapted their religion to new goals of social justice, Mary and others involved in the Sanctuary movement rearticulate Catholicism. Later, as the couple's premature baby hovers between life and death, Mary's godmother, Soledad, advises her to "offer it up" (90). But the traditional resignation to God's will encouraged in orthodox Catholicism is rearticulated here for Mary as a newly learned political solidarity. Soledad's words, "Offer up your pain for the mothers whose children are disappeared," enable Mary to get through her son's crisis and to remember the narrative she is reconstructing: "What I cannot remember, I will invent, offer up my tales for those who were not granted time enough to recall, to mend" (91). The writing of the text we are reading becomes, then, both a political and spiritual project, a collage-novel parallel to the practice of liberation theology. In this revolutionary re-reading of traditional Christian doctrine in the years following Vatican Council II (1962–65), theologians and community groups focused attention on the growing scandal of massive poverty in the modern world. Liberation theologians in Latin America developed alternative re-readings of the Bible as a means of understanding and remedying the causes of poverty and the "social sin" it represents. The essence of Christianity, they argued, is to be concerned about the poor and how they might be helped to better their circumstances. (See, for example, Gutiérrez [1994, 1996] and Romero [1985].)

Traditional and nontraditional elements of material religious culture give solace and strength to Martínez's characters. While Soledad asks Mary to bless José Luis' shoes with holy water because they formerly belonged to a gunned-down *compañero* in El Salvador, José Luis himself recalls the image of holy water in the context of Salvadoran liberation theology: "Father Gustavo helped us to see that it was not God's will that we cross ourselves with holy water and die of thirst. . . . We decided that as a church project we would put in a communal well" (19). On the incubator holding Mary's premature baby, Soledad tapes holy cards of the Virgin, Saint Joseph, Saint Jude, and Rafael the Archangel along with rosary beads blessed in Lourdes. This "ad hoc committee of divine intervention" (88) gives her comfort, just as the *santos* and candles in a dark cantina reassure José Luis. Both the darkness and the *santos*, he believes, will prevent him from being detected as an illegal.

Although Mary's home altar is eclectic before she meets José Luis, it is transformed further with symbols of her personal and political knowledge by the end of the novel. Mary travels to El Salvador twenty years after the main events in the novel and photographs a Church file photo of José Luis as a *desaparecido* with his full name. On her return she modifies her home altar. Behind it she places a large poster, given to her by a bishop in El Salvador, depicting reconfigured Christ and Virgin figures as a Salvadoran mother and her disappeared son. In the lower corners of the poster she superimposes the reproduced photo of José Luis and one of herself at age seven when she was sexually abused; her act of lighting a candle before these three images above her reconfigured altar puts closure to her victimization mode, paralleling her telling the story of her painful life moments to her adult son, whom we learn is the diegetic narratee of the text we are reading. Fulfilling the *promesa* she made to God twenty years earlier in a plea to save her premature son's life, Mary with great difficulty reveals to her adult son (in a figurative or projected future moment in the year 2002) the political and personal pain underlying the story of his origins.

At the beginning of the narrative, the nineteen-year-old Mary rebels against orthodox Catholicism but at the same time envies the deep faith of the older women she sees leaving daily Mass. By the end of the novel, however, the thirty-nine-year-old Mary, at this time in the twenty-first century, combines Chicano religious practices with a reconfigured Catholicism linked to social justice, the legacy of solidarity between U.S. Latinos and Central Americans in the turbulent 1980s.

Caribbean Syncretism

Several U.S. Latina fiction writers of Dominican, Cuban, and Puerto Rican origin draw from both Catholic religious imagery and other popular practices such as Santería. Although ample narrative space is accorded to traditional Catholic motifs, elements of syncretic Yoruban-Christian imagery appear as well. The syncretic images are either the legacy of the slaves' attempts to hide the worship of their indigenous deities from the Spaniards beneath the images of Catholic saints (in the view of some theorists) or simply the worship of the same gods under different names.[6] Despite the secrecy that traditionally surrounds these nonofficial practices—a strategy of religious survival for generations of practitioners in the New World—writers such as Alvarez, Garcia, and Ortiz Cofer embed descriptions of these practices in their fiction from the perspective of insiders who are at the same time outsiders.

The primary religious motifs in Alvarez's *How the García Girls Lost Their Accents* involve the Catholic culture in which the girls were raised. Their grandfather, for example, is said in common family parlance to be so good and saintly that "he pees holy water" (227). Jealous of this praise for her husband, the grandmother allegedly serves him a whiskey mixed with holy water brought home from the cathedral, playfully endeavoring to make literal the figurative image. Just as Alvarez shows no reticence in mixing the sacred and profane in this scene narrated by Yoyo, she links religious imagery and sexuality in another story, "Still Lives," in which the second daughter, Sandi, narrates her own artistic awakening. Here, however, the triad of art, religion, and sexuality is imbricated with both Catholicism and non-orthodox beliefs.

Some perceive Sandi's early artistic talent as the site of magical powers. After she draws a crayon picture of the child of the nursemaid, Milagros, the boy takes ill; when candles, holy water, and a High Mass at the cathedral fail to revive him, Milagros insists that Sandi release the child from the spell by destroying the drawing. Burning the image ostensibly cures the child in Milagros' reading of the events. But the García family is equally susceptible to such beliefs. Punished for drawing a cat on the front of their house by having to scrub the image off the wall and eat a supper of bread and milk, Sandi allegedly causes the pantry to be overrun with rats the next morning, now that her cat has been removed. Deciding to take her talent more seriously, the family enrolls her in art lessons, but more profound aesthetic experiences occur for Sandi in an off-limits shed behind the teacher's house, where an imprisoned artist works, and later in the cathedral.

Don José, a Dominican sculptor rumored to be insane, has been commissioned to create statues for the new cathedral. Sandi unexpectedly finds him at work in what functions as a primal scene for her. Naked and attached to a ball and chain in the back shed, Don José intensely sculpts a wooden statue of the Virgin, sexually aroused and straddling the statue while he works. Distracting him by screaming just as he is about to carve the Virgin's face, Sandi then becomes integrated into his work, his vision of the child's face serving as his model as he finishes the sculpture. In an epiphanic moment at midnight Mass in the cathedral the next Christmas, Sandi recognizes herself in the face of the new statue of the Virgin in the Nativity scene Don José has completed. The power of art, religion, and sexuality have afforded Sandi a sense of identity and self-worth, replacing her previous feelings of inferiority as the second-born who is only valorized by relatives for the parts of her face that resemble those of other García family members. The reifying gaze of "some aunt or other [who] would take hold of my face in her hand . . . exclaiming that my eyes were those of my great-aunt Graciela" (241) is replaced at the end of the narrative by Don José's aesthetic, religious, and sexually sublimated vision of her, now publicly displayed and given a modicum of immortality in the religious sculpture. A second signification of the story's title comes into play so that "still" now means "continuing" and "lives" functions as a verb. The title thus refers to "still lives" not only as the aesthetic objects that the characters in the story create but also as Sandi's image living on in Don José's sculptures in the church.

Syncretic religious motifs of Yoruban and Christian origin also appear in Alvarez's narrative both as part of its realistic impulse and as expected elements of exotic Latino culture that will help to sell books. In depicting elements of Santería, Alvarez is simultaneously an insider and an outsider; that is, characters in the book such as Doña Tatica and Chucha who engage in non-official religious beliefs and practices represent an Other with respect to the privileged main characters in the García family and, by implication, to Alvarez herself. Perhaps this accounts for the narrative's occasional inaccuracy, as, for example, when Doña Tatica worships an apparently male *santo*, "Candelario" (204), who in fact is female both in Yoruban and Christian traditions.

Oyá, the Yoruban goddess of the cemetery, is frequently syncretized in Santería with the Catholic virgin Nuestra Señora de la Candelaria, Our Lady of Candlemas or the Purification. As is this Catholic virgin, Oyá is associated with fire. Ancient tradition recounts that as the first wife of the god Changó, Oyá sees him drink a potion before battle that enables him to spout fire from his nose and mouth; she herself then secretly drinks the potion and thereby acquires power over fire. As owner of the cemetery, Oyá is the guardian of the passage from life to death; in González-Wippler's words, "She is not death but the awareness of its existence" (4).[7] Alvarez selects this *orisha* in her syncretized Christian form as the appropriate devotional object of the character Doña Tatica, an ordinary Dominican woman who exhibits extraordinary strength and, in a sense, presides over the life and death of the García family in her small way.

Doña Tatica, who runs a brothel and is a minor but crucial player in the family's dangerous last day in the Dominican Republic, invokes Candelario to ease the burning pain in her belly; she has made a *promesa* to the *santo* to wear red, believing that when doctors removed part of her stomach and reproductive organs, Candelario remained inside "filling that empty space with spirit" (204). As Tatica struggles despite her severe pain to notify the American agent Vic Hubbard, who is in a bungalow with a prostitute, that the García family needs him immediately, she calls out *"Urgente"* as she knocks, "meaning her own condition now, for her whole body feels bathed in a burning pain as if her flame-colored dress were itself on fire" (205). Although it appears that Hubbard is responsible for saving the family from Trujillo's police, Alvarez makes the point that the family's survival is as much due to ordinary people like Doña Tatica who exhibit inordinate strength in such emergencies, perhaps with the help of their devotion to syncretic *santos*. Hubbard may term her and fellow Dominicans of her class "riffraff" (206), but Alvarez hints that perhaps the term better applies to Hubbard himself.

The second major nonofficial religious practice in Alvarez's narrative is Haitian voodoo, which has some similarities to Santería, including the common deities Changó, Oggún, and Elegguá with slightly different names. However, as González-Wippler points out, the two religions are very different, primarily because the Yoruban influence rather than that of other tribes is the most predominant in Santería, and because the French influence in Haiti differed from the Spanish culture in other areas of the Caribbean. In Alvarez's narrative, the black servant Chucha has been employed by the García family for decades, since the girls' grandfather gave her refuge in 1937 when Trujillo ordered the execution of all the black Haitians on the Dominican side of the island. In various sections of narrative testimony about the family's last day on the island in "The Blood of the Conquistadores," we see Chucha through several perspectives. Her fellow maids look down on her and are disrespectful because she is "so black and Haitian" (219). She defends herself against their insults by giving them one of her "spelling looks," living up to their belief that she "got mounted by spirits" (219) and casts spells on the other members of the household. In her narrative about Chucha, Fifi, the youngest daughter, describes the Haitian woman's engagement in voodoo rituals throughout the house, including the "miracle" in which the mother finally allows Chucha to sleep every night in a coffin after Chucha burns a votive candle for a week and offers mints to a picture of the mother as a baby.

On the day the family departs for the United States, Chucha brings a wooden statue into the girls' room and places a cup of water above its head. As Chucha prays over the girls, drops begin to run down the statue's face when condensation occurs in the heat; then, like the statue that "cries," the girls themselves start to cry, "as if Chucha had finally released her own tears in each of us" (221). Chucha engages in her nontraditional religious practice from the perspective of an exile offering solace to other imminent exiles. The wooden statue is the only material object she has brought from Haiti, just as her ancestors brought their deities with them when exiled from Africa centuries earlier; its "miraculous" powers not only mark the ritual of a blessing at departure but also serve Church worshippers as a connection to the lost homeland. Chucha's wooden statue has been semiotically embedded with centuries of exile. And importantly, Fifi notes, a picture of a similar statue serves to evoke memories of Chucha years later, as the madeleine did for Marcel Proust.

Chucha's own narrative about the family's departure is heavily punctuated with voodoo images such as hearing the voices of her *santos* in the empty rooms, and of a *loa* telling stories of what will happen in the future to the family. She has a vision of the *loa* of Don Carlos all in black, and after it departs, she hears his car start outside. This vision contrasts with the deathlike whiteness she perceives in the American military men who come to drive the mother and children away to the nation of "zombies . . . the color of the living dead" (221). She burns incense and lights six candles for the family members, performs her bedtime cleansing ritual, and climbs into the coffin she sleeps in each night to prepare herself psychologically for her future burial. It is as if Chucha has foreseen this moment when the entire house would become like a coffin and has taken control of her own exile by burying herself each night in the real coffin she has chosen for herself.

Figure 4.7. Seven African Powers, popular holy card

Syncretic religious motifs are also developed in Cristina Garcia's *Dreaming in Cuban*. Garcia's description of the alternative religious practices of Santería in Cuba and among Cuban immigrants in the United States is respectfully critical but at the same time deploys an ethnographic tone sensitive to U.S. readers who have little or no knowledge of these cultural practices. The visual depiction of the Seven African Powers syncretized as Christian saints on one popular holy card (fig. 4.7) is especially relevant to Garcia's novel. Although verbally anchored by the corresponding names of *orishas*, the predominant visual images on the holy card are of Catholic religious figures, allowing it to be sold in Catholic stores. However, because it is doubly encoded, those who so wish may engage in an interpretation through the optic of Santería.

At the top center of the chain is the largest of the medals or charms, a visual depiction of Santa Bárbara syncretized in Santería as Changó, the deification of an ancient Yoruban king. The god of thunder and lightning, Changó is frequently portrayed near his castle with a double-edged ax symbolizing his power and a mortar in which he prepares his magic spells and thunderbolts. González-Wippler notes that Santa Bárbara was most likely identified with Changó because she also holds a cup or chalice parallel to Changó's mortar, a sword comparable to his ax, and sometimes is depicted with a castle (fig. 4.8); her colors, like Changó's, are red and white, and she also is associated with fire and lightning. Consequently, worshippers can read their preferred text in the doubly encoded visual image of the Seven African Powers, even though Catholic imagery appears to predominate in the holy card. Although this visual representation depicts a white Santa Bárbara, Garcia alludes to the common image of the saint as black in her syncretized form. In *Dreaming in Cuban*, when entering La Madrina's house, Felicia sees that "an ebony statue of Santa Bárbara, the Black Queen, presides" among the other *santos* (13).

To the left of Santa Bárbara/Changó on the holy card is "Ochun," the deity of the river, named for the Oshún River in Nigeria. This female *orisha* is syncretized with the patron of Cuba, Nuestra Señora de la Caridad del Cobre (Our Lady of Charity) (fig. 4.9). This virgin and *orisha* are associated with copper (*cobre*) because it was the most valuable metal in ancient Yoruba. She is frequently represented with a golden-yellow halo and with three men in a boat in the sea below her. According to legend, she appeared to the men, who were shipwrecked outside Havana during a violent storm.

The two other female figures on the holy card also appear on the left of the chain. Yemalla (Yemaya), the mother goddess, is syncretized as Our Lady of Regla (a region in Cuba). Obatalá, an androgynous male-female *orisha* who is the oldest and wisest, is depicted as Our Lady of Mercy. On the masculine side of the chain are images of Saint Francis of Assisi, here called "Orula" (Orunla); Saint Peter, named "Ogum" (Oggún); and Saint Anthony, syncretized with "Elegua" (Elegguá).[8] In the center of the circular chain is an image of the crucified Christ with the title "Olofi." The highest deity of Santería, "Olofi" is understood as creation, "a manifested force that is in charge of creation, being creation itself" (González-Wippler, 25–26) and worshipped syncretically as Christ. At the bottom of the chain are the work implements linked with Oggún, and inside the chain, surrounding the cross, are images

Figure 4.8. *"Santa Bárbara," wooden* retablo *by Margarito Mondragón, Las Vegas, New Mexico (courtesy of Margarito Mondragón)*

associated with the Passion and Crucifixion of Christ, some of which have additional encodings relevant to Santería.

In Garcia's novel, Felicia del Pino, the second daughter of Jorge and Celia, is the character most involved in the practice of Santería. She had been exposed to syncretic religious artifacts and beliefs early in childhood when she collected the "paraphernalia of faith" left in church, including prayer cards, rosaries, missals, holy water, and crucifixes, which she used to bap-

Figure 4.9. Nuestra Señora de la Caridad del Cobre, popular holy card

tize chickens and bless her baby brother. Her mother, although ostensibly not a believer in Santería, locks the children in the house on December 4, the feast of Changó, the god of fire and lightning, with warnings that "they'd be kidnapped and sacrificed to the black people's god if they wandered the streets alone" (76). Here Celia invokes race, sifting out half of the syncretized religious image of Santa Bárbara/Changó on the Catholic saint's feast day to induce fear in her children. Felicia's older sister Lourdes engages in a similar tactic of intimidation on a secular level during the enforced confinement by terrorizing the child about a tin peddler who abducts children, scoops out their eyes, and drinks their blood. And just as Felicia may not witness any of the public celebrations of Changó's feast, she is forbidden to visit her best friend, Herminia, whose father is a *santero*.

Felicia is fascinated in her youth with San Sebastián, who underwent a kind of "double death" by being shot through with arrows, surviving, and then being beaten to death. When she meets her first husband, she has been hearing the saint speaking in her head in jumbled rhymes and follows the man she will marry out the door "as if commanded by Saint Sebastian him-self" (78). Already in these early stages of mental instability, her madness is associated with religious practice. Not only does she become a *santera*, but she also assumes a semidivine role when she kills, or attempts to kill, two of her husbands. The first, whom San Sebastián had led her to, beats and chokes her on the first night they are married and gives her syphilis. Five years later, in 1966, she tries to murder him, "standing over him like a goddess with a fiery ball in her hand" (82)—the rag she has soaked with oil from the skil-let and ignited. Fire is also involved in the death of her second husband, a restaurant inspector, and Felicia suspects it is a vengeance killing. She herself pushes her third husband from the top of a roller coaster, "and watche[s] him die on a bed of high-voltage wires"; according to Herminia, "his body turned to gray ash" (185–86). The fire and burning motifs involved in the deaths or attempted murders of all three of her husbands evoke Changó, the *orisha* of fire and lightning who wields power for both good and bad ends.

As Felicia's madness progresses, she becomes obsessed with coconuts one summer, excessively consuming the fruit commonly used in Santería ceremonies. She trades her food coupons for the entire grocer's bin of coco-nuts and begs door-to-door for more of them, promising manicures and hair-cuts in return; she feeds her family only coconut ice cream the entire summer. Eventually, in that "summer of the coconuts," Felicia attempts suicide.

After burning and almost killing her first spouse, Felicia approaches a *santero* to read her future in the cowrie shells in the hope of finding another husband. When the holy man is only able to predict misfortune after several attempts at reading the shells, he prescribes a cleansing ritual in which she is to rub herself with a specially cured piece of meat in a paper bag and re-turn to him for a follow-up cleansing. Although describing the session with the *santero* in minute detail, Garcia does not engage in exotic, uncritical nar-ration. Instead, she has Felicia fail to follow the *santero*'s instructions because the character falls in love on her way home. Garcia, in a sense, has it both ways here; Felicia gets her wish even though she disregards the *santero*'s advice, but tragedy befalls her shortly thereafter when her new husband is killed in a hotel fire. Audiences may choose to read the events either as validating Santería's power or debunking it.

In April 1980, when Pilar visits Cuba, she and her nephew Ivan speak to Herminia Delgado, a lifelong friend of Felicia and fellow practitioner of Santería. Herminia narrates a *testimonio* about Felicia's life, discussing her third marriage, her induction into Santería, and her subsequent death. In 1978, after killing her third husband, Felicia returns home and asks to be taken to see La Madrina, who initiates her into the *elekes*, the necklaces of the saints intended to protect the wearer from evil. Felicia undergoes an *asiento*, the major initiation in which one is said to "*hacer el santo*" [make the saint]; in this rite, saints are believed to take possession of their initiates and literally "to mount" them (González-Wippler, 14). Garcia describes in much detail the three-day ritual in which Felicia is inducted as a novice *santera* of Obatalá, who as the "owner of all heads" is believed to control the mind and thought.[9] Syncretized with the Catholic Our Lady of Mercy, Obatalá shares her feast day, September 24.

Garcia presents a sympathetic yet partially critical portrayal of Felicia's induction and subsequent death in which she is buried, as she requested, in her induction garments. Flores-Peña notes the importance of the beautiful garments sewn for the induction ceremony, which allow new *santeras* the function of "speaking without a voice." The garment "visually educates everyone who participates by summarizing the most important events in the life of the deity" (16) and is worn on only three occasions—in the last instance, when one dies. Although Felicia's body is visually eloquent after her death in Herminia's account, the fact that she dies interjects a critical realism into Garcia's account of Santería. Felicia's saint failed to take care of her as expected during the year after her initiation. Despite sacrifices, bringing offerings to the mountains where Obatalá is believed to live, and placing white flags around Felicia's house, her fellow *santeros* are unable to prevent her death. Consequently, her mother, Celia, knocks the image of Obatalá off its altar and destroys the *orisha's* sacred shells and stones.

Garcia focuses on both the positive and negative elements of Santería, portraying it as a contested space in revolutionary Cuba as well as in the United States, where thousands of Caribbean Latinos practice it. When Pilar purchases herbs and holy objects in the *botánica* and they fail to protect her in a dangerous alley in New York City, Garcia engages in the same critical realism with which she portrays Santería in Cuba. Like Alvarez, she is an insider who is at the same time an outsider in depicting Santería:

I knew very little about it, just a few odds and ends from an aunt who grew up in the countryside. My family was Catholic and thought that Santería was mumbo-jumbo African rites. They were disdainful of it. So I had to send away for books on Santería to Miami, and read as much as I could. Once I became exposed to it, I was completely fascinated. It's part of our cultural landscape and, as Pilar says at one point, it makes a lot more sense than more abstract forms of worship. (" '. . . And There Is Only My Imagination," 610)

As a result, Garcia portrays the important religious and cultural practices of Santería both sympathetically and critically. She does not present a firsthand personal knowledge of these religious beliefs but recuperates this element of her culture in a highly accurate and unromantic fashion.

The alternative religious practices of Puerto Rico complement those of the Dominican Republic, Haiti, and Cuba critically narrated in the work of Alvarez and Garcia. In *The Line of the Sun*, Judith Ortiz Cofer narrates a battle between official and popular religious practices and elaborates a realistic social critique of both. The practitioners of popular religion in the novel include the Mesa Blanca spiritist Papá Pepe, the transgressive "Sister Rosa" in Puerto Rico, and the *santera* Elba La Negra in New Jersey. In a 1992 article, Bruce-Novoa makes an excellent case for the important homology between ritual practice, bifurcated identity, and narrative structure in the novel; however, gender is another optic through which to view religion and ritual in the text. Although Papá Pepe's alternative religious rituals enable him to "divine" the location of the missing Guzmán twice in the novel, Cofer focuses more narrative attention on the relation of various women to religion.[10] Another instance of men's connection to religion is also quickly whisked away in the novel: the important transgression against prescribed male gender roles that takes place in the rectory between El Padrecito César and Carmelo is "punished" by the reassignment of the priest and military enlistment and death for Carmelo. Gay transgression peeks briefly out of the closet in the novel but undergoes a kind of narrative repression; homosexuality is ultimately a kind of political unconscious in the novel that surfaces only in attenuated form, as also occurs in Castillo's *So Far from God*. Instead, Cofer develops much more fully the "safer" transgression of the brother Guzmán, who remains within the heterosexual order even as he transgresses.

Women's competing reappropriations of religion receive greater narrative development. Figures such as Doña Tina, Doña Julia, and the members of the Holy Rosary Society become more vigilant than the Catholic Church in fighting transgressive sexuality and stand in stark opposition to the popular religiosity of Rosa. They attain guardianship of Rosa's daughter, Sarita, and raise her to be a religious fanatic who ultimately tries to tame Guzmán by marriage. Rosa—whose various interpellations include "Pura Rosa," "Sister Rosa," "La Cabra," and "puta"—practices an alternate spiritism infused with unconventional sexuality. She "works causes" in the *centro* in her isolated home with *agua florida*, cigar smoke, and "passes" to purify her clients of evil influences. Her purification of the rebellious Guzmán involves not only spiritist rituals and teaching him about herbal cures, but also, later, a sexual relation he initiates during the novena and carnival for the town's patroness, "Our Lady of Salud."

Rosa functions as an alternative or competing religious power to the town's namesake. The miracle she is to perform on Guzmán parallels that attributed to the Virgin for whom the town was named.[11] According to the legend, after a bull wounded a woodcutter in his side, as Christ had been wounded on the cross, the Virgin appeared above the very tree the man was about to cut down. Pronouncing the single word "*salud*" (health), the Virgin cured him, and the bull became tame as a lamb. After other miracles were reported at the site, missionaries built a large church there. In recounting the perhaps too numerous coincidences of the legend directly after telling the story of Rosa's spiritist rituals on Guzmán, Cofer subtly suggests that the supernatural powers attributed to both Rosa and the Virgin share a homologous narrative structure. The battle in the novel between competing religious practices to tame the figurative bull, Guzmán, is left unresolved by Cofer's postmodernist ending, even though he marries the religious fanatic Sarita in the final scene.

The Black Virgin is also a locus of popular religious reappropriation within the official church shrine in Hormigueros. In *Silent Dancing* Cofer describes the *promesas* her grandmother made to the Virgin for the safe return of her sons after climbing the one hundred steps to the shrine on her knees each week. Believers left crutches and baby garments in a room beside the nave in petition or thanksgiving for help with medical problems, fertility, and domestic crises. "Being a woman and black made Our Lady the perfect depository for the hopes and prayers of the sick, the weak and the powerless" (42), Cofer notes. Some women elaborated their alternate mode of petitioning for intercession by wearing sackcloth, or *hábitos*—plain dresses in the color of the favorite saint, with a cord tied at the waist to represent Christ's Passion. In "San Antonio al Revés," a poem in *Silent Dancing*, Cofer highlights the popular practice of turning statues of San Antonio backwards or upside down. The virgins who pray to the saint for help in finding husbands promise hymns and prayers "as dowry"; married women, in contrast, ask that their husbands be protected from "the rum-slick bodies of *putas*" (104). Because Rosa, in *The Line of the Sun*, practices prostitution and learned her spiritism from a pimp, her alternate religious practices stand in contrast to, and compete with, both official and popular versions of Catholicism.

Although Cofer uses the term "spiritist meeting" to describe the ritual ceremony of Elba La Negra in New Jersey in *The Line of the Sun*, the syncretic images of Santería predominate in the rite.[12] With critical distance, the narrator expresses pity for her mother, who participated "in this silly game of spiritism" (251). Spatially reconfigured with preparations for the evening ritual, their kitchen is now filled with flowers and ribbons in special colors: "red roses for the adherents of Santa Barbara, whose favorite color is red; white and blue carnations for the mild mannered La Mercedes [Obatalá]; greenery in glasses filled with water colored according to the saint or orisha whose favor they sought" (250). With ominous symbolism, Cofer prefigures the conflagration that will kill Elba and destroy the building in the middle of the ceremony: the women are dressed "in the incendiary colors of their patron saints" (254), her mother wears a "fire-engine red dress" (255), and each time the narrator describes the objects collected in the kitchen for the impending rite, she ends ominously with an allusion to the lighter fluid for the ceremonial flame that will summon the spirits. Cofer emphasizes both the syncretic aspects of the ritual itself and those that the narrator, Marisol, constructs because of her familiarity with both Catholicism and Santería. As her mother prepares for the alternative evening ritual, Marisol studies rote answers from the Catholic catechism. Later, Elba La Negra jumps over the flaming pail four times, forming the sign of the cross and invoking a saint's name in each direction. Marisol reads her mother's face during the ritual in montage with a Catholic image: with a golden halo around her head, her mother has "a beatific smile I recognized from a cheap print of Our Lady of Salud that hung above my parents' bed" (265).

Despite the allusion to "silly" spiritism, the novel points to the strength many Caribbean women take from these alternative religious practices. Elba sits on a chair raised above the crowd "like an African queen in their midst" (260), dressed in a red gown and cape. Santa Bárbara's aggressive nature attracted many young women. Under the saint's spell, Elba denounced many straying husbands. In the form of Changó, the spirit of fire, Santa Bárbara would make even timid women "strut across a room puffing on a cigar, often demanding a shot of rum" and ordering the other women about (261). Re-appropriating traditional male gestures, the women use the religious ritual to reverse their usual subordination.

Cofer emphasizes that Puerto Ricans such as her mother see no conflict between Catholicism and *espiritismo* for both are central to their lives. *Espiritismo* is ordinary and everyday to most Puerto Ricans and, like Santería, enables them to feel in control of their world. Everything in her grandfather's practice of Mesa Blanca *espiritismo* can be explained naturally—people voluntarily make themselves go into a trance and play ordinary tricks of the mind on one another. Immigrants further adapt the popular religious practice of the homeland; in *The Line of the Sun*, people have a Santería meeting because the men have no work, marriages are disintegrating, and the women are dissatisfied and lonely.[13] This alternate religious practice offers some modicum of control over the troublesome new surroundings.

Cofer offers a realistic critique of both official and popular religious practices, suggesting that larger political concerns are often played out on the terrain of religion. The religious ritual that results in Elba La Negra's death is less the cause of the tragedy than are the crowded, unsafe living conditions of El Building and the lack of public space in which to practice alternative religion. Women are not only empowered to various degrees in both popular and official religions, but they sometimes abuse power under the guise of religion, as do Doña Tina and her cohorts.

The Seen and the Unseen: The Disrupting Body in Visual Religious Culture

Both official religion and popular alternative practices have focused on the body as a site of both control and recuperation. Official Catholicism simultaneously valorizes and devalorizes the body. On the positive end lies the anthropaphagic symbolism and valorization of Christ's corporeality in the Eucharist, additional metaphors of community in which members constitute a large social body, and the strong role of the senses in liturgical ceremonies and pedagogical narratives designed early on to draw in illiterate worshippers. If the sacred word could not be read firsthand, visual, auditory, olfactory, tactile, and gustatory means of representation would communicate religious tenets. But the Church simultaneously devalorizes the body as the site of sin and self-denial, even as it argues for respect of the body as the figurative "temple of the Holy Spirit."[14]

Several Latina writers emphasize a recuperation of the denied or repressed body in their ample religious imagery. While all five senses come into play in their narrativized religious remembrances, voice and vision predominate, often in transgressive recuperation of official religious verbal and visual culture. The work of Mary Helen Ponce, who emphasizes vision, complements the narrative of Denise Chávez, who foregrounds voice, and that of Sandra Cisneros, who focuses on visual and verbal hybridity.

For Ponce, the remembrance of religion is overlain with images of the disrupting body—its refusal, even within the sacred site of church ceremony to remain within set social constraints. In *The Wedding*, as I will argue in chapter 5, grotesque eruptions of bodily functions turn the church ceremony inside out in a parodical, carnivalesque simulacrum in which nature overpowers culture; Ponce's narrative humorously celebrates the persistence of the centrifugal against the official forces that attempt to constrain and control transgression. She disturbs one Chicano literary critic by this irreverent portrayal, and by a parallel instance in the autobiography *Hoyt Street*, when she remembers having to take the public blame for an elderly woman's passing gas in church, a sacrifice of the self related to Christ's that allows the dying woman a modicum of respect.[15] Although Ponce is denied the power of speech as a child (and, by extension, by the critic who would prefer she not write about such inappropriate themes), she will assert her right to do so now as an adult writer, recuperating the word for her own ends. In this adult narrative she dares to utter the unspeakable—words such as the Spanish and English terms for the transgression "*pedo*" (fart) that will highlight in both languages the intrusion of the body into the space of the sacred.

In stories such as "Rose," "Sacrifice," and "El Mes de Mayo" [The month of May], Ponce (I use "Ponce" to refer to the adult author and "Mary Helen" to refer to the child in the narrative) recounts the eruption of banal elements of everyday life into church ceremony. She feels demeaned when another girl who also claims the affection of Mary Helen's godmother wears the same style veil at Confirmation, and when she is forced to take the blame for the sick woman in church. In a scene reminiscent of *The Wedding*, Ponce recounts in "El Mes de Mayo" eruptions of vulgar language and gesture during the nightly church processions of *ofrecimiento* in which flowers are brought to the Virgin Mary. Two sisters quarrel aloud during the ceremony using the derogatory epithets "*babosa*" and "*hocicona*," just before the priest and others intone holy utterances; one girl gives another "the finger" while marching in the procession. Ponce remembers both wanting to distance herself from such transgressive behavior and yet admiring it because it appeared to earn respect from boys and represent courage. Unlike the disruption of bodily functions in *The*

Wedding, the false stigma of "*el pedo*" in the story "Sacrifice" is a vehicle of maturation whereby Mary Helen learns that her embarrassment was a sacrificial gift that allowed an elderly woman near death to preserve her dignity.

The numerous segments on religion in Ponce's *Hoyt Street* attest to the rich community involvement in religious activity in Pacoima, California, in the 1940s—both official religious ceremonies and alternative Mexican practices sometimes integrated into them. A number of Ponce's remembered religious images involve the interplay between the seen and the unseen and the underlying repressed sexuality of some religious display. She describes her pleasurable memories of Holy Week ceremonies, especially the washing of the feet ritual, which allowed her a rare opportunity to view the priest's and the altar boys' usually concealed feet; her desire to see the hidden parts of the Other's body is heightened by the excessive clothing of priests and nuns, and she and her classmates, with an excitement parallel to that displayed at the baring of the priest's feet, try unsuccessfully to dislodge the elaborate head-covering of one sister on the playground. She elaborates the tension between the seen and unseen again in describing her role in the daily church processions in May in honor of the Blessed Virgin and, finally, in her account of the covering and uncovering of the church statues during Holy Week, embeds more direct sexual signification into her account:

> The candles flickered, the bells filled the room, the flowers shone bright. Suddenly Don Crispín, dressed in a spotless white shirt, appeared from inside the sacristy; in his hands was a long pole. He approached the Guardian Angel and lifted the purple covering; then he did the same with all the other statues. . . . I stared at my friends who had been in hiding, delighted with how refreshed and happy they looked. Even Jesus, his bleeding heart still dangling to the side, appeared less sad. (153–54)

In this passage and elsewhere, Ponce emphasizes the corporeal and visceral nature of much visual religious display as it oscillates between the seen and the unseen to heighten the religious experience.

Deploying an ethnographic tone with a visually detailed description of customs by an insider addressed to outsiders, the section Ponce devotes to Doña Magda focuses on alternative religious practices such as *altares*, shrines to nonofficial religious figures, and the repaying of *mandas* to saints. In addition to wearing numerous medals and scapulars, Doña Magda prays novenas and fulfills *mandas* in person in return for "miracles" received. Ponce describes in rich visual detail the three altars in Doña Magda's bedroom to

Figure 4.10. La Virgen de Guadalupe, popular print

El Santo Niño de Atocha (see figure 4.1), La Santísima Virgen del Perpetuo Socorro, and La Virgen de Guadalupe (fig. 4.10), including the numerous votive candles, framed santos, rosaries, and other religious artifacts displayed there. As Turner has argued, the display of visual representations of religious figures on home altars is a deployment of the body as a central metaphor for the relation between the supernatural and the earthly; altars rely on such bodily representations to bring the spiritual and physical realms together ("Mexican American Home Altars"). In effect, Doña Magda's statues reinsert bodily representations of holy figures she has chosen herself into her alternative, nonofficial religious practice.

When Doña Magda's alternative religious practices enter the public visual space of the official Catholic Church, the new priest tries to quash them. As many in the neighborhood watch Doña Magda coming to church on her knees to fulfill the vow she has made for her son's safety in World War II, Father Mueller stops her at the church door, insisting that her custom is out of date. As a result of this rebuff, the parishioners sneak off to the Los Angeles Placita and the shrine of the Virgin of San Juan de los Lagos in Sunland to engage in their customary alternative religious practices.

But Father Mueller is not an entirely negative figure. A young priest who replaces the elderly Father Juanito, he brings a new energy to Ponce's parish in the late 1940s, playing jazz on the new church organ, displaying a picture of Duke Ellington on his dresser instead of a religious image, and shouting the transgressive phrase "Orale cabrones" to loud *pachucos* who have taunted him with the disrespectful interpellation "Orale, Mickey" (265). Mary Helen reads the image of the new priest through visual signifiers such as his red ears that stick out and his sunburned skin when he returns from a day at the beach. With ethnographic explanation that will help readers born after 1960 negotiate the text, Ponce focuses on Father Mueller's revival of pre-Vatican II religious cultural practices that had lost viability during World War II. In this transitional moment before the postconciliar reforms, the new priest revives the traditional *cofradías* (confraternities) and organizes parish *jamaicas*, or bazaars, which Ponce describes through visual motifs. Father Mueller encourages the young girls to form a Stella Maris confraternity, but instead of engaging in charity work in the community, their role is to appear as a group once a month at Sunday Mass. Relegated to this visual role, the girls fight among each other to be in the front of the procession—in effect, to be the one seen first, and march in public display down the church aisle to the front altar where Father Mueller plays the role of the male surveyor, "beam[ing] his approval" (259).[16]

Ponce focuses further on the tension between the seen and unseen and the role of the male surveyor in her religious experience in describing her role in the daily church processions in May. The pleasure of self-display underlies her enjoyment in marching in the procession, which "was like being onstage, with the whole town watching" (162). To be selected for the front of the procession afforded the opportunity to be seen by boys; yet this lucky position represented a repressed mode of self-display, a concealed visibility. The lead girl had to look "pious, humble and pure" (165), with her head veiled like the nuns, the Virgin Mary, and other female saints: "Dressing up to look like the Virgin Mary was fun. Each time I covered my head with a veil I felt holy, special, like a 'little bride,' or even a child saint" (163). Mary Helen practices attaining this ideal vision of herself in the bathroom mirror at home, engaging at a young age in the process Simone de Beauvoir described of women imagining the implicit approbation of an ideal male surveyor when viewing themselves in the mirror.

Ponce's autobiography depends on a rich intertextual system of verbal and visual narratives about religious figures. In "Catechism," Ponce recounts some of the narratives that fascinated her from the book *The Lives of the Saints*. Especially important to her were the stories about female saints, which, with a kind of protofeminism, Mary Helen recognized as countertexts to the predominant male figures of the Church. Here also her experience of religious narrative is closely tied to visual representation.

In an intertextual homology that privileges the visual, Ponce allows the physical appearance of the childhood book about the saints to structure her present narrative. In effect, her readerly experience as a child shaped her preferences for certain saints, her views of her own physical appearance, and ultimately the narrative structure of this section of *Hoyt Street*. Her description of *The Lives of the Saints* begins with its cover image—a beautiful rendering of Saint Teresa, whose narrative then becomes her favorite. Ponce's remembrances are structured through the cover image much as her childhood reading experience of the book was. In effect, she has her readers first "see" the cover image as she did as a child so that the visual description of Saint Teresa appears first, accounting for half of Ponce's narrative about the saint: "Saint Teresa . . . was my favorite. She had creamy white skin, blue eyes, and rich auburn hair that fell below her slender shoulders in long, thick waves. She wore a pretty blue robe, which I knew was made of silk, over what resembled a white nightgown. . . . On her delicate feet were tiny slippers, which must have been of silk too" (190).

Similarly, this image will structure Mary Helen's self-perception in later years. On her Confirmation day, measuring herself against the idealized saint, she describes her feelings of inadequacy in her ill-fitting white dress, which she purposely bought a size too small because of embarrassment about her weight: "I wanted to look like St. Teresa of Avila, known as the Little Flower. I felt pious, holy, and fat" (273).

Visual description predominates in Ponce's narratives about religious figures, much as it did in the early catechistic instruction she depicts here. The nuns taught the biblical narratives using large easel pictures of the stories. Ponce's retelling structures itself homologously: "In the first illustration, Adam and Eve looked young and healthy on their tropical island. In the second picture, Eve ate an apple, while Adam hid behind a branch; at her feet was the slimy snake. Next we saw Eve crying, while a troubled Adam held her hand; in a corner the sly snake smiled. The lesson ended with Eve clinging to Adam, her blue eyes full of fear and her dark hair flying as they fled the Garden of Eden" (197). Here Ponce's retelling progresses image by image, much as the classroom story had, so that the visual predominates despite the verbal mode of representation. As in other religious practices, both the seen and the unseen, the told and the untold, structure these narratives; Mary Helen and her friends, like most narratees, perform work themselves to fill in the gaps with images from movies and their own oral counternarratives:

> "Gosh, God sure is mean! He chased Adam and Eve from the pretty garden for nothing!"
> "Yeah."
> "Do you think they were kissing?"
> "Hmmmm, maybe . . ."
> Years later Nancy alluded to what Adam and Eve had *really* done but I never believed her. I thought they were a fine-looking couple who had been unfairly treated. (198)

The numerous embedded narratives in *Hoyt Street* about Mary Helen's participation in Church events reveal an integral sense of community and belonging that characterize her religious upbringing. While there are occasional moments of embarrassment or youthful rivalries experienced at religious events, overall Ponce's autobiographical narrative depicts the Catholic Church positively and her parish as the site of pleasurable experiences: "I came to realize how much I enjoyed the silence, the mystery, the beauty within our church. Unlike our noisy household, our church was quiet, peaceful, empty. I studied the shadows cast by the statues atop the altar, whom I knew by heart and greeted like best friends: Guardian Angel, Saint Joseph, the Virgin Mary, and the fat Niño de Atocha. Church for me was a wonderous, silent place" (101).

Ponce also recounts the strong community participation in church bazaars, religious organizations, official religious ceremonies and the family celebrations that developed around them, as well as alternative Mexican practices integrated with those of the Church. The religious experience Ponce recounts takes on a certain nostalgia given the half century separating the publication of *Hoyt Street* and the period she describes; post-Vatican II readers need the writer's ethnographic explanations for several of the rituals and practices that are no longer common. Ponce's narrative focuses to a large degree on the centrality of vision and denied vision in religious practice, and through ethnographic presentation, it allows readers a picture of the traditional and popular elements of Mexican American immigrant religion in the 1940s.

Performative Voice in the Reconfigured Novena

Although Denise Chávez's experimental one-woman play "Novena Narrativas y Ofrendas Nuevomexicanas" deploys many visual signifiers, it recaptures voice as its predominant textual strategy, especially in its published form. When performed, the play adds visual bodily display to its strong emphasis on voice as it recuperates the denied or repressed body of official religious culture. In presenting the oral prayers of nine New Mexican women, Chávez eschews for the most part ethnographic explanation that would help to orient outsiders, choosing instead to present the direct locutions of strongly bilingual characters who often employ Chicano slang. So important is an accurate rendering of voice for Chávez that readers without the requisite cultural and linguistic competence are simply out of luck, clearly not the primary addressees of this work. While briefly mentioning that a novena is a nine-day prayer cycle, Chávez seems not to be concerned that many of her readers outside of New Mexico will be unfamiliar with this pre-Vatican II religious ceremony, no longer widely practiced by U.S. Catholics.[17] In effect, Chávez is transforming a religious rite with both traditional and nontraditional characteristics. The preservation to this day of this religious practice in New Mexico, despite the official Church's canonization of updated liturgical practices, affords it a nontraditional character; this viability of the novena in New Mexico is reminiscent of the way that non-official pre-Tridentine versions of Christianity survived throughout the colonial period and beyond in the Americas, as Espín and others have argued.

The narrator, Isabel, an artist who represents Chávez herself as both playwright and actor, begins the hybrid ceremony-performance with a kind of overture in which she articulates key phrases from various characters who will follow. Since the play bares the device from the beginning, showing the process of its own construction, these lines are on one level Isabel's public rehearsal of phrases she will shortly utter. At the same time, they serve a pedagogical function similar to the rehearsal of songs with a congregation before a religious liturgy begins; Chávez's audience will learn to recognize the idiosyncratic speech patterns of the characters about to utter their narrative prayers. "Adrede iba a bailar!" (I was determined to dance!) (88), for example, previews a key phrase of Corrine, the lesbian who invites another woman to dance at a senior social. And later, other key phrases punctuate the speech of this "aging, very tough bag-lady" (for example, "Corrine got it covered, ésa! Ssss" [98]) along with oral New Mexican and Chicano slang that invites audiences to learn regional utterances such as "the pinta in Santa" (the penitentiary in Santa Fe) or "una pinta jotita" (99) (a lesbian ex-con). In this way Chávez closes the gap that the mainstream sees between the sacred and the profane by portraying characters who speak in their own ordinary language as they pray rather than with the official utterances that the Church prescribes.

Chávez's text is an important contestation and re-reading of official and non-official religious practices. The central altar to the male deity here becomes a private altar fashioned in alternative sites and honoring, instead, the Virgin as a kind of female deity. As Turner has argued, the home altar reverses the official Church altar—"the stage for . . . the central canonical drama of Catholicism . . . the symbolic focusing point of male privilege and authority"—allowing women to function to a certain degree as their own priests at home ("Mexican American Women's Home Altars," 30). Similarly, Chávez's alternative drama opens a discursive space for a number of women whom the Church has previously denied the power to speak. As discussed further in chapter 5, several transgressive acts enter into the public domain here, among them those of the lesbian Corrine, the nonmonogamous Magdalena, the "marked" Minda (whose father has sexually abused her), the "nativa" *curandera* Juana with her indigenous religious practices, and the alienated, illiterate teen Pauline, whose tattoos, like Corrine's, reappropriate the sacred symbols of the Virgin and Jesus. While adding important transgressive significations to the dominant icons of the Church, Chávez allows the characters to speak in their own, forbidden language. "Novena narrativas" transgressively reconfigures several religious signifiers while at the same time using them as unifying cultural symbols.

Visual-Verbal Hybridity: Fictional *Retablos*

Earlier in the chapter, I discussed several religious motifs in Sandra Cisneros' *Woman Hollering Creek* (1992); here I will focus on a central diptych in the collection, "Little Miracles, Kept Promises," and the gateway story that precedes it, "Anguiano Religious Articles." Although voice is the predominant narrative strategy in the two stories, an implicit intertextual visuality underlies all of the characters' profoundly oral utterances. Like Chávez, Cisneros does not bother with ethnographic explanation for various "outsider" readers, although through certain real names she undergirds her writing as that of an insider.[18] As a result, those unfamiliar with the rich visual system underlying these stories function as partially incompetent readers, similar, for example, to readers of Joyce's *Ulysses* who are unfamiliar with *The Odyssey*.

The gateway story "Anguiano's Religious Articles Rosaries Statues Medals Incense Candles Talismans Perfumes Oils Herbs" spatially displays its title in linear segments that amass the names of religious objects without punctuation, as if it itself were the sign above a religious goods store across the street from San Fernando Cathedral. Narrated as a second-person cautionary tale told to an unspecified interlocutor, the story's diction suggests that the narrator is a nontraditional religious devotee. The transgressive utterances of this tough-talking woman who enters Anguiano's store to buy a gift for a sick friend suggest a recuperation of the denied speech of orthodox Catholicism, in which worshippers repeat prescribed liturgical phrases and songs and children are taught to retell their sins according to the proper rubric of the sacrament of Reconciliation. When the "crab ass" owner, as the narrator terms him, tells her loudly in Spanish to leave the store after other customers have come in, the woman argues that *he*, in fact, is the utterer of ugly speech, given the content of his directive.

Along with the orality of the story, however, visual imagery plays a central role in understanding the owner's actions. The woman's trip to the religious goods store is the occasion for Cisneros to descriptively present to readers several items of non-official Mexican material religious culture. The woman is fascinated by the "pretty 3-D pictures" of religious figures that allow one to see different saints depending on the angle of vision (114); the image of the Santo Niño de Atocha is transformed into La Virgen and then into "Saint Lucy with her eyes on a plate" (fig. 4.11). But revealing a traditionalism within a non-official religious practice, the narrator negatively describes the statues of the Virgen de Guadalupe with long fake eyelashes that make her look, in the narrator's view "*bien* mean, like *los amores de la calle*" (215). Although she rejects these statues that give the Virgin the look of a streetwalker, the story hints ironically that the owner is performing the same visual reading of her, anxious that she leave because her "streetwalker's" look forms an oxymoronic combination with the holy images in the store.

Like this character whom the store owner directs to the San Fernando Cathedral across the street, readers who turn the page and begin reading "Little Miracles, Kept Promises" are made to "see" the popular religious culture on display in this church in San Antonio, where Cisneros now lives (fig. 4.12). The story presents twenty-four fictional ex-votos; that is, *promesas*, or vows, made to religious figures in exchange for favors requested or granted. Again,

Figure 4.11. "Santa Lucía" (photograph reproduced from Mexican Folk Retablos, 1974, *courtesy of Gloria Fraser Giffords)*

although the story is entirely constituted by verbal utterances, images such as the display of votive offerings under the crucifix of the Black Christ of Es-quipulas in San Fernando Cathedral are the necessary visual intertexts for a competent decoding of the text. The story depends on the larger public visual system of non-official religious practices in Latino communities, including such material culture as *retablos*, small paintings of religious figures (fig. 4.13) or illustrated narrative scenes with handwritten verbal texts giving visual and verbal testimony to a miracle received (fig. 4.14); *santos* and *bultos*, carved wooden religious figures (some with hair, clothing, and jewelry) placed on

Figure 4.12. Ex-votos beneath the crucifix of the Black Christ of Esquipulas in San Fernando Cathedral, San Antonio, Texas

home altars or in churches and sometimes carried in public religious processions (fig. 4.15); and the display at shrines and in churches of synecdochic signs of "miracles" received such as crutches and *milagritos* (small replications of body parts [fig. 4.16]), photographs, and small notes narrating the favor requested or granted. Each of these practices has its own embedded narrative that overcodes those of Cisneros' fictive petitioners.[19]

Among the figures to whom Cisneros' petitioners pray is the Santo Niño de Atocha, the patron of prisoners and travelers, whose image and narrative are widely known to Latinos (see figure 4.1). During the Moorish invasion of Spain, in response to prayers of the Christian prisoners' families, a child dressed as a pilgrim and carrying a basket, staff, and gourd of water is said to have entered the Atocha prison outside Madrid and miraculously fed all the prisoners with his basket and gourd never emptying. As Elizabeth Kay has noted, for many years at the Capilla del Santo Niño de Atocha in El Potrero, New Mexico, the proprietors gave baby shoes to worshippers who wished to leave them for the Santo Niño, presumed to have worn his out each night

Figure 4.13. Tin retablo *of Nuestra Señora de los Dolores, Mexico*

doing good deeds. Cisneros' hybrid rearticulation of this image and narrative revolves on the motifs of travel, transportation, and imprisonment; the verbal *milagrito* is offered by an ex-prisoner's parents, thanking the Santo Niño for help when the son's truck was stolen. The mode of transportation is linked to sustenance, for it enables the wayward son to get to work. It might be argued that in Cisneros' fictive ex-voto, two multitemporally heterogeneous narratives intersect: the pilgrim's staff in the traditional visual images of the Santo Niño is replaced in the postmodern narrative by the figure of the truck as transportative aid, while the basket is replaced by the motif of working to feed one's family.[20]

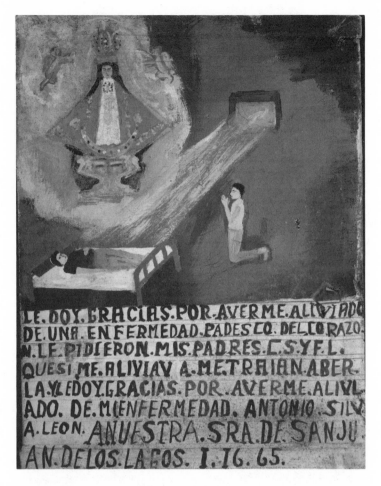

Figure 4.14. Retablo *to La Virgen de San Juan de los Lagos, Mexico, 1965*

In several narrative segments, Cisneros carries the already non-official religious practices even further toward the pole of the nontraditional and transgressive. One of her more confrontational feminist characters invokes San Antonio de Padua (fig. 4.17), who is traditionally petitioned for help in finding lost articles, obtaining a husband, and becoming pregnant and bearing children. As mentioned previously, Cisneros' character, who signs herself "Ms. Barbara Ybañez," demands from the saint help in finding "a man who isn't a pain in the nalgas," "a man man" whose mother didn't ruin him with "too much chichi" (117–18).

Even though the popular narratives about San Antonio de Padua contain references to his unconventional speech and his powers to facilitate marriage

Figure 4.15. La Conquistadora, a revered bulto, *Santa Fe, New Mexico*

and childbirth, Cisneros encases Ybañez's petition in code-switching so that sexualized and transgressive words are uttered in Spanish. Further, just as Latino Catholics often reward statues for favors granted with special cloth-ing or jewelry, they likewise punish statues who fail to grant favors. Statues are turned backwards, put away, or stood on their heads. In Cisneros' story, Ybañez threatens San Antonio with punishment by turning his statue upside down if he fails to grant her petition. Cisneros deploys the grammatical and plot elements of the visual tradition of San Antonio *santos* in her verbal re-articulations of the religious practice. In contrast to the traditional religious rite — which even though it is a non-official, alternative religious practice em-

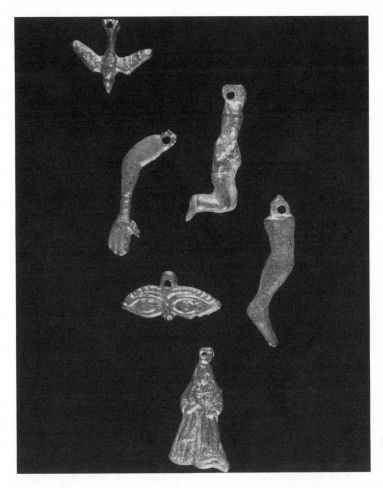

Figure 4.16. Milagritos, *Michoacán, Mexico*

phasizes the accepted values of marriage and childbearing—Cisneros links the practice to contemporary feminist ends, often at odds with officially sanctioned behavior for women.

A parallel postmodern temporal and cultural hybridity is harnessed to an incipient feminism in the ex-voto to the Santisima Señora de San Juan de los Lagos (see figure 4.5), a small triangular statue often brought from the popular shrine in Jalisco to sites in the U.S. Southwest such as the shrine at San Juan, Texas, where Chicanos pray to her. As the Mexican cultural theorist Jorge González has noted, the official Church hierarchy and those engaged in these alternate religious practices "read" the same signs differently. While the Church interprets these icons as devotion to the mother of Christ, the

people see a more personalized "nuestra Sanjuanita de los Lagos" (67). In Cisneros' story, the supplicant, Tere, and her family travel to San Antonio twice to see the statue. In an example of Cisneros' wry humor and the confrontational stance some worshippers take toward the saints, Tere's sister, Yoli, prays for help in losing weight, "<u>because I don't want to wind up like Tía Perla, embroidering altar cloths and dressing saints</u>" (122)—this precisely as she participates in just such a religious ritual, praying to the Virgin. The cultural and temporal hybridity of the prayer is evidenced in parodical references to contemporary images such as "Grasa Fantastica, guaranteed to burn away fat—It really works, Tere, just rub some on while you're watching TV" (122)—and the contemporary incipient feminism as the petitioner prays to the Virgin herself for help in finding a boyfriend. On the second visit, after the petition for the boyfriend has been granted, Tere asks the Virgin to "[l]ift this heavy cross from my shoulders and leave me like I was before, wind on my neck, my arms swinging free, and no one telling me how I ought to be" (122). Sanjuanita de los Lagos is rearticulated to contemporary social concerns, often far removed from the priorities of the official Church.

Several of Cisneros' *milagritos* are addressed to the "Miraculous Black Christ of Esquipulas" (122) (fig. 4.18), whose powers of healing in locales as far apart as Guatemala and Chimayó, New Mexico, are allegedly transmitted through material contact with or consumption of the earth at the shrine.[21] In Guatemala a type of narrative geophagy is practiced wherein clay tablets called *bultos* or *tierra del santo* are stamped with narrative icons of the Virgin, saints, or the crucifix of Esquipulas. These mininarratives are then blessed and eaten to produce a *milagrito*, or to cure ailments, especially those of menstruation and childbirth. Whereas indigenous people of the Americas more easily identify with the dark skin of the suffering Christ figure, one of Cisneros' petitioners additionally identifies with this version of Christ from his position of marginalization as a gay man. As I will discuss in chapter 5, "Benjamin T." writes his entire message in code, engaging in what Hebdige terms "hiding in the light." His sexual transgression both displays and hides itself in this public space, puncturing the sacred aura of the church setting with its poignancy and transgression. I would argue that the intertexts of this narrative include the images and legend of Santa Librada (fig. 4.19), who allegedly grew a beard to escape marriage to an unwanted suitor and who is often portrayed as a transgender figure, bearded in a woman's clothing, while undergoing martyrdom on the cross.

In a parallel syncretism to that of the Black Christ of Esquipulas, one petitioner in Cisneros' story invokes the "Seven African Powers" to influence the Illinois state lottery in his favor. The words with which the character begins his prayer verbally re-create the picture on the popular holy card discussed above in which seven circular images of each of the powers encircle the image of the cross (see figure 4.7): "Seven African Powers that surround our Savior—Obatala, Yemaya, Ochún, Orunla, Ogun, Elegua, and Shango— why don't you behave and be good to me?" (119). The circles representing each of the named African powers on the holy card contain visual mininarratives, as does the large image of the crucifixion in the central circle. Additionally,

Figure 4.18. *Black Christ of Esquipulas, San Fernando Cathedral, San Antonio, Texas*

they function as enlarged versions of the charms, or *dijes*, on a chain necklace or bracelet that encircles the central image of the cross, setting it off as the main visual text, itself also in the shape of an enlarged circular charm or *dije*. Although African motifs underlie these syncretic representations, Christian images predominate: the card's visual layout places the image of Christ at the center, and the surrounding images are those of Christian saints, despite the small-print African names in the captions. Nonetheless, as discussed earlier, the double encoding of these syncretic representations permits a variety of interpretative engagements with the holy card so that practitioners of Santería can engage in their own readings of the card's officially sanctioned religious images. Like the Black Christ of Esquipulas and the Virgin of Guadalupe

Figure 4.19. "Santa Librata" (photograph reproduced from Mexican Folk Retablos, 1974, *courtesy of Gloria Fraser Giffords)*

herself, these syncretic Christianized images represent a non-official visual iconography within Latino religious practice, even though the Church also encodes them within its own pictorial prayer cards.

Cisneros' rearticulation of the Virgin of Guadalupe figure as an image of feminist strength in the final metatextual passage of the story continues the strong transgressive thread present in both the story and its visual inter-texts. The prayers to Guadalupe invoke the many visual representations of the Virgin in which the four apparitions are recounted pictorially in circular insets in the four corners (see figure 4.10), as well as the self-referential rep-

Figure 4.20. "Juan Diego with the Tilma of the Virgin of Guadalupe" (photograph reproduced from Mexican Devotional Retablos, 1994, courtesy of Gloria Fraser Giffords)

resentations in which Juan Diego himself displays his *tilma* to viewers as he did to the doubting bishop (fig. 4.20). In much the same way, the petitioner Chayo tries to assuage readers' doubts about the possibilities of rearticulating *la Guadalupana* to feminist concerns. As discussed in chapter 1, the typeface of Chayo's narrative ex-voto matches that of the book as a whole in a metatextual reference to Cisneros herself. Like the Juan Diego figure shown holding his *tilma* for viewers to see in some representations of the Guadalupe narrative, the Chayo-Cisneros figure strives self-consciously to convince the reader or viewer of the value of the reconfigured religious image.

Among the numerous visual intertexts of Cisneros' resignification of

Figure 4.21. Yolanda M. López, "Portrait of the Artist: Tableau Vivant," Guadalupe series, 1978 (photograph by Susan R. Mogul; courtesy of Yolanda M. López)

the Virgin are the handkerchief and tattoo art produced by prisoners[22] and the militant, modern Virgins portrayed by Chicana artists, perhaps the most transgressive of which is the montage between the title and painting on the cover of the book *Chicana Lesbians*. Yolanda López's 1978 installation "Portrait of the Artist: Tableau Vivant" closely parallels the Chayo section of "Little Miracles." In the installation, López poses in front of a re-creation of the Virgin of Guadalupe's aura as a self-assured, active woman in her jogging clothes, confidently displaying paint brushes in both hands (fig. 4.21). Like the artist Chayo-Cisneros who is the subject of her own narrative *retablo* to the Virgin at the end of Cisneros' story, López resyncretizes the image of Guadalupe using contemporary feminist images of women's strength and creativity. Both López and Cisneros reinterpret their grandmothers' and mothers' devotion to the Virgin, as is evident in López's series *Our Lady of Guadalupe* depicting her grandmother, her mother, and herself as contemporary Guadalupes (del Castillo, McKenna, and Yarbro-Bejarano, 64, 326). In much the same way as Chayo begins to understand her grandmother's and mother's devotion to Guadalupe as a sign of strength rather than submission, López describes her intention in the three Guadalupe paintings: "I feel living, breathing women also deserve the respect and love lavished on Guadalupe. . . . It is a call to look at women, hard working, enduring and mundane, as the heroines of our daily routine" (qtd. in LaDuke, 121).

While most of Cisneros' fictive petitioners pray to official and syncretic religious images, the entirely non-official folk healer Don Pedrito Jaramillo plays a central role in the story. Cisneros credits a visit she made to Jaramillo's shrine in south Texas as her inspiration to write "Little Miracles."[23] From his arrival in the United States from Mexico in 1881 until his death in 1907, Don Pedrito dispensed folk cures and food to hundreds who journeyed to his home on Los Olmos Creek. He also traveled to Corpus Christi, San Antonio, and Laredo to cure people. Many of his followers wrote to him, and these petitions, which sometimes numbered two hundred per week, became the precursors of the written notes that supplicants would leave at his shrine after his death. Elevating him to the level of an unofficial folk saint, people believed he would intercede on their behalf in obtaining divine favors. Many placed his photo or a statue of him prominently on their home altars, either alone or with images of other, official saints. Octavio Romano describes in detail the appearance of the shrine at Jaramillo's grave site and reproduces several of the written petitions left there in 1957. The petitions are homologous in structure and content to those of Cisneros' fictive petitioners, including one that asks for help "to pass English and graduate" (Romano, 130.)[24]

Cisneros approximates the appearance of the handwritten notes to Don Pedrito Jaramillo left at the shrine by using a typeface of all block letters in her character's petition. She employs a double-voiced narrative in which a grandmother writes in childlike letters, ostensibly re-creating the voice of her seriously ill two-year-old granddaughter. The block lettering refers not only to the grandmother's perceived notion of childlike discourse but perhaps as well to her own limited orthographic abilities. The fictional voice of the child (who in real life can only be uttering beginning words and syllables at this age) continually interacts with the grandmother's diction and the imagined "child talk" she incorporates into her note. Although the medical condition appears tragic and almost unbelievable in its severity with both the loss of a kidney and the discovery of a tumor, the petition insists on its own truthfulness, openly referring to the grandmother's authorship both in the "child's" note and in a testimonial metatextual note beneath it. The petition is designed to become part of the display at the shrine in the hope that "everybody who sees this letter will take a minute to ask for [the granddaughter's] health" (118). It contests its own fictionality precisely as it appears in a work of fiction.

A second important *curandero* invoked in the story is Niño Fidencio (1898–1938), whose shrine in Espinazo, Nuevo León, in northeastern Mexico continues to be visited by thousands of pilgrims from Mexico and southern Texas. An especially charismatic *curandero*, his widespread reputation for miracle healings is said to have attracted a visit in 1928 by Mexican President Calles, whom Fidencio reportedly cured of a chronic illness. Turner points out that oral narratives recounting El Niño's powers, as well as testimonial photographs taken during cures, served to widen his reputation, helping to sustain it to this day (" 'Because of This Photography' "). Some of these photographs are deployed as hybrid forms of *retablos*, with written testimony added to the photo to document the miracle. In the story, the written message that Cisneros' fictive petitioner leaves might represent the verbal portion of such an ex-voto, with an implicit intertext of one of Niño Fidencio's many photographs evoked mentally in those of Cisneros' readers with such visual competence.

Indeed, visual representations of Niño Fidencio reveal another of his departures from orthodox religious status: his crossing of gender boundaries. He is said to have been soft and effeminate, to have been called "Mamá," and to have disguised himself as a woman to escape crowds. Turner places this aspect of Fidencio within a widespread tradition of gender manipulations in world religious practices. One widely circulated representation pictures him inside the aura of the Virgin of Guadalupe and displaying the Sacred Heart of Jesus (fig. 4.22). As occurs in the syncretic holy card combining Christian saints and the Seven African Powers, viewers here have access to two semiotic strategies. Turner has argued that in this image of Fidencio, his femininity becomes less troublesome by being associated with the Virgin, while at the same time he can appear more acceptably masculine through the association with Christ as the Sacred Heart (" 'Because of This Photography' "). Certainly the hybridity of this image evokes the syncretism evidenced in the Virgin of Guadalupe herself, in the Black Christ of Esquipulas, and in the transgender aspects of the visual representations of Santa Librada. But the words

Figure 4.22. *Niño Fidencio, popular holy card (photograph by Doré Gardner; reproduced from Doré Gardner's* Niño Fidencio: A Heart Thrown Open, 1992, *courtesy of the Museum of New Mexico Press)*

of Cisneros' petitioner from Pharr, Texas, to Niño Fidencio are an especially apt evocation of the multitemporal hybridity discussed by García Canclini ("Memory and Innovation"): "I would like for you to help me get a job with good pay, benefits, and retirement plan. I promise you if you help me I will make a pilgrimage to your tomb in Espinazo and bring you flowers. Many thanks" (118). Although informed about and desirous of the modern bene-fits accorded to some U.S. workers under advanced capitalism, the petitioner promises to travel to a tiny Mexican village accessible only by a small dirt road to repay the folk healer's assistance.

In addition to the embedded narratives and visual icons implicit in the saints and religious figures invoked, Cisneros' story is imbricated with a larger system of material religious practices with particularized inflections of the official Church grammar. The system includes clothing statues of saints, promising the saints rewards such as jewelry or other ornamentation, punishing the saints if favors are not granted, and even betting with the saint, as is the practice with San Caetano, the patron of gamblers.[25] *Milagritos*, photographs, and other sundry representations of the self are placed beneath the Black Christ of Esquipulas in San Fernando Cathedral in San Antonio, Texas (see figure 4.12). Decades ago in New Mexico Passion re-enactments during Holy Week, large wooden *bultos* of the crucified Christ had plastic bags of blood spilled on them or were made with a hole in the back through which the Sacred Heart was made to palpitate. Cleofas Jaramillo describes a wooden *bulto* of Christ in her church whose jaw was articulated so that it could move to show the agony of death on Good Friday. In some Passion play processions, an *acompanante* or *rezador* walking alongside the man carrying the cross or the woman representing the Virgin reads a scriptural account of the Passion in a narrative voice-over to the visual representation.[26]

In addition to her visit to Don Pedrito Jaramillo's shrine, Cisneros particularly credits as inspiration for her story the public display of *milagritos* (see figure 4.16).[27] Three-dimensional, miniature representations of real-life objects, these iconic signs metonymically symbolize the miracle requested or granted; the small metal hands, feet, breasts, or eyes eschew the verbal, speaking of or for the miracle in spatial rather than temporal terms. The explicit narrative of *retablos* is occluded in favor of a concentrated representation of the corporeal or material, a metonym for the larger narrative of the miracle. The specular predominates over the discursive as these *milagritos* publicly signify the religious figure's power both as individual artifacts and as the semes of a larger system of visual representation in which thousands of them cover the garments of saints and sometimes entire church altars.

In a variation of this practice, everyday material objects are placed at shrines as an offering for, or testimony to, the miracle sought or received. Crutches and braces can signify both the original affliction and the "miracle" of its cure. Shoes and clothing are left for the Holy Child of Atocha, and even though the narrative of the Child of Atocha is not verbally recounted, it implicitly undergirds the symbolic objects that the faithful leave as offerings. Just as *milagritos* or crutches metonymically signify a miracle, the baby shoes offered to the Child of Atocha are lexemes complete in themselves in the visual system that gives testimony to the miracle. For believers and those familiar with the culture, the baby shoes are a shorthand to recount the miracle, as words and lengthier syntagmas might do for the uninitiated.

Cisneros' story relies entirely on the verbal to convey these predominantly visual practices. Through the voice of Chayo in her lengthy petition we "see" the miscellaneous material objects placed at the Virgin's shrine, including hospital bracelets, business cards, notes on scraps of paper, fluorescent orange crocheted roses, and photos; these signs offer viewers the initial elements of a compressed narrative about the individual petitioner: "Caramel-skinned woman in a white graduation cap and gown. Mean dude in bandanna and tattoos. . . . Teenager with a little bit of herself sitting on her lap" (124–25). Although relying on the verbal, Cisneros directs us to visually peruse these displayed images so central to her story. Chayo, who leaves her braid of hair at the shrine as a *milagrito*, establishes for readers the visual context in which her offering is placed: "So many *milagritos* safety-pinned here, so many little miracles dangling from red thread—a gold Sacred Heart, a tiny copper arm, a kneeling man in silver, a bottle, a brass truck, a foot, a house, a hand, a baby, a cat, a breast, a tooth, a belly button, an evil eye. So many petitions, so many promises made and kept" (125). Although "Little Miracles" only specifically invokes its central visual intertexts, the *milagritos* here in Chayo's section, in an important sense several of the verbal notes by supplicants in the story function as a variety of *milagrito*, publicly displayed in the San Fernando Church which the protagonist of the previous story perhaps has entered.

A special variety of votive offering that, like some Passion re-enactments, employs a visual image and redundant yet amplifying narrative verbal text, is an additional key visual intertext of Cisneros' story. These popular paintings, called *retablos* or ex-votos, are displayed in churches, shrines, and even ordinary spaces such as outdoor fences and usually employ rich narrative detail (see figure 4.14). Although the painting dominates spatially in most *retablos*, the verbal text is lengthy and moves beyond the traditional function of a caption by amassing numerous narrative syntagmas. There is the sense in these verbal/visual texts that the pictorial portion is insufficient, but neither would a verbal text suffice on its own. The verbal narrative performs a more fully developed function of anchoring in which the diegesis within the expanded caption moves into excess and takes on its own life; while redundant to some degree, it moves beyond mere repetition. If space is the predominant rhetorical strategy of the pictorial part of the ex-voto, time is the dominant narrative element of the verbal text. Time serves both a documentary and sequential function, establishing the date on which the miracle occurred and delineating the temporal move from the disruption of the initial narrative equilibrium to the final return to a new state of balance. In many *retablos*, however, long narrative syntagmas are enchained in the verbal portion, and the resultant orality of the *retablo* parallels the lengthy verbal utterances of Cisneros' petitioners.[28]

Cisneros extends these popular religious practices to a further dimension of popular recuperation, for now they are also linked to issues of social justice for U.S. Latinos, feminist liberation, and gay oppression. Although the visual intertextual system that undergirds the story is immensely important, the verbal utterances of the characters in the text allow a greater discursive development of social issues than is usually possible in the popular religious practices themselves. For example, one petitioner's request for $253.72 of unpaid wages for "67½ hours that first week and 79 hours the second" (120) offers readers a clear example of the egregiously substandard wages paid to some migrant workers in the United States. Along with the rich narrative detail of this twenty-two-line petition to the Virgencita de Guadalupe, this precise information connects devotion to the Virgin to issues of social injustice.

Instead of including photos or illustrations in the story, Cisneros requires supplemental visual work by readers, deploying her skill as a writer to enable us to hear her characters' rich speech. Although readers must look beyond the text to envision the image of San Martín de Porres if they are unfamiliar with this important black Latin American saint (fig. 4.23), they can clearly hear the distinctive voice of the petitioner who prays to him: "Please send us clothes, furniture, shoes, dishes. We need anything that don't eat. Since the fire we have to start all over again and Lalo's disability check ain't much and don't go far. Zulema would like to finish school but I says she can just forget about it now. . . ." (117). Another message thanking Saint Sebastian for helping to get a petitioner's extended family out of his house further exemplifies this orality: "Here is the little gold milagrito I promised you, a little house, see? And it ain't that cheap gold-plate shit either. So now that I paid you back, we're even, right? Cause I don't like for no one to say Victor Lozano don't pay his debts. I pays cash on the line, bro. And Victor Lozano's word like his deeds is solid gold" (121).

Father Virgilio Elizondo, former rector of the San Fernando Cathedral in San Antonio, has noted the seriousness with which such *promesas* or bargains with God are made and repaid: "People know that it requires more than just promising to be good. It requires some action, a sacrifice of sorts, made for God. It requires commitment. You can't just send in a postcard or use your

Figure 4.23. Statue of San Martín de Porres, San Fernando Cathedral, San Antonio, Texas

Visa card. It has to be personal" (qtd. in McLemore, 12-E). Cisneros' character has developed an elaborate metaphor in praying to San Sebastian in which his in-laws represent the arrows in the saint's chest; he repays his *promesa* with an expensive gold *milagrito* that gives testimony to his self-sacrifice to keep his end of the bargain and at the same time iconically represents the house now once again his. Cisneros' language enables readers to both hear the character's voice and visualize the images to which he refers.

Cisneros has elaborated a unique visual-verbal hybridity in these two stories although only verbal signifiers appear on the pages. Underlying the rich orality of the utterances is a particularized system of primarily visual religious intertexts. For readers in possession of, or willing to attain, the cultural competence that the stories demand, the narratives constitute an intricate imbrication of the verbal and the visual in which popular Latino religious practices are linked to contemporary social issues.

Ponce, Chávez, and Cisneros recuperate the repressed body of official Catholicism in a variety of ways. I have focused here on the interplay of the visual and the verbal in these texts as a mode of reclaiming the controlled vision and speech of orthodox religious practice for use in popular and neo-popular religious practices. As do other Latina narrativists, Ponce, Chávez, and Cisneros deploy forbidden speech and repressed vision as a means of reclaiming religion in their struggle for social justice and a new moral vision. While writers such as Corpi and Martínez link specific political events to religious imagery, Cisneros and Chávez focus on more general political issues such as low wages, inadequate housing and schooling, child abuse, and issues of gender and sexuality. All three writers emphasize popular religion and syncretism in addition to official religious practices. And although there is an ethnic inflection in many of the practices they include in their narratives, the writers move beyond the stereotypical representation of postmodern ethnic commodification, revealing the deep connection of religion in Latino communities to spirituality, tradition, and issues of social justice.

CHAPTER FIVE

Transgressive Narrative Tactics and Subcultural Expression

Transgression and rupture have long been the chosen modes of representation of countercultural groups. Retaliating against a variety of sites of power and control, and at the same time fashioning a distinct group identity, subordinated groups often wage cultural battles against the dominant modes of representation rather than attempt to radically change social relations of power through the exercise of force. As Dick Hebdige has argued, subcultural groups frequently play with their power to discomfit, engaging in rhetorical contestation and "resistance through ritual" that challenges the symbolic order through transgression with an underlying logic (18).

The literary production of Latinos in the United States is a vital and varied form of subcultural production; that is, a key means by which a subordinated group works to invert its institutionalized negation. As theorists from the Birmingham school in England have argued, a scale of cultural power exists whereby the dominant sociocultural order represents itself as the primary culture and invokes normative definitions by which other cultures are to be evaluated and contained; both dominant and subordinated groups struggle to produce their own "maps of meaning" through culture as a mode of rendering the world intelligible to both members and nonmembers (Clarke et al., 10). In a myriad of cultural forms that reflect the wide heterogeneity of Latinos in the United States, some in this diverse group have attempted to map out territorial spaces through a particularized subcultural expression.

The term "subculture" carries a number of negative signifieds, implying an inferior culture or subdivisional elements of a larger, more valuable culture. Theorists at Birmingham note that the prefix "sub" refers to the culture of a subordinated group, not a culture that is substandard or inferior. They thereby foreground the relations of power that obtain in the production and reception of culture, and the social divisions that affect all cultural practices in a given society. Further, although subculture is often a hybrid of "high" and "low" forms, it can nonetheless function as an important political contestation; it is not simply a variation of high cultural models that defines itself within the terms that dominant groups establish. Amplifying the theories of Bakhtin, Stallybrass and White have lucidly demonstrated as well the inaccuracy of viewing subculture as mere play, as a form of "low" knowledge with no serious political import: "one of the most powerful ruses of the dominant [group is] to pretend that critique can only exist in the language of 'reason,' 'pure knowledge' and 'seriousness.'" The logic that underlies certain forms of subculture can "unsettle 'given' social positions and interrogate the rules of inclusion, exclusion and domination which [structure] the social ensemble" (43).

Feminist critiques of subcultural theory have questioned the ostensible redundancy of women in subcultures. Early theorists viewed the style of a subcultural group, for example, as primarily that of its men—in the case of Latinos, the hyper-masculinized figures of the *pachuco*, or the lowrider. In light of this critique we might classify the recent fiction of U.S. Latina writers as a sub-subcultural movement that contests both the "dominant" culture of the U.S. mainstream as well as the "parent" culture—the patriarchal blindspots of the Latino cultural "renaissance" of the late 1960s and beyond. Here I will focus on a series of transgressive narrative tactics in which some Latina writers engage as doubly counterhegemonic practices, with particular attention to a critically neglected text written by Mary Helen Ponce.

Sexual Transgression and the Socially Constructed Individual

The ruptural narrative strategies of contemporary Latina writers are an essential element of the battle for control of signification discussed in chapter 2. However, certain narrative transgressions combine more successfully with the elements of group struggle than do others. Some writers, in an attempt to reassert agency in a society that marginalizes them through gender, ethnicity, and to varying degrees through class, map out these narrative tactics on the grid of an exaggerated individualism. Other narrative renderings of subcultural transgression either shatter the mystique of individualism or allow the apparently individualist attempt to reestablish agency to be almost involuntarily drawn into the social.

The issue of individualism surfaces, for example, in three distinct narrative renderings of female autoeroticism in the texts of Alma Luz Villanueva, Ana Castillo, and Nicholasa Mohr. All three writers create narrative ruptures with direct and indirect portrayals of women masturbating, which, like lesbianism, constitutes one of the most serious affronts to patriarchal authority. In each narrative, the transgressive, usually private act ruptures to one degree or another into public space—both on the published page of the text and on the diegetic plane.

Rosa, in Villanueva's *The Ultraviolet Sky*, masturbates at 7:30 A.M. on a city beach in San Francisco, where, we are asked to believe, no one is about; the protagonist of Castillo's narrative poem "Coffee Break" uses the public/private space of a storeroom in her office building for her transgressively autoerotic "performance"; the private acts of resistance to achieve sexual autonomy of Mohr's Zoraida in "Aunt Rosana's Rocker" (*Rituals*) are forcefully brought into the public sphere both by the couple's cramped living conditions and by the husband's desperate attempt to regain patriarchal control by revealing details of her transgressive sexuality to others. This interplay between the public and the private, crucial to subcultural expression, as Hebdige has argued, connects closely to the mode in which each of these writers renders individualism narratively.

Although Villanueva's character transgresses in a public place allegedly privatized by the temporary absence of the public, Castillo's character finds a semiprivate space within the public workplace. In both cases, the fear and excitement of discovery permeates the transgression: someone else may appear on the beach in the first instance, and in the second, "A tiny streak/of sun leaks/through a space/of unpainted glass," creating a spotlight to reveal the forbidden act (Castillo, "Coffee Break," *Invitation*, 19). Hebdige has noted that "[s]ubculture forms up in the space between surveillance and the evasion of surveillance, it translates the fact of being under scrutiny into the pleasure of being watched. It is hiding in the light" (35). Besides "hiding" in the streak of sunlight, Castillo's character further inscribes her transgression within the public sphere by imagining an audience applauding her "performance," and even envisioning the male and paternal approval conflated in the song "Isn't She Lovely," which she sings to herself as she returns to work. Villanueva's Rosa terms her subversion "[making] love to one's self" and a mode of "self acceptance" (*Ultraviolet Sky*, 41, 42), yet she fantasizes about a man she has recently met and previous lovers in addition to female goddesses. Thus, while Villanueva and Castillo aim to glorify individualistic cultural expression in these narratives, the transgressive acts they describe ultimately require a minimal narrative grounding in a wider social space.

Mohr, in contrast, appears almost to deny the protagonist of "Aunt Rosana's Rocker" a narratively autonomous presence. The scenes of Zoraida's sexual transgressions are recounted through her husband's disapproving optic, narratively rendered primarily through his visual and auditory perceptions. But surprisingly, Mohr's narrative gives her character greater social agency than do Castillo's and Villanueva's full descriptions of sexual transgression.

Mohr's narrative politically reappropriates Zoraida's act of resistance by delineating the turmoil it establishes for the traditional male power and the extended family with whom he forms a loose group of cohorts. Where Villanueva's and Castillo's renderings of transgressive autoeroticism attempt to deny the Other, Mohr reveals more about the act's disruptive force by encoding it within the surveillance of the male Other and those who temporarily share his subject position.

As an autonomous agent of sexual transgression, Zoraida stands in marked contrast to the weak male figure of her hypochondriacal husband, who constantly takes vitamins, tiptoes around the apartment, and futilely tries to re-establish in his home the power denied him in the workplace. Unable to exercise his proprietary rights over his wife's sexuality, he works to establish a type of hegemonic bloc made up of his and Zoraida's relatives, who temporarily become his allies in order to solve the problem of the protagonist's alternative sexuality. Women become part of this temporary hegemonic alliance to defend the patriarchal authority of husband over wife; together the husband and Zoraida's well-meaning father exercise leadership in the group, and all come to agree that the "commonsense" solution to the problem is simply to remove from the couple's bedroom the great aunt's chair in which Zoraida enjoys sexual fantasies—her form of resistance to her husband's demands for sex. As Gramsci has noted, the notion of "common sense" is unstable and continually transforming itself even though it may appear to be a rigid form of knowledge at a given time. Here, the husband's struggle to articulate a commonsense, apparently logical solution to the crisis of the patriarchal authority has succeeded in establishing a temporary alliance of people formerly at odds with one another, who adhere for the moment to their solution as if it were an obvious and correct form of knowledge. Mohr disarticulates this "commonsense" view of the situation, recoding the rocking chair as the bearer of female familial tradition and the site of a temporary sexual liberation, all the while overcoding as futile the solution that the temporary hegemonic group decides upon.

Mohr's social positioning of an individual act of transgression in this story parallels her narrative rendering of ruptural strategies in the final story in *Rituals of Survival*, "The Artist." Here, as in "Aunt Rosana's Rocker," she demonstrates that the social antagonisms that underlie populist rupture cannot be reduced to essentialist notions of gender difference. The protagonist, Inez, is antagonistically opposed to both her oppressive aunt and the violent man she marries to escape the aunt. Mohr's narrative functions as an initial preparatory stage for the kind of "populist rupture" Laclau discusses; the story collapses the spurious gender differences between the aunt and the man she encourages Inez to marry (both in fact share the authoritarian ideology of patriarchy) and shows that the two are equivalent in their attempts to deny Inez her autonomy. This new system of equivalences allows social antagonisms to become ruptural, as Laclau has theorized.

The transgressive strategies in which Inez engages move beyond Zoraida's lone, yet socially situated ruptural tactics. Indeed, these two stories frame the collection and point to a path for women's development beyond Zoraida's initial mode of resistance (a "making do" through fantasy) to Inez's strong and effective contestation of patriarchal dominance. Even within the outward confines of patriarchal control—for example, when Inez's husband sends her to a female physician to prevent a male doctor from having contact with his "property"—Inez obtains access to birth control that enables her to engage in another series of transgressive acts that will salvage her autonomy. Free from the burden of bearing and raising children at the young age of eighteen, Inez secretly studies art, paying for her lessons by working as a model for other students. In her husband's mystified patriarchal consciousness, her art lessons are greatly transgressive, but worse is her posing nude. Her public nudity invokes the antithesis of the patriarchal possession of one's wife, away from the view of others. And worse, the entrance of his privatized vision of his marital property into the public sphere will be reproduced in the studio on dozens of canvasses, moving interminably beyond his control as they enter the public domain outside the studio as well.

The transgressive tactic of the lie surfaces in "The Artist" as a double structure. In one instance, Inez lies to a friend from a position of weakness, and in another, she lies to an enemy from a position of strength. Still in the process of establishing her autonomy, Inez tells her friends at the art school that her husband is away on military duty, elaborating more precise details of the lie in conversations with Aldo, one of her closest friends at the school. When finally breaking away from her husband, Joe, at the end of the story, however, she deliberately shatters the ideology of romance in a ruptural lie about herself; in this especially transgressive lie she wages a battle for discursive and narrative dominance in a struggle between competing ideological views of reality. Inez counterposes an invented, defiled picture of herself to Joe's romanticized vision of her as the virginal object to be possessed, telling him a doubly transgressive lie about premarital sex and incest. "Uncle Generoso was my lover," she tells Joe, a lie that readers easily decode because of the prior positive portrayal of Generoso and the denotation of his name. Thus, Inez refuses Joe's interpellation of her as a wife-object and substitutes an ostensibly denigrated image that she herself controls. The ruptural narrative she invents about herself parallels the transgression that her nude posing represents for Joe's patriarchal consciousness.

In contrast, Mohr shows the raw power of the patriarchal order when it engages in its own transgression in another scene in "The Artist" where Inez's aunt allows her son, Papo, to masturbate freely in the public spaces of the family's apartment while others observe him with disgust, powerless to stop him. Unlike Zoraida's autoeroticism in "Aunt Rosana's Rocker," Papo's transgression does not threaten the patriarchal order. Forced to undergo this form of visual violence in her living space, Inez retaliates with a series of transgressive drawings of her cousin "resembling his own penis, . . . eating his penis, or . . . as a rat with the body of a penis." Finally she draws a caricature especially pleasurable for her, "of Cousin Deidre beating Papo to death with his penis" (*Rituals*, 112). In her drawings, Inez turns the oppressive motifs of patriarchal sexual violence back on themselves, just as she will later reverse the terms of Joe's romantic, possessive vision of her in her transgressive lie about her incestuous premarital experiences.

In Cristina Garcia's *Dreaming in Cuban* sexual transgression enters the public sphere both intra- and extradiegetically through writing. In a first-person section early in the novel, the young Pilar Puente describes the auto-erotic experiments she enjoys in the private sphere of the shower, which are dragged into the public sphere when her mother reads her hidden diary. Two instances of writing are overlain in this narrative of revealed transgression, that of the diary and of the text we are reading. Where having written about transgression is ultimately a source of betrayal for the diegetic character Pilar, writing implicitly empowers the more mature Cuban American narrativist Garcia, who freely writes about the private in the published book we are reading.

Like Zoraida's transgressive acts, Pilar's sexual experimentation incurs the redoubled repression of the authority figure, who desires control at all costs. Pilar's mother beats her, pulls out her hair, limits the time she is allowed to spend in the bathroom, and forces her to work in the bakery for twenty-five cents an hour. And like Mohr, Garcia emphasizes the double standards at work in sexual repression and permissiveness. Pilar's father freely walks the streets of New York with an illicit lover, and even her repressive mother engages in exaggerated sexual behavior, exhausting her husband with persistent demands for sex each night that loudly pervade the entire house. In the face of these public sexual displays, Pilar has difficulty accepting her mother's calling her "*desgraciada*" while beating her for having masturbated in the shower. Garcia successfully situates this involuntary revelation of private sexuality in the social context of patriarchal double standards and authoritarian control.

Sexual, religious, and gender-role transgression are linked in Pat Mora's 1982 story "Hands." On one level, the story's primary moral or lesson involves the politics of signification. Mora foregrounds the arbitrariness of a sexual signifier such as women's breasts, revealing the roots of erotic desire to be closely connected to personal rather than socially predetermined semiotic systems. Besides the transgressive strategy of deconstructing the arbitrary cultural significations of women's breasts, the story critiques the sexual repression of traditional mainstream religion and portrays alternative popular practices such as *brujería*.[1]

The protagonist, Cuca, a devout churchgoer, had married years earlier "seeking a union more spiritual than physical" (223). To her surprise she discovered a sexual desire for her husband yet continued to suffer from the conflict between her sexuality and its repression by Catholicism. Speaking about sex to her husband "cause[es] her pain" (223), and as she tries to unlearn the religious repression, he urges her to "let go" during sex. After discovering he is having an affair with another woman, Cuca visits a *bruja*, or sorceress. Although popular rumor has it that the *bruja* can "shrink a man's private parts," Cuca asks instead for magical remedies to shrink the breasts of her husband's lover, to "make her flat like a boy" (224). Smart enough to ask for a remedy that will preserve her own sexual pleasure at the expense of her husband's with his lover, Cuca hopes to defeminize her rival while preserving her husband's masculinity for her own ends.

As she engages in the two-week ritual of snipping off pieces of a cotton doll's breasts and sprinkling a powder outside the lover's door, her rival's breasts gradually disappear. But as the *bruja* had predicted, this "masculinization" of the lover does not achieve the husband's return. As the story ends, he rejects his wife's voluptuous breasts in order to caress her bony back, which reminds him of his lover's new body. Large breasts are not inherently erotic objects, guaranteed to produce male desire, despite widespread social conventions to the contrary. Personal rather than socially predetermined semiotic systems are at work in the construction of objects of desire. Mora only subtly alludes to the homoerotic level of the husband's desire for the transformed body of his lover, but the brief incursion into the transgressive space of gender reversal allows readers to question received social conventions about sexual difference and desire.

The transgressive ritual Cuca engages in is, of course, shortsighted— misdirected competitively against another woman rather than to the source of her problem with her husband. On the positive side, however, Cuca transcends the expected wifely passivity and the constraints of Catholicism ("one didn't ask the Lord to remove a woman's breasts" [225]). To satisfy her desire to feel her husband's hands once again caressing her breasts, she takes action with her own hands, engaging in the rituals the Church forbids as "black, evil, smelling of the devil" (222). The transgressive activity not only marks her initial steps into agency and autonomy but serves to foreground the semiotic construction of women's bodies into desirable objects, sometimes even in homoerotic terms.

Gendered Youth Subculture

Angela McRobbie has criticized Hebdige's concept of style for its structural exclusion of women; as a signifier of desire and the starting point for fantasies and the sorting out of friends from enemies, style for Hebdige is a "desirable mode of narcissistic differentiation" in which women appear as static objects such as "girlfriends, whores or 'faghags'" (McRobbie, 43). Hebdige, McRobbie says, fails to study the distinct modes in which girls engage in subverting and reassembling semiotic codes through subculture.[2] Contemporary writers such as Julia Alvarez and Mary Helen Ponce, in contrast, emphasize the subculture of young U.S. Latinas. As I will show in greater detail, Ponce in *The Wedding* reveals the modes in which *pachuco* subcultural expression constitutes a leak or rupture in the mainstream culture that it sometimes parodies; more importantly, however, her novel centrally pivots on the contestatory figure of "*la pachuca*," who confronts, quotes, and parodies the intertext of male *pachuco* culture.

Alvarez's "A Regular Revolution" (*García Girls*) examines the strategies of resistance of four sisters who have recently immigrated with their parents to the United States from the Dominican Republic. The girls struggle between two worlds both culturally and materially, for even as they try to adjust to life in the United States, their parents send them back each summer to the island, in part to control the daughters' sexuality. Transgressions such as smoking, using hair removal cream, reading the book *Our Bodies, Our Selves*, and staying out all night require that the girls be resocialized by spending the summer back in the Dominican Republic. And when Fifi, the youngest, admits to using marijuana, her punishment is an entire year in their homeland.

Alvarez compares the parental authority to the state authority and argues that the girls' subcultural tactics constitute as real a revolution as the one the girls' father engaged in against the dictator Trujillo. The elaborate tactics for hiding each other's transgressions from their parents in the high school years develop later into more effective, although still only protofeminist, subversion. The central narrative thread recounts a key "revolutionary" tactic that allows them to "take open aim and [win]" (111) so that their lives become their own; it involves, however, an apparent betrayal of subcultural solidarity. "A Regular Revolution" reverses this surface appearance to show that the tactic is based on a strong protofeminism as it astutely redeploys one of the oppressor's strategies of containment for its own ends.

The narrative turns on a series of primary and secondary subcultural transgressions. While the sisters take pleasure in talking about and appearing to break the social taboos against "incest, group sex, lesbian sex, and virgin sex" (125), Alvarez ultimately shows these to be of secondary importance in the "revolution." Similarly, while the three older sisters are at first happy that Fifi's boyfriend on the island is a transgressive figure because he's an illegitimate cousin, they soon realize that he is "quite a tyrant, a mini Papi and Mami rolled into one" (120). The elaborate pretense of leaving and returning to the house as a group so that the parents will think Fifi is chaperoned while with her boyfriend is similarly shown to be a secondary, less important transgression—one that in fact runs the danger of cementing Fifi more firmly within the patriarchal order.

Upon discovering that Fifi is engaging in unprotected sex with her macho boyfriend, the sisters move from secondary to primary subcultural transgression. Realizing that pregnancy will close Fifi's options by forcing her to marry immediately, securing her firmly within the patriarchal authority, the sisters break the agreed-upon rules of youth subculture. They transgress against their own youth group's transgression, appearing on the surface to uphold the parents' attempts to control Fifi's sexuality. In a protofeminist recuperation of an oppressor's strategy, they prevent her from sleeping with her boyfriend because he refuses to use birth control. As a result, all four girls are allowed to return to the United States, where their lives are less restricted, because the parents' plan for straightening out the transgressing Fifi have failed.

Three of the girls move from secondary to primary transgressive tactics, believing that they have won a "real revolution." Fifi, however, not having been allowed a voice in these efforts to save her, regards her sisters as traitors.

Indeed, Fifi continues to suffer from patriarchal oppression once back in the United States, and even after she marries, she still engages in youthful transgressive tactics against patriarchal authority. In the chronologically later events of "The Kiss," she publicly embarrasses her father by sexualizing a party game in which the rules allow the participants only to play at being sexual. The blindfolded father is to guess which family member is affectionately kissing him; Fifi, whose name he refuses to utter in his guesses, and who has worked long hours to give him this party, decides to assert her presence by giving him a transgressively sexual kiss that violates the incest taboo. The sexuality he had previously tried to repress in her throughout her adolescence returns with a vengeance to contest patriarchy here. Just as he had made her vulnerable years earlier by reading her private love letters and thereby exposing her sexuality in the public sphere, so does she fight back now by exposing his sexual pleasure in public. Her tactic remains at the level of protofeminism, though, as did her sisters' transgressions in "A Real Revolution"; such youthful subcultural ploys offer therapeutic pleasure but direct themselves to the symptoms rather than the causes of patriarchal repression.

Parody, the Carnivalesque, and Pachuco/a Subculture

Like many U.S. Latina narratives, Mary Helen Ponce's 1989 novel *The Wedding* has not received the mainstream recognition accorded to such writers as Sandra Cisneros, Cristina Garcia, Julia Alvarez, and Ana Castillo; instead it has been the subject of only a few and very mixed reviews. Alejandro Morales, a first-rate novelist and critic himself, deems Ponce's characters stereotypical, unidimensional, and lacking in history. Another critic accuses the novel of insincerity, being laden with clichés and Chicano stereotypes, and crippled by bad writing; in authoritarian fashion, he insists that the novel "doesn't belong in most bookstores" (Lazaroff, 28). A reviewer for the *Albuquerque Journal* accuses Ponce of employing a condescending tone and of being embarrassed by her characters, and another for *Kirkus Reviews* argues that the speech of Ponce's characters is not only flat but of the wrong ethnicity.[3]

I would like to suggest another way of reading the novel, however, that both incorporates and goes beyond these criticisms. To a certain degree, these reviewers engage in monological appropriations of the book. In fact, throughout much of *The Wedding*, Ponce engages in a double-voiced quotation of the speech and gestures of *pachuco* subculture and ends the book with a carnival-esque parody of the traditional mainstream wedding as it is reconfigured by this subcultural group. Bakhtinian theory, in conjunction with the Birmingham school's theories of subculture and the feminist responses to subcultural studies, enable a more dialogic understanding of Ponce's novel. Ponce reveals the modes in which *pachuco* subcultural expression constitutes a leak or rupture in the mainstream culture that it sometimes parodies. The contestatory figure of "*la pachuca*" in the novel parodies the social intertext of male *pachuco* culture, as do the other gender issues and the bodily functions that surface in the final wedding scene.

Pachucos have long been stigmatized in the press, in academic studies of deviance, and in large sectors of the popular imagination. In interviews conducted by Laura Cummings, however, older Mexican Americans in the Southwest remember the *pachuco* culture of their day in different terms; *pachuquismo* for them involved clothing styles, music and dances, good times, occasional fights, work and jobs, police roundups and beatings, incarceration in prisons and reformatories, and punitive shaving of ducktail hairstyles. Nevertheless, the negative media images of *pachucos* had affected the family life of those interviewed; sons were forbidden to wear baggy pants, and sometimes parents cut up their zoot suits with scissors; one woman's uncle called her "*pachuca*" to belittle her to other family members. Like the interviews Cummings conducted, Ponce's novel offers an alternative view of *pachuco* subculture; in contrast to the academic models and popular images of deviance and stigmatized identity, Ponce humorously critiques from within the subculture she grew up with, presenting what might be termed a narrational "thick description" that reveals both the pleasures and internal contradictions of *pachuco* subcultural practices.

Without romanticizing *pachuco* culture, Ponce shows the logic with which it operates and the ways in which it uses signs to interrogate the rules of the social ensemble. Early on, Ponce delineates the material roots of the group's social alienation: the failure of the schools to educate;[4] limited employment alternatives such as garbage collection, farm labor, or turkey processing; and the destructive attempts to ameliorate social powerlessness with compensations in the private sphere through gender relations. The subgroup's economic deprivation leads to the excessiveness of subcultural display—elaborate clothing, make-up, bodily poses, decorated cars, language patterns, and the culmination of the ritual spectacle of the wedding. This semiotic display necessarily foregrounds the visual, "hiding in the light," as Dick Hebdige has argued (35), transforming surveillance into the pleasure of being watched. Ponce deftly describes the signs that this subgroup employs in its attempt to question social and class hierarchies; at the same time, however, the novel's unromantic realism and humor reveal the limitations of these semiotic elaborations.

Sammy-the-Cricket López, the main male figure, has dropped out of elementary school at age thirteen and lives in a reconverted toolshed with his widowed immigrant mother and his brother, who is frequently in trouble with the law. Cricket fails at several of his early attempts to work, most notably at a machine shop where he cannot read the directions on the soldering iron, thinking the "on" switch says "one." He finally gets what he terms "clean" work as a garbage collector, where he learns from his fellow workers that "*yesca*," or pot, will enable him to get through each day's heavy labor. His affiliation with, and eventual leadership of, the *pachuco* group Los Tacones (The Heels) relates directly to his social and economic marginalization. An elaborate system of vestimentary semiotics — including custom-made suits and the three-inch heels for which the group is named — joins the implicitly parallel totems of a remodeled '44 Ford and the desire to make the protagonist, Blanca Muñoz, his "old lady." The wedding that Cricket imagines he and Blanca will have is a site of symbolic reversal of his subgroup's social marginalization through public semiotic display.

John Clarke's study of the youth subculture of the British skinheads offers parallels to U.S. *pachuco* culture. "The kids inherit the oral tradition of the area from the parent culture," he notes, referring to the class or social group from which the skinheads come, "especially that part which refers to the community's self-image, its collective solidarity, its conception of masculinity, its orientation to 'outsiders' and so on" ("Skinheads," 101). The group's preoccupation with territoriality and identification of masculinity with physical toughness and the refusal to back down in the face of trouble represent what Clarke terms the "magical recovery of community" — the modes in which the skinheads "attempted to recreate the inherited imagery of the community in a period in which the experiences of increasing oppression demanded forms of mutual organisation and defence" (102). We might ask, then, if Ponce's representation of *pachuco* subculture in the Southern California of the late 1940s and early 1950s shows that the subgroup's attempts to recover a sense of community are magical and imaginary solutions to social problems.

Ponce employs several narrative strategies in *The Wedding* to offer just such a critique, among them double-voiced quotation, parody, the carnivalesque, and the central figuration throughout the novel of a sub-subcultural group of *pachucas* or "pseudo-Pachucas," as Ponce has termed them.[5] The reviewers who have disliked Ponce's writing have characterized it in odd terms. The dialogue is called "flat" and "even laughable," with all the characters speaking at "the same, low linguistic level." One reviewer has even decided that the speech in the novel is of the wrong ethnicity, that of Brooklynites or Chicagoans. Seemingly unaware of the practices of narrative heteroglossia, another accuses Ponce of abandoning and ridiculing her characters because she "energetically affects the speech and cadence of the pachuco Spanglish then abruptly steps out of it into grammatically correct English, as though she wants no part of the world she has created" (Brown, "Novelist"). These readings represent a crisis in what Todorov terms the "little drama" (49) of the utterance, which, according to Bakhtin, is played out between the speaker, object, and listener of a discourse: Ponce's narrative utterances are ineffective for these reviewers because of the absence of a "common horizon between speaker and listener" (85). For Lazaroff, for example, the intertextual resonances of Ponce's dialogue are the previously produced utterances of the Brooklynites or Chicagoans he is familiar with, not those of *pachucos*.

Voloshinov's concept of reported speech, or "speech within speech," is a more effective way of understanding the language in Ponce's novel. When using this narrative strategy, an author signals that the linguistic patterns he or she employs are the utterances of someone else; the speech is transposed into an authorial context and retains the rudiments of its own linguistic integrity. It is crucial, Voloshinov notes, that reported speech be linked to the reporting context; "the true object of inquiry must be the interaction of these two levels" (119). Consider, for example, Ponce's deployment of *pachuco* speech patterns in this third-person description of the rival gangs fighting at the final wedding scene.

> When the two Planchados that were with Skippy saw Los Tacones making fun of their leader, they started to punch away. The first one to get it in the kisser was Tudi the Best Man. His face became a bloody mess. Next, Frankie tried to hit a Planchado with his brass knuckles, but instead of hitting the guy, he hit Blanca's Tio Ernie, who hated Frankie's guts. That was a big mistake. Tio Ernie let Frankie have it with a left to the jaw, just like Joe Louis! By this time it was a free for all. (196)

If we remain aware of the reporting context here as Voloshinov advises, Ponce's critical perspective interacts dialogically with the reported speech she integrates into the passage. The narrative voice is that of the critical insider who tells the events using certain subcultural clichés shared with the larger parent culture of the time. Brooklynites or Chicagoans may indeed have used similar turns of phrase, as members, along with *pachucos*, of a particular "parent" or working-class culture of the 1940s and 1950s. Just as many people today incorporate language patterns currently in vogue into their everyday speech, so, too, did *pachucos* reappropriate colloquial sayings of the time. The speech Ponce reports here represents this common sociolinguistic phenomena rather than being of the wrong ethnicity, as Lazaroff suggests.[6]

Ponce's implicit feminist critique of Cricket's machistic values is the reporting context of the following passage, read as a dialogical utterance:

> By eighteen Cricket . . . got in with Los Tacones, a gang of Pachucos that hung around Kiki's Pool Hall on Saturday nights. He began hanging around with Tudi, a neighbor whom Cricket considered too square, because Tudi gave his mother half of his pay. Worse, Tudi sometimes ironed his own pants! That Tudi's too stuped, Cricket thought. The moola he earns ain't his mudder's. Ain't nobody gonna make me give em my pay. Not even my Ma. Mostly, he hated to pay for the food and cigarettes his brother Sully took with him when running from the cops. (34)

Ponce quotes *pachuco* behavior and speech patterns in this passage not to "stereotype her own people" as the *Los Angeles Times* headlined the review by Morales, but as a parodical, humorous critique of some elements of working-class subculture, here deploying the reporting context of contemporary feminism.

There is a double-voicing as well in the structural organization of the novel, which parodies an ethnographic account of the rituals of a subgroup. Like the novel's title, sparse phrases announce the chapters: "Blanca and Cricket," "Lucy," "The Bridesmaids," "The Cushions," "The Dress," "The Wedding Mass," "The Wedding Breakfast," "The Pictures," and "The Dance." When Ponce ethnographically describes the wedding cushions, for example, it is to lay the ground for the defiling they will undergo during the ceremony, when the more profane aspects of everyday life intrude on the sacred and ceremonious: "The small pillow-like cushions were made to order to match the material and style of the bride's dress. They were always white . . . [and] trimmed with an abundance of lace, ribbons and soft-pink rosettes. Oftentimes, the bridal couple's initials were embroidered on the cushions with tiny seed pearls. After the wedding, the cushions were stored as a memento" (64–65).

When Blanca first sees the cushions her aunt has made, however, she engages in a quiet verbal defiling that prefigures the final degradation of the junior bridesmaid's vomit during the ceremony: "[Blanca] put her hand to her head and softly moaned. Shit! Them cushions look just like dish towels. Just like the stuff sold in Tijuana. . . . Like most chicks in Taconos, Blanca and her friends hated stuff that they thought was too low-class Mexican, such as embroidered pillowcases and dishtowels" (68). With irony, Ponce juxtaposes Blanca's "low-class" language here to Blanca's attempt to distance herself from the low-class "Tijuana" appearance of the cushions. Additionally, this "tough" language participates in broader sociolinguistic contestation.

Cummings has argued that much of the stigma attached to *pachuco* language stems from its violation of the mainstream conventions of politeness and propriety. Especially in the 1930s, '40s, and '50s, the graphic sexual metaphors and flaunting of conventions in *pachuco* diction were considered appropriate only for certain closed, male-sphere interaction. Female appropriation of *pachuco* speech was especially stigmatized for violating the gender-segregated spaces of which the language was a marker. Yet women adopted it in an attempt to gain a position of strength through the appropriation of a dominant form; the women's strategy was much like that of the early Hopi "chucos" interviewed by Cummings who adopted *pachuco* dress and language to defend themselves against violence and extortion from Mexican American *pachucos*.

The double voicing evident in the speech of the *pachuco* characters in *The Wedding* interacts dialogically both with mainstream conventions of proper speech for women and with the male subcultural linguistic preserve that seeks to exclude women, denying them the "tough" language of men's own attempted empowerment. The *pachucos* criticize Lucy Matacochis, for example, (whose surname means "pigkiller," as Vásquez has pointed out) for "act[ing] too tough fer a dame . . . always want[ing] to give orders" (43). Lucy's speech and actions in the novel exhibit this subcultural strategy of transgressive re-appropriation of male toughness. "Every other day she painted her nails a bright purple or hot magenta, determined not to look like a hick. Ain't nobody gonna take this from me, Lucy vowed. My nails gotta look cool, or my life ain't worth a shit" (44). Lucy redeploys the long painted nails to fend off unwanted sexual advances: "I told him to take me home or I'd knock the shit outta him. He thought I was kiddin, so I scratched his fat face wid my nails. I chipped 'em good, but scared the piss outta him" (48). Lucy's tough language allows her to be a successful waitress at her aunt's bar; as her aunt advises, "Ya gotta drink and cuss like a man, so's ya can call the shots" (46). Lucy's dual transgression against mainstream linguistic codes of expected female politeness and against male subcultural linguistic exclusion is executed both in diction and action.[7]

In Ponce's frequent use of reported speech, ethnographic description, and *pachuco/a* diction, one is reminded of Bakhtin's "Discourse in the Novel": "Within the arena of almost every utterance an intense interaction and struggle between one's own and another's word is being waged, a process by which they oppose or dialogically interanimate each other" (357). Indeed, Bakhtin's description applies not only to the linguistic utterances that Ponce textually recuperates but to the larger behaviors and displays of *pachuco/a* subculture.

Central to *The Wedding* is the contestatory figure of "*la pachuca*," part of what might be termed a "sub-subculture," who confronts, quotes, and parodies the intertext of male *pachuco* culture along with mainstream cultural rites of passage such as wedding ceremonies and the elaborate preparations for them. Rather than occupying satellite or decorative status in the novel, Blanca and her friends are the main characters. Crucial to their sub-subculture are the elaborate preparations for entering the public sphere, whether for a dance or a walk to church. Max Factor pancake makeup, Maybelline and Tangee Real Hot Red lipstick, hair styled high in a pompadour, and a clinging dress prefigure the elaborate accoutrements for the wedding day, especially the gown, which becomes tighter and tighter because of Blanca's advancing pregnancy; her condition is never directly spoken of in the novel, paralleling the characters' own self-censorship and repression about this matter.

Some of the female figures offer an unpleasant quotation of aspects of male *pachuco* subculture. Lucy, for example, "enjoyed nothing more than a good fight . . . even liked to throw a few punches" (6). "[She] used her quick temper to intimidate everyone . . . [and] won most arguments by . . . snarling and shaking her fists" (43). She engages in a raucous fight with another *pachuca* at the wedding dance. Importantly, Ponce allows the female subcultural figures in the novel to present a critique of the "magical" recuperation of community of the larger subcultural group at the same time that she shows the limitations of the *pachuca* strategy of quoting, copying, and reappropriating certain behavioral practices of male *pachuco* culture.

Ponce's double-voiced portrayal of *pachuco* subculture and *pachuca* sub-subculture uses mainstream U.S. culture as one of its intertexts. In a similar fashion, Blanca and Cricket's wedding—although attempting to mark with proper seriousness and decorum the accepted mainstream ritual of the church marriage ceremony and its one-day mimicry of the accoutrements of aristocratic culture—degenerates into a carnivalesque parody of that mainstream intertext. Ponce foregrounds the profanation and debasing of the sacred church ceremony Blanca is attempting to reproduce. Despite Blanca's efforts to achieve the perfect wedding, centrifugal or "unofficial" forces upset the intended imitation in Ponce's parodic rendering of the events.

For the protagonists themselves, the wedding is not enacted as carnival; rather, Ponce's narrative account of it foregrounds the carnivalesque. Recounting events with what Bakhtin terms a "slum naturalism," Ponce focuses on profane disruptions of the sacred—scandal, debasing, bodily transgressions, and blasphemy. Cricket is so sick from his drunken spree the night before that Blanca must hold him up during the ceremony. The junior bridesmaid vomits on the satin wedding cushions, and the ringbearer has to go to the bathroom in the middle of the ceremony. On his way out, he leaves "a long trail of snot on Cricket's black pants"; Cricket utters the profanation "Son-ava-beesh" in response, just as the priest and congregation speak the sacred words of the religious ceremony, "Go in peace, Amen" (113). Blanca's enlarged belly presses uncomfortably against the tight, safety-pinned wedding gown. In Ponce's humorous account, bodily functions erupt against the centripetal forces of containment and control in the prescribed sacred ceremony, and even against the subcultural adaptations of the mainstream rite of passage ceremony. The debasing of the revered subcultural "drapes" by the young boy's mucous is perhaps the most serious transgression in Cricket's value system.

Bodily excretions turn the church ceremony inside out, disrupting the safe boundaries between the body and the outer world. Blanca's enlarged womb epitomizes the struggle between the constraints of official culture and the doubling or expanding body of grotesque realism—the move to fuse the body and the world rather than to constrain and hide it and its natural functions, as Bakhtin has argued (*Rabelais*). The uterus protruding against the satin wedding dress parallels the vomit on the wedding cushions, the mucous on Cricket's pants, and the other threatened eruptions of bodily fluids into the sacred space: the ringbearer's urine, Blanca's own vomit from morning sickness, and the blood of her imminent miscarriage.

The stage had been set earlier in the novel for the grotesque eruptions of the bodily functions of the ringbearer and the junior bridesmaid. Under protest, Blanca accepts her nephew Petey as ringbearer, calling him "that little snot" and insisting that "somebody better wipe his nose" (70). Although his mother "wipe[s] his nose clean" before he visits Blanca, these efforts at centripetal containment will never entirely succeed; nature overpowers culture during the church ceremony, and Petey leaves a trail of mucous on Cricket's pants.

The doubling or expanding body of the junior bridesmaid parallels Blanca's own, but beneath the grotesque description of the young bridesmaid's enlarging body parts is the serious issue of the eating disorder. Porky, age twelve, wears size fourteen Chubby dresses and "throughout the day and night . . . munched to her heart's content, stopping only to sleep"; often she would eat an entire loaf of French bread made into a sandwich and a half gallon of milk, "indulg[ing] her expanding stomach" (73). Her mother is complicitous: "I let her eat all she wants, except when she gets sick, then she takes Milk of Magnesia and in two days eats more than ever" (71). Ponce foregrounds porcine imagery in her grotesque description of the girl, who weighs more than her mother and whom the neighborhood kids call "Oink! Oink!": "Porky's thick round arms, which literally burst from her dress sleeves, were almost the size of her mother's thighs. . . . her round belly . . . each year grew more prominent. Her thighs, like huge pink hams bulged from beneath the summer shorts. . . . Her squinty eyes gleamed wickedly above a small snout" (74).

Like Blanca's expanding body, Porky's bodily protrusions will cause her dress for the wedding to have to be altered several times. Blanca's desire for one of the shiny consumer commodities that Porky's mother is known to give as wedding gifts overpowers her desire to exclude grotesque bodily images and functions from her wedding ceremony: "instinct told her [Porky's presence] was a mistake; but the thought of a gleaming two-slice toaster won out" (73). Ponce emphasizes the parallels between the acquisitiveness fostered by the burgeoning consumer society and the eating disorder, as does Cristina Garcia with the character Lourdes in *Dreaming in Cuban*. In Ponce's text, however, the eating disorder is also linked to a carnivalesque disruption of the sacred; Porky's episode of vomiting during the wedding ceremony occurs precisely at the moment of Communion, evoking a bodily reversal of the religious ritual of eating the sacred bread.

The dance after the wedding and dinner is a scene of gang fighting and drunken revelry, followed by the bride and groom being taken away in separate ambulances. Blanca is in the midst of a miscarriage although her exact ailment is never uttered. In this case, Ponce moves the problem of bodily eruptions into the private sphere for a time, the previous tone of carnivalesque bawdiness erased:

> Inside the bathroom stall, Blanca spread out her Scarlett
> O'Hara dress, trying to keep it from getting dirty. The bathroom
> smelled, as did her armpits. She flopped onto the black toilet seat,
> breathing in and out, hoping the sharp pain that had forced her to
> stop dancing would go away. Just then she felt her stomach cramp,

then a sticky wetness run down her thigh. Her round face froze in fear, her heart about to burst through her white bride's dress. She sat quietly, hoping someone familiar would walk inside the bathroom. She took a deep breath, then with one sweep of her hand, brought down the orange blossom crown, crushed it in her hand and slung it on the floor. (185)

Blanca's longing for community here and her violent gesture of disillusionment with the wedding situate her in an interplay with the public sphere even though they occur within the private space officially designated for lower-stratum bodily functions.

The scene of Blanca's miscarriage unleashes a series of ironies and sets the stage for her final portrayal as an unfinalizable character. When Lucy shouts to her, "Now ya don't havta stay with him," Blanca responds, "But he's my honey! He's gonna change! You'll see" (198). As she is being wheeled into the emergency room, the nurse remarks that it must have been a beautiful wedding. "'Yeah,' Blanca answered, 'The best wedding, in all of Taconos.' Then she passed out" (199). Do these final words of the novel represent Blanca's uncritical recuperation of the debased ceremony, dinner, and dance? I would argue that Ponce leaves us with an unfinalizable character here, rather than with the closed, stereotypical portrayals that some reviewers have attributed to the text. Reading these final lines intertextually with all that has preceded, I cannot help but hear a sardonic tone in Blanca's words.

The Reappropriation of Sacred Space

Denise Chávez's experimental "Novena Narrativas y Ofrendas Nuevomexicanas," as we have seen, employs a variety of strategies to disrupt narrative individualism. Simultaneously, the play engages in subcultural transgression. Like the scenes of autoeroticism discussed earlier, this feminist reappropriation turns on the interplay of the public and the private; the public sphere of the patriarchally configured Catholic church with its central altar to the male deity is rearticulated here as the private home altar honoring the Virgin. The play then relocates this privatized domestic space of worship to another public arena constituted not only by the public performance of the modified religious ritual—the nine days of prayer of the novena—but also by the nonprivatized, almost communal use of the altar by the nine women in succession.

The altar, a floating signifier, occupies various "home" sites in the play:

Esperanza, for example, comes home to check the mail and eat a can of peas for lunch, while Corrine talks to the Virgin on an altar in a church that she temporarily uses as a home. This heterogeneous "familia de mujeres" (100), each with her transgressive or subcultural character, collectively and, to a certain degree, counterhegemonically replace the male deity with the "madre-cita" figure of the Virgin with whom they are more comfortable. Minda, the seven-year-old victim of paternal child abuse, asks the Virgin not to tell "God the Man" the secret she is about to reveal (91–92), while the promiscuous figure of Magdalena exhibits a persevering devotion to the Virgin, to whom she makes regular pilgrimages and directs her monologue, pretending to ad-dress as well her imprisoned husband, as if he were with her in the room.

Although Alvina Quintana, in her 1989 study of Chicana discourse, asks Chávez for a more radical reappropriation of the Virgin figure that would verge on sacrilege in order to challenge the Church, I would argue that Chávez's text is an important first stage of contestation. The play opens a discursive space for a number of women to whom the Church has previously denied the power to speak. Several transgressive (indeed, from some perspectives, sacri-legious) acts that represent the diversity of human experience enter the public domain here, among them those of the lesbian ex-convict Corrine, the pro-miscuous Magdalena, the "marked" Minda whose father has sexually abused her, and the alienated, illiterate teen Pauline, whose tattoos, like Corrine's, re-appropriate the sacred symbols of the Virgin and Jesus. Through these charac-ters, Chávez allows the subaltern to speak in their own, forbidden language. While one can certainly conceive of more radical contestations of the ideol-ogy of the Virgin, Chávez adds important transgressive significations to the dominant icons of the Church without entirely challenging them. As Bakhtin, Stallybrass and White, and other theorists of subculture have shown, trans-gressive cultural production is often characterized by hybridity, redeploying elements of the dominant culture precisely as it contests dominant practices.

We might compare Chávez's text to previous reappropriations of the Vir-gin of Guadalupe during Mexico's wars for independence and later by the United Farm Workers Union in the United States. Like the Indians under the Spanish conquest, as de Certeau reminds us, who subverted the imposed ritu-als and representations by using them for oppositional ends while outwardly remaining subjugated, "Novena Narrativas" transgressively reconfigures sev-eral religious signifiers while at the same time using them as unifying cultural symbols. It succeeds in combining a series of tactical reappropriations with counterhegemonic interventions in the politics of signification.[8]

Sandra Cisneros' "Little Miracles, Kept Promises" similarly focuses on everyday reappropriations of sacred religious sites. As we have seen, the story is about ordinary men and women from both sides of the border who offer prayers, mementos, *retablos*, and *milagritos* to Christ, the Virgin, and various Catholic saints. Whereas Chávez's characters in "Novena Narrativas" offer more lengthy narratives of the self in each dramatic scene before the altar, readers extrapolate larger narratives even from the brief notes left by many of Cisneros' supplicants. The characters in "Little Miracles," whom we know only through the linguistic and implicit visual messages they have left for these religious patrons at various shrines, link their everyday and sometimes extraordinary problems to the realm of the sacred. Many of the problems emerge from the conditions of poverty: a man on parole whose truck has been stolen, preventing him from getting to work; a tortilla factory worker who desperately needs the back wages he is owed; a family with a disabled breadwinner that has lost all of its belongings in a fire; another worshipper's need of a job with good pay and benefits; an overcrowded living situation in which a man's sister and her family become for him "arrows" that pierce him and his family in the small domestic space; and a plea for an income tax refund to help pay bills. Some prayers are for psychically painful yet less vital problems such as the relief one boy begs for from his "face breaking out with so many pimples" (121) and another's request to the patron saint of lost causes for help in passing "English 320, British Restoration Literature" (124). But more life-threatening problems are also conjoined to the sacred here, such as a fatal bus accident that a family miraculously survives and the cancer and kidney disease from which a two-and-a-half-year-old girl suffers.

As in "Novena Narrativas," the transgressive "hides in the light" (Hebdige, 35) in several instances. A message written in code reveals homosexual love to readers who succeed in deciphering the substitution of numbers for vowels. Decoded, the prayer reads as follows:

> *Miraculous Black Christ of Esquipulas,*
> *I ask you, Lord, with all my heart please watch over Manny Bena-*
> *vides who is overseas. I love him and I don't know what to do about all*
> *this love sadness and shame that fills me.*
>
> > *Benjamin T.*
> > *Del Rio, TX*

The simple poignancy of love, transgression, and shame motivates the postmodernist literary device; the character Benjamin articulates his forbidden feelings for a man in the sacred space of a prayer, writing about his transgression in the public sphere, yet hiding to a degree beneath the coded, although decipherable, language.

Similarly, various expressions of feminist transgression enter the public sphere here, although those who engage in them, on one narrative level, utter them privately to the religious figures to whom they pray. Sometimes the feminism involves simple wisdom gained from lived experience. One woman, who signs herself only with an initial, evidences suffering and guilt like that of the man who wrote about his homosexual love: "Father Almighty, Teach me to love my husband again. Forgive me" (119). Another woman recounts her disillusionment with having been granted her request from the previous year for "a guy who would love only me" and put his arm around her neck. Now she prays, "Please, Virgencita. Lift this heavy cross from my shoulders and leave me like I was before, wind on my neck, my arms swinging free, and no one telling me how I ought to be" (122). These public yet private prayers reveal subjectivity intimately, liberated from the public masks that usually disguise gender inequality.

The feminism of these narrative prayers moves beyond timid statements about unhappy love relations. The character of Barbara Ybañez, as discussed previously, uses transgressive language to petition San Antonio de Padua for a liberated man who will do his share of cooking and cleaning and taking care of himself to earn the title "adult." Confident and self-assured, Ybañez transcends the usual humbleness of supplicants and the second-class status of women in the institutionalized Catholic Church. Transgressive both in content and diction, her petition insists on equal rights for both sexes in domestic life and in access to forbidden linguistic codes. Just as it reverses the usual humbleness expected of worshippers in making requests to deities and other supernatural figures, it eloquently shatters the officially accepted sacred language of religious ritual.

"Little Miracles" ends with a strong statement of feminist transgression, one that also rearticulates the figure of the Virgin of Guadalupe in a mode similar to Chávez's. Chayo, an artist, has transgressed by eschewing marriage and motherhood, courageously desiring to live alone. Her family denounces her with epithets such as heretic, atheist, loudmouth, traitor, and white girl. Her current transgression is that of having cut off her long braid, which others view as a product of her mother's labor rather than as Chayo's own bodily possession. Chayo has previously rejected the Virgin, whose folded hands remind her of all that her foremothers have "put up with in the name of God." She transgressively wishes for a Virgin "bare-breasted, snakes in [her] hands. . . .

leaping and somersaulting the backs of bulls. . . . swallowing raw hearts and rattling volcanic ash" (127). Finally she realizes that the Virgin is not "Mary the mild, but our mother Tonantzín" (128), a powerful figure who has rallied a people during the wars of national independence, a civil war, and a farm-workers' strike in California. This reconfiguration of the Virgin allows her to see the power and strength in her mother's patience and her grandmother's endurance—marks of their ability to understand the pain others undergo and thereby to begin healing them. Her female ancestors thus reveal the role that the religious figures play in the larger story—that of understanding, healing listeners to whom those who suffer can reveal their intimate burdens. Thus when Chayo lays her braid as a "*milagrito*," or "little miracle," at the Virgin's shrine, it is in tribute to the strength of the rearticulated Virgin figure and her own independence.

Cisneros carries this reconfiguration of the Virgen de Guadalupe further in her 1996 essay "Guadalupe, the Sex Goddess," de-emphasizing the traditional virginity associated with the image and using transgressive language that will seem sacrilegious to some. Against the sexual repression of her youth, Cisneros reinvents the image of "La Lupe" as a positive "*cabrona*"—a strong, sexualized woman who is God rather than the mother of God. Contrasting Guadalupe to the "neuter" Barbie dolls of childhood, Cisneros notes, "When I see la Virgen de Guadalupe I want to lift her dress as I did my dolls, and look to see if she comes with *chones* and does her *panocha* look like mine, and does she have dark nipples too?" (46). For Cisneros, the sanctity of the Guadalupe figure must be redefined to include her sexuality in order for modern women to see her as a role model. Holy because of her sexuality, "La Lupe" extends her sanctity to contemporary women as comfortable with their sexuality as Cisneros is: "Blessed art thou, Lupe, and, therefore, blessed am I" (46).

In reappropriating sacred spaces in their narratives, both Chávez and Cisneros are recognizing that culture is a site of battle for competing defini-tions and visions of reality. Powerful religious symbols need not necessarily be left to those who enjoy patriarchal privilege. History has shown that the tools of oppression are not entirely monolithic and sometimes even mis-takenly appear to be liberatory. By the same token, cultural workers engaged in the politics of signification can recuperate certain powerful symbols for more progressive ends, providing, of course, that the new signifieds they ar-ticulate clearly replace the traditional signifieds, which are sometimes slow to disappear in the process of cultural lag.

Lesbian Transgression

Unlike Nicholasa Mohr's narrative rendering of a lesbian re-entering the heterosexual sphere ("Brief Miracle," *Rituals*), Ana Castillo's and Denise Chávez's portrayals focus on lesbians in more transgressive moments. Chávez's reappropriation of a sacred space for the doubly Othered Corrine in "Novena Narrativas" contrasts with Castillo's realistic portrayal of the profane prison setting as the site of her protagonist's transgressive sexual experience. Both writers render the subordinated culture of lesbianism on its own terms.[9]

The figure of Corrine, doubly Other for many readers because she is both homeless and a lesbian, foregrounds another doubled alterity in her narrative description of herself as *"una pinta jotita,"* an ex-con who is also a lesbian, denied access to her children and a place to live after leaving prison because of this double transgression. Reminiscent of a sub-subcultural figure of a previous historical period, Corrine addresses her audience with the tough talk of *la pachuca*. Repeated phrases such as, "Corrine got it covered, ésa! Ssss" (98), feminize the standard male addressee of *pachuco* slang by changing "ése" to "ésa," a term that frequently punctuates her oral narrative. Thus she centers the female members of the audience as a primary constituency. As does the protagonist of Mohr's story "Brief Miracle," Corrine reminds her audience that family life is "never as good as it looks" (99). However, Corrine's narrative begins where Virginia's left off by recounting Corrine's lesbian relationship with Sophia in prison, their marriage "in our hearts" (99), Sophia's unfaithfulness, her own family's rejection when she leaves prison, her transgression at a Senior Citizen's dance when she asks another woman to dance, and her ultimate reappropriation of a church as shelter for an evening. Her free-flowing bilingual speech, like her reappropriation of *pachuco* diction, is a key strategy of her subcultural expression.

Ana Castillo also encases in a second-person narration her rendering of a lesbian experience in chapter 38 of *Sapogonia*, marking the events off from the rest of the novel with a technique previously employed by canonical writers such as Michel Butor and Carlos Fuentes.[10] Like these writers' use of "you," the second-person signifier slides into several signifieds. Castillo's primary anchoring of the second-person pronominal addressee signifies the protagonist of the novel, but it also at times refers to readers, both singular and plural, and at other times is decoded in the impersonal sense in which the casual storyteller employs it.

The self-referential narrator highlights the prison as a site in which cosmetics are discarded as signs of the "world of men," an observation that parallels the exclusionary threat that lesbian sexuality poses to men. The transgressive figure of Mary Lou Acevedo, whose children will not forgive her for having "left their father to be with a woman" (190), becomes for the narrator "the one familiar object [in prison] that reminds you of where you come from" (188). The narrator's initial attraction to Mary Lou, then, involves the "magical recovery of community," as John Clarke has argued occurs in certain subcultural expression ("Skinheads"). The Chicago slum in which they both grew up becomes an idealized space around which to re-create a lost sense of community within the profane site of the prison. Mary Lou's lover outside prison is the antithesis of the male antihero who predominates in the novel as a whole; in the lesbian utopian space that is narrated but not seen here, this lover "was like a mother sometimes, when Mary Lou needed mothering, and she was a loyal sister when Mary Lou needed a confidante" (190). The protagonist's own friendship and sexual experience with Mary Lou will retain these positive traits. And like Chávez, Castillo transgressively reappropriates religious symbols, among others, in which to couch the beauty and intensity of the experience for the protagonist: "pink and white roses offered to the Virgin the month of May; Christmas pilgrimages which taught you the hymns that gave you the gift of song" (193).

The bilingualism of both texts is essential to the transgressions they invoke. Chávez joins English, Chicano Spanish, and *pachuco* slang so that her character moves naturally among all three. Castillo's expressions in Chicano Spanish are fewer but employed in an equally naturalized mode along with numerous terms of prison subcultural slang that parallel Corrine's use of *pachuco* diction. Both narrators display their previously concealed subordinated cultural experience, using their language of resistance in public forums such as the printed page or the stage as if it were completely natural to do so. It is now their interlocutors who must make the cultural leaps, not they. On the diegetic plane, the narrators hide to a certain degree, recounting their experiences either privately in prayer or through the second-person narrative device of talking to oneself; on the page of the text, however, their subcultural transgressions enter the public sphere.

Aurora Levins Morales narrates lesbian transgression as an innocent childhood experience with her friend Tita in Puerto Rico. Here the second-person interlocutor is Tita, whose sexual intensity is recounted as lived experience in counterposition to mass-cultural stereotypes about lesbians. "*Kiss my mouth* you said, and wondered if you'd get pregnant / and said you didn't care" (59). The poetic "I" cannot remove from her mind, however, the *Ladies' Home Journal* photograph of "skinny, stringy haired, gaunt eyed" women that is anchored with the caption "Lesbian Junkie Prostitutes in Jail" (59). Instead of denying the mass-cultural distortion, Morales establishes a parallel structural opposition between two signifying realities; the utopian lesbian moment of the childhood experience in Puerto Rico stands in contradiction to the mass-cultural portrayal of lesbians, just as an imagined future moment of lesbian pleasure with her childhood friend opposes Tita's life with her "thieving husband" (60). The two girls' childhood experimentation with transgressive sexuality has been subordinated and tamed by traditional patriarchal modes of adult sexuality, exacerbated by poverty, multiple pregnancies, and the death of several of Tita's children. Further, as an intertextual reading with the previous narrative segment, "Class Poem," reveals, Tita's early talent for scientific inquiry was truncated by her marriage at eighteen, numerous pregnancies, and her current work in a douche bag factory in Maricao.

In the parallel structural oppositions that Aurora Levins Morales has established, alienated labor to produce douche bags replaces scientific research; patriarchal sexual and social formations replace lesbian love; and mass-cultural distortions of lesbianism as a degraded form of existence compete with the positive utopian space of lesbian moments in "Tita's Poem." These narrative poems establish continua, then, between such phenomena as douche bags, youthful marriage, repeated pregnancy, a "thieving husband," and the *Ladies' Home Journal* version of lesbianism at one pole, and a young woman choosing a professional career in science, experimenting with lesbian sexuality, and being unimpeded by the demands of a husband and children at the other.

Abortion and Life

In her unconventional essay on the Virgin of Guadalupe ("Guadalupe, the Sex Goddess"), Sandra Cisneros recounts a youthful sexual experience in which she was too timid to deal with the issue of birth control. In the succeeding days she experiences the "torture" of a feared pregnancy, and when her period comes on Mother's Day, she "celebrate[s] [her] nonmaternity by making an appointment with the family planning center" (44). Although Cisneros does not discuss the issue of abortion here, the reversal she enacts functions as an important preliminary estrangement device that calls abstract ideals of motherhood into question.

Rosario Morales' transgressive motif of serving a platter of placenta garnished with parsley to her unsympathetic mother-in-law in the segment "Birth" expresses sadness at the miscarriage of a desired pregnancy. But in

"The Grandmother Time," the segment that directly follows, a parallel image reveals the alienation also present in the work of raising children: *Sweet and pungent child served / on a bed of tired toys, garnished / with blanket à la baby pee, topped / with sour milk sauce, redolent / of society, redolent / of deep sleep*" (102). By juxtaposing realistic details of mothers' unpaid and often unappreciated labor to the sorrow experienced at a miscarriage, Morales presents a balanced account of pregnancy and mothering—the underside along with the idealistic expectations before the experience.

Where Morales rearticulates a miscarriage as "Birth," Helena María Viramontes goes one step further by recoding the day a woman has an abortion as "Birthday" (*Moths*). Here the subject is not a symbolic birth in a desired but unsuccessful pregnancy but a pregnant woman's own birth as she terminates an unwanted and unsupported pregnancy. Images of birth, baptism, and naming structure the story, foregrounding the importance of language and the politics of signification: "Would I like to stay Alice, or become a mama?" the protagonist asks herself (41), highlighting the opposing modes of self-identity that such interpellations signify. The woman called "Alice" instead of "Mama" will be born and baptized (named) on the day of the abortion. As Alice struggles with moral issues about life as she makes the painful decision to end her pregnancy, she emerges as a critical, thinking subject who asks alternative moral questions centered on self-identity. She transcends the popular aphorisms and religious doctrines about virginity that circulate in her consciousness by reminding herself, "Virgins have babies too" and "God isn't pregnant" (43).

Another of Viramontes' female characters also engages in a critical hermeneutic process of decoding patriarchal attempts to control women's sexuality and reproductive functions. Decades before Alice's experience, during the 1910–17 Mexican Revolution, Amanda, the protagonist of "The Long Reconciliation" (*Moths*) defends her abortion to her husband by counterposing two contradictory moral orders. When he argues to her that he killed another for honor, she replies, "Then I killed for life. It's the same thing isn't it? Which is worse? You killed because something said 'you must kill to remain a man'—and not for this honor. For me, things are as different as our bodies. I killed, as you say, because it would have been unbearable to watch a child slowly rot. But you couldn't understand that, because something said 'you must have sons to remain a man'" (79). Contesting his attempt to anchor signifiers to his preferred meaning ("killed, as you say"), she highlights the opposing moral orders by which they lead their lives precisely by showing the parallels between the two orders. Their actions are both "the same thing" and entirely opposed to one another. Amanda is doubly transgressive in this narrative because she also offends her husband's honor by engaging in adultery. Viramontes narratively recodes what begins as a reifying relationship with a landowner into a moment for Amanda to exercise her own sexual autonomy. These two affronts to her husband's masculine honor serve as moments for Amanda's fulfillment and autonomy during a very different historical period than that of Alicia.

Heterogeneous Audiences

Thematic narrative transgressions run the risk of alienating and offending various audiences at the same time that they link writers to other segments of their subcultural community. Unlike some youth subcultural expression that strives to shock the establishment and often remains within the subgroup's own set of rules for cultural play, Latina narrativists transgress against the mainstream, their ethnic subgroup, and the received views ideologically sustained by both. In reappropriating sacred patriarchal spaces, contesting male subculture, and breaking taboos through public narrative renderings of women's autoeroticism, lesbian sexuality, and abortions, these writers act against the silence and naturalness behind which much patriarchal power has hidden. Because they treat such topics nonexploitatively, their narrative transgressions may decrease their readerships rather than render their books hot, marketable commodities. Their transgressive themes, then, represent to various degrees a series of courageous statements of principle and alternative moral questioning that may, indeed, estrange them from some readers, both within and outside of the subordinated group. As Denise Chávez has noted, U.S. Latinas have followed the path paved by African American writers such as Alice Walker in breaking taboos against interdicted topics: "You don't have voices talking about sexuality. . . . you grow up in a culture where everything is in whispers. But Latinos can be risqué and honest, and there's a need for them to be portrayed that way" (qtd. in Mena, 2).

As we have seen, however this contestatory artistic production is also subject to both marginalization and attempted commodification. Some writers who deploy transgressive themes have succeeded in the mainstream, while the experiments of others have received less national attention. Although publishers choose certain works that they will market as "minority commodities," heterogeneous readers will ultimately pass judgment on the books.

CHAPTER SIX

Gender, Ethnicity, and Political Truth(s): Narrative Harmony and Dissonance

The Gendered Construction of Ethnic Identity

Crucial to the initial stages of oppositional movements, identity politics function to consolidate the constituents of a subcultural group through commonality and difference. Group identity is forged both through internal shared experience and oppositionality to the Other. In its positive moments, it is affirmational, contestatory, and begins to achieve social reform. In its negative stages, however, it is exclusionary, individualist, and essentialist.[1]

Because they are intervening into what has been a largely male-dominated ethnic literary movement, Latina fiction writers in the late twentieth century frequently emphasize the gendered construction of ethnic identity. Many of these narratives strive for a dual oppositionality and often constitute a doubly subordinated culture. As theorists of the Birmingham school have argued, subcultural groups function in opposition both to the dominant culture and to the "parent" culture, the class from which they come (Clarke et al., 55). It might be argued, then, modifying this model somewhat, that Latina writers work not only in opposition to dominant U.S. cultures but also often contest the patriarchal blind spots of the Latino cultural "renaissance" of the late 1960s and beyond. My temporary occlusion of class here is intended to highlight both the cultural nationalist trends of this "parent" culture and the ethnic ties that continue to unite many Latinos who engage in identity politics. Although a number of these Latina narratives ultimately emphasize the role of gender politics in the construction of identity, they often pass through the mediations of class, race, ethnicity, and, sometimes, sexual preference.

In his study of contemporary African American women writers, Elliott Butler-Evans argues that a narrative violence is generated by the unresolved textual struggle between the separate, totalizing discourses of race, gender, and the aesthetic. Despite the attempted synthesis of racial issues, gender politics, and the concern with the aesthetic, Butler-Evans believes that efforts to achieve narrative closure often fail in these texts, and one of the discourses assumes privileged status. The fiction of Toni Cade Bambara, for example, is overdetermined by the ideology that writings by blacks are necessarily oppositional; consequently, feminism can intervene only in a violent mode in her texts as the secondary pole of a set of unresolved, competing ideological discourses (Butler-Evans, *Race, Gender, and Desire*, 3–12).

I will argue, in contrast, that certain Latina writers, present gender, ethnicity, social justice, and the aesthetic as elements of a continuum. These issues are integrated noncompetitively in such texts as Cisneros' *The House on Mango Street*, Helena María Viramontes' *Under the Feet of Jesus* and "The Jumping Bean," Carmen de Monteflores' *Cantando Bajito*, and Cherríe Moraga's *Giving Up the Ghost*. Sometimes, as in the case of Julia Alvarez, for example, a writer foregrounds one or the other discourses but without producing the narrative violence that Butler-Evans sees in the texts he examines. In some instances, however, this foregrounding produces occlusions and blind spots so that the absences or obsessions in the text enact the kind of dissonance to which Butler-Evans refers.

Noncompeting Narrative Discourses

In a 1991 interview broadcast on National Public Radio, Sandra Cisneros, when asked if she was a feminist, responded proudly, "Oh, yes. Fiercely."[2] Her unhesitating reply gives some sense of the unity in her artistic production between the discourses of feminism and ethnicity. In writing *The House on Mango Street*, a coming-of-age story about a Chicana in Chicago, Cisneros found it imperative to emphasize the gendered construction of ethnicity and its corollary, the ethnic construction of gender. As Ramón Saldívar has pointed out, Cisneros engages in "a clear-sighted recognition of the unavoidably mutual overdetermination of the categories of race and class with that of gender in any attempted positioning of the Chicana subject" (182).

I have argued elsewhere that *Mango Street* delineates the continuum that links sexual desirability, male power, and violence in patriarchal society ("Community-Oriented Introspection"; "Latina Narrative"). In "The Family of Little Feet," for example, the protagonist learns that the ostensibly flattering male gaze that valorizes the young girls' feet as they play dress-up in high heels is, in fact, reifying. Cisneros elaborates the public sphere of Esperanza's Chicago barrio as the site in which this transformative moment of the protagonist's rite of passage occurs. The corner grocer who threatens to invoke the order of the Repressive State Apparatus by summoning the police as a means of controlling the girls' sexuality, the drunken bum who proposes a kind of protoprostitution by offering to pay the girls a dollar for a kiss, the cat calls of the barrio boys, and a competitive encounter with female cousins who pretend to ignore the girls' experimental, public display of the accoutrements of adult sexual expression—these are the primary figures in the ethnic space of Esperanza's barrio through whom the underside of male sexual reification of women is revealed. These figures move from positive to negative actantial positions within the narrative (Greimas; Greimas and Courtés, 5–6) as the girls discover the negative nature of the apparent flattery of these onlookers. The gender issues that the story develops—among them, the thesis that sexual flattery, male power, and the potential for violence are elements of a continuum—are inextricably linked to the ethnic social space in which the protagonist undergoes her transformation.

The culture of the barrio structures other elaborations of gender issues in *Mango Street*. When Rafaela's husband locks her in the apartment during his absence because "she is too beautiful to look at" (76), the neighborhood children send papaya and coconut juice to her in a paper bag tied to a clothesline. Metonymic symbols of the island she has emigrated from and the good times other women are enjoying at the dance hall down the street, these elements of Latino culture are only modes of making do, Cisneros suggests. In fact, the sweet drinks are among the figurative "silver strings" (76) that patriarchy offers women in exchange for submitting to control.

The practice of verbal interpellation throughout the collection reveals the interconnection of ethnicity and gender. Esperanza's sexual assailant in the story "Red Clowns" incorrectly interpellates her Otherness by saying, "I love you, Spanish girl" (94) as he rapes her behind the carnival booth. The form of racism that views all Latinos as the same, and that conflates language with national origin, is linked here to the eruption of patriarchal violence. Earlier in the text a parallel instance of male possessive power is connected to interpellation and the importance of self-naming in the struggle for autonomy. As Esperanza ruminates about her name, she remembers the great-grandmother for whom she was named, who was "so wild she wouldn't marry until my great-grandfather threw a sack over her head and carried her off. Just like that, as if she were a fancy chandelier" (12). Where her great-grandmother ultimately acquiesced to patriarchal possessive violence, Esperanza reconfigures the interpellative sign she has inherited: "I have inherited her name, but I don't want to inherit her place by the window" (12). Renaming oneself is connected to rejecting the image of the passive Esperanza, the great-grandmother waiting by the window; instead, the protagonist envisions names for herself that sound stronger and more transgressive: "Lisandra or Maritza, or Zeze the X" (13). The discourse of gender is intimately linked to that of ethnicity throughout this coming-of-age narrative.

Issues of gender, ethnicity, and social injustice are also noncompeting narrative elements in Helena María Viramontes' *Under the Feet of Jesus* (1995). The coming of age of Estrella, the Chicana protagonist of the novel, is inseparable from the crossing of gender barriers, ethnic solidarity, and standing strong against such social evils as substandard wages, poor living conditions, pesticide contamination, and lack of access to adequate health care. Early on she defends her nontraditional family against an Anglo girl who calls her "Star" and makes derogatory comments about the sexual practices of Estrella's mother and Perfecto, the man who now lives with the family and works to provide for them. Although language has been Estrella's strong suit in her relationship with this companion, to whom she reads comic books, on this occasion she resorts instead to physical violence, beating up the girl in a rage over the comment and causing her family to be evicted from the migrant camp. At the novel's climax, however, Estrella harnesses language to a more controlled use of violence, this time directed to a broader issue of social injustice.

In a more mature replay of the earlier confrontation, Estrella again rejects the traditional female role by making an unconventional ethical decision and taking the initiative to carry it through when everyone else in her family is literally immobilized and completely without money. Alejo, a fifteen-year-old migrant worker, is near death after having been aerially sprayed with pesticides as he worked in the fields. Although Estrella's family has taken him in because, in her mother's words, "If we don't take care of each other, who would take care of us?" (96), the traditional home remedies are unsuccessful; Viramontes invokes ethnic identity here and at the same time shows its limitations. In the face of Perfecto's despair on the journey to secure medical care for Alejo, Estrella painstakingly scoops dirt and lays stones to try to get the car out of the mud and then assumes a leadership role in the ensuing ethical dilemma that the family faces. After an uncaring nurse in a makeshift clinic in a trailer takes the family's last nine dollars for only having diagnosed that Alejo is very sick, and they are left with no money for gas to get him to the hospital, Estrella brandishes a crowbar and demands the return of the unearned money. She now uses words and controlled violence to achieve a small degree of social justice, where earlier, with her Anglo companion, she could only deploy enraged violence; this time she smashes inanimate objects rather than the offending person in order to illustrate the seriousness of her demand for the money. Knowing she is acting outside the law, she engages in what Kierkegaard terms a teleological suspension of the ethical to attain the higher good of getting Alejo to a hospital.

In the same way that she substitutes one moral order for another, Estrella offers an alternate model of the ideal feminine to the nurse's perfect makeup, perfume, patent-leather purse, and photos of her children on her desk. And once back at the camp after getting Alejo to the hospital, Estrella climbs to the top of a dilapidated barn, standing proudly among the other stars, "an angel on the verge of faith . . . powerful enough to summon home all those who strayed" (176). Her strong femininity and leadership are an alternative model to the traditional strategies of her family, who now stand below, outside their bungalow, holding the broken statue of Jesus and wondering when the police will come to arrest them for the violence.

The particular ethnic religious practices of Petra, Estrella's mother, center on prayers and offerings to a plaster statue of Jesus displayed on a home altar that is disassembled and reassembled each time the family moves. The civil identities of the family members are safeguarded beneath the statue's feet in the form of documents that prove U.S. citizenship. Viramontes suggests that a new model of female empowerment and strength can replace the traditional ethnic strategy of prayer and recourse to the protection of a deity. Just as the home remedies were powerless against the modern pesticide, so too are Petra's traditional practices unlikely to save the family from the trouble they expect from the authorities at the end of the novel. Instead, the statue breaks, and Estrella herself symbolically replaces the image as she stands tall atop the barn she has been forbidden to enter.

Estrella's retaking of the barn at the end of the book concludes a quest begun with the first sentence of the novel. The barn is a contested space, the site in which a deformed child appears (perhaps the result of his parents' exposure to pesticide), an image later connected to Estrella's incipient sexuality and the fear her mother tries to instill in her of a child born "sin labios" [without lips] (69) because of female sexual transgression. The barn becomes materially important when Petra tries to control both Estrella's sexuality and Perfecto's coming and going by demanding his keys to the bungalow; he then tries to earn money to escape by tearing down the barn. Estrella reclaims the barn at the end as a symbol of her autonomy and strength, her rite of passage into adulthood, and the new forms of ethnic religiosity that women of her generation will employ.

Viramontes does not develop ethnic solidarity, feminist strength, and the critique of social injustice in this novel by reductionist oppositions between good and evil. Conscious that she has moved beyond the almost entirely negative portrayal of men in *The Moths and Other Stories*, she notes that the male characters in the 1995 novel "are more complicated" ("Interview," 10). Perfecto, for example, makes many sacrifices to help Estrella's family but is about to leave when he senses her mother is again pregnant. He lies to Estrella to enlist her help in tearing down the old barn, but Viramontes portrays him as a complicated human being who has been worn down by the conditions under which migrants must work. He helps to get Alejo to the hospital and gives his last nine dollars to pay the nurse. And most importantly, he teaches Estrella to use his tools; like language, they empower Estrella, as Perfecto changes them for her from empty signifiers ("as foreign and meaningless to her as chalky lines on the blackboard" [25]) to the vehicles of pride in one's ability to "build, bury, tear down, rearrange and repair" (26). At this point Estrella also learns to read, beginning a two-pronged strategy of female empowerment with both tools and language, preparing herself for the courageous action in the medical trailer. In the end, Perfecto remains torn between leaving while he can and staying with the family, revealing a thoughtful indecisiveness and self-control that are a credit to his character.

Viramontes situates the ethnic and gender issues of the novel in the context of the dismal social conditions in which migrants live and work in the United States. Issues of social justice are as important as those of gender and ethnicity; no single issue is foregrounded at the expense of the others in the novel. In imagining how the nurse will narrate the traumatic events of the day to her husband, Perfecto also implicitly offers a picture of those readers who have the most to learn from this book: " 'You won't believe what happened to me today . . . ,' she would probably say to [her husband] while he lay on the couch, because that is how Perfecto imagined people who had couches and living rooms and television sets and who drank coffee even at night" (162). Viramontes' novel cannot be displayed innocuously on the coffee table of a middle-class home, for the narrative violence it evokes is far from the metaphorical one to which Butler-Evans refers. Like the work of Cisneros, Martínez, Limón, and several other U.S. Latina writers, Viramontes' novel brings the true story of ordinary people like her parents and their fellow migrant workers into the social conscience of the mainstream U.S. public.

In a similar vein, Viramontes harmoniously integrates the concerns of ethnicity, gender, social justice, and the aesthetic in her 1995 story "The Jumping Bean." She has noted that writing the story functioned as a kind of exorcism because it helped her to understand her father's sociological and economic situation and the source of the rage he took out on the family

("Interview," 10); as we have seen, because of having written this story, she was able to craft the male characters in *Under the Feet of Jesus* in more complicated and less reductionist terms. Thus, "The Jumping Bean" represents a particularly important moment in her writing for the integration of the competing discourses of ethnicity, gender, and the aesthetic.

Although the tightly crafted story offers an honest portrait of the father, emphasizing both his strengths and shortcomings, it makes space as well for the daughters' and mother's concerns. The father, for example, resignifies one of the instances of the ethnic ridicule he suffers at his job; instead of throwing away the bag of jumping beans that an Anglo worker has tauntingly placed in his lunch box, he brings them home for his children to play with. But his eldest daughter carries the resignification one step further, against his wishes, by biting the beans to release the caterpillars trapped inside. The father is both oppressed himself and an oppressor of the women and children in his family—not the jumping bean that his fellow workers call him in the ethnic slur, yet a kind of jumping bean that controls and attempts to contain the women/caterpillars in his family. Viramontes insists in the story that the struggles he engages in to move beyond ethnic hatred at the workplace must be augmented by the symbolic and literal rebellion of those under his control at home.

At the positive end of their polysemy, the jumping beans represent speech and empowerment as well as the potential to overcome ethnic slurs and patriarchal silencing. For María de la Luz, the older sister in the story, the life-giving direct rays of the sun that activate the caterpillars to make their outer shells appear to jump symbolize her own move into selfhood and autonomy. She speaks forbidden words to the truant officer and to her father, both of whom do not understand her wisdom and logic. Without seeing the irony, her father tries to silence her by slapping her severely across the mouth for having said a bad word to explain the meaning of the bad word he has uttered. Both she and her younger sister cover their mouths with a hand or fingers in fear or pain at moments in which they are silenced, symbolically placing themselves in the dark interior of a jumping bean. Whereas María de la Luz cracks open the shells of the beans against her father's will, the younger sister bravely swallows the last bean whole, overcoming her fear of magic and the dangerous visions that have plagued her and directly confronting the father, who is engaged in a battle with María over the disposition of the last bean.

At the end of the story, Viramontes symbolically transmutes the beans into watermelon seeds, which the girls spit out like words and imagine to be playful confetti in sweet red juice. Viramontes thus connects the girls' struggle to their father's struggle as a talented but alienated worker trying to find a succession of jobs to support his family. The watermelon juice at the end reconfigures the image of the "sweat that bled like torrents" (103) over the father's eyes as he carried 160 pounds of cement on his back up a three-storey scaffold. Similarly, the red watermelon juice happily consumed at the end replaces the younger sister's image of the window and ceiling bleeding tears when she overhears that her hospitalized mother will not be coming home for Christmas. Instead of merely longing to possess María's "capacity to walk barefoot on broken jagged words" (108) and wishing she could free a trapped moth in her room that symbolizes language, the younger sister at the end swallows the especially symbolic last jumping bean and happily spits it out in transmuted form—the seed-words of the watermelon. Together, the two sisters savor the sweet red juice that replaces the alienated images of bloody tears and sweat.

Viramontes has suggested that in some of her earlier stories in *The Moths* she in effect "screamed" and "shouted" against the pain that her female characters experienced, creating the type of narrative violence that Butler-Evans has attributed to a writer's preoccupation with a single totalizing issue. In later narratives such as this one, Viramontes develops male characters more fully, together with her emphasis on gender, ethnic, and aesthetic issues. Whereas an earlier story might have focused entirely on the mother and daughter to show the effects of the father's domestic rage, "The Jumping Bean" makes the father's story central, emphasizing his extraordinary efforts to work and support his family. She grounds his authoritarian behavior at home as a product of his workplace alienation, itself further tainted by the ethnic slurs and bigotry of some of his fellow workers. When he worked as a fisherman, he felt connected to his work and the product of his labor, but as a day laborer he becomes ashamed of even the momentary pride he experiences when the building is complete. The visceral description of his backbreaking physical labor is joined to the poignant account of the emotional suffering he experiences as another worker compels him to listen to a racist joke about "spics" and "drunks." He exhibits heroic self-control in response, mentally remembering an image of the crowd of men who gather on a central Los Angeles street corner every morning to try to secure a day's work (104–5). In Viramontes' narrative, the characterization of the father is overdetermined by several factors, including his physical and emotional strength at work, and his both affectionate and authoritarian behavior at home.

The politics of race are central to the configuration of gender, class, and ethnicity in Carmen de Monteflores' *Cantando Bajito: Singing Softly*, and together these elements constitute a single, integral problematic in the text. The narrative about Pilar's first encounter with Don Juan, a wealthy Spaniard who eventually fathers her children, emphasizes the conflation of desire, gender politics, and Pilar's sense of class and racial inferiority. Ashamed of her old clothes and dirty feet, she becomes especially aware of how dark her mother looks in comparison to the white Juan. And although Monteflores clearly establishes Pilar's own sexual desire in this scene, the agency of the rich, white Spaniard predominates. "She felt caught in his fixed gaze. . . . he looked . . . steadily, as though once he wanted something he wouldn't let go until he got it" (47). Owner of the local store, he gives her mother free cloth to make Pilar a new dress, attempting to refashion Pilar's exterior appearance to enable her to enter his own social circle so that he may possess her. The race and class issues cannot be cosmetically disguised, however. Juan tries to prevent Pilar from seeing her family after they begin to live together, and his mother dislikes Pilar because her mother is black. Furthermore, Juan wants their daughter, Luisa, to stay out of the sun so that her skin will not darken.

Monteflores shows that the modes in which Puerto Rico's colonial history continues to affect women in the private sphere are related to the structures of patriarchy that also prevail. Speechlessness and illiteracy contribute to Pilar's disempowerment in her relationship with Juan. His facility in the colonial language gives him discursive power: "[Pilar] felt foolish talking like the Spaniards and ashamed of talking like the *country people*, the jíbaros. Juan was very angry when the children spoke like that. . . . So Pilar tried to correct herself and correct them. She tried every day to pay attention" (76). When Pilar enters Juan's house for the first time, she immediately lapses into speechless disempowerment, which Juan occludes with patriarchal flattery: "A beautiful girl doesn't need to say anything" (98–99). And Juan intimidates their daughter into speechlessness by correcting her utterances, telling her she sounds stupid, and garnering his patriarchal authority to force her to answer him: "Luisa tried to speak but only sounds came out of her. She gasped as if she were drowning" (72).

Pilar's illiteracy not only disempowers her but makes her more susceptible to the male-defined interpellative order. Unable to read Juan's secret notes to her in the beginning of their relationship, she deduces that the last word of the various letters he writes to her is the spelling of his name and that the first is hers. For years she believes her name is spelled "*querida*," a signifier that delimits her within the male enunciator's discourse to others who are literate—in this case, the readers of the text. Pilar tries to learn to read and write while chaperoning her children's lessons with a private tutor;

ashamed of what she views as a transgressive activity, she hides the note-books in which she practices writing. Entering Juan's study after his death to use the dictionary, she conceives of herself as an interloper: "She didn't want anyone to know she was there. She felt as if she were breaking into a church. She feared she was going to be punished" (124). Her "punishment" includes her discovery in the study of a note from one of Juan's other lovers. And soon thereafter, she is humiliated when her daughter must help her to read a letter from Juan that has arrived after his death, for in it the daughter learns that her mother and Juan had never been formally married. At the root of this en-tire series of humiliations is not merely illiteracy but Juan's patriarchal power, which overcodes her experience of her verbal disempowerment.

Monteflores uses the theme of the written word to accent the homolo-gous structures that underlie the historical legacy of colonialism and the patri-archal oppression in women's everyday life. Pilar's only experiences of books as a child are those that she sees in church, the purpose of which is to shape proper speech to God. Similarly, she suspects that she needs such a book to speak to the king of Spain, whose statue she has seen in church as well. Feeling kindly toward the king, who, she believes, has generously shared his road (El Camino Real) with the people of Puerto Rico, Pilar feels sorry that he had to suffer the U.S. invasion of his territory in 1898. And when Pilar meets Juan, she very much wants to ask him if he knows the king, but her shyness in the face of her suitor's patriarchal and class standing prevents her from uttering the question. Similarly, she is afraid to speak to Juan's parents because she cannot reproduce their Castilian Spanish—the same language of the books that his parents read to her, even though she is now an adult. Juan forbids her from entering the rooms in which he keeps books so that he may remain in control of the written word. When Juan sometimes reads one of his books to his children and Pilar listens on, he does so in a dominating, impa-tient fashion. Pilar's illiteracy, her lack of direct access to the written word, is the site in the private sphere of everyday life in which the historical legacy of colonialism is played out as continuing patriarchal control.

When Seña Alba tells the story of her rape by a white priest at age eleven or twelve, she uses the words of her own jíbaro dialect as a reconfig-uring weapon against the written word of the Church and patriarchy with which she associates this violent event. Her narrative reveals to Pilar the modes in which the Church sometimes participates in patriarchal violence and attempts to invoke ideological closure by an inversion of guilt and in-nocence:[3]

He say he have to put his hands on me to cure me, that God's power
pass through his hands. . . . Well, he take off my clothes and he
begin to touch me and to pray at the same time, and later he say
he have to lie on me so that all God's power can go from him to
me . . . and right there he rape me.

  . . . I start screaming and he cover my mouth . . . I hurt a lot.
He tear me up. When he finish he clean the blood with a handkerchief and he kneel to pray . . . and he tell me to kneel and pray
for my sin. That what we do is a sin. . . . And that God is going to
forgive me if I pray a lot and don't tell anybody about it. (187)

Now able to speak the words "rape" and "*ultrajó*" rather than euphemisms,
Alba begins to dismantle through popular speech the attempted ideological
closure of the Church. In the continuation of her narrative, the Church's explanation of the events stands in stark contradiction to Alba's firsthand account;
the nuns label both her and her mother whores and accuse her mother of
being in love with the priest. Monteflores shows ideology to be a site of contestation among competing narratives about reality; Alba's oppositional narrative—encased within the story Pilar tells to her granddaughter, Meli—and the
larger narrative we are reading are constituents of this struggle; each is rooted
in the struggle against the homologous legacies of colonialism and patriarchy.

  Graciela Limón harmoniously integrates issues of ethnicity, ethnic nationalism, and gender in her latest novel, *The Day of the Moon* (forthcoming).
While the narrative frame begins in Los Angeles in 1965 before the Chicano
movement, certain problematics of the movement leave their mark on the
text, as the novel re-elaborates the question of *mestizaje* examined by many
Chicanos during the late 1960s and 1970s. The novel moves backward and
forward in time, revisiting the battles over racial and gender identity in the
trajectory of the first half of the twentieth century in Mexico and Los Angeles.
Focusing on the painful rather than the celebratory aspects of *mestizaje* for
Chicanos and Latinos across the Americas, Limón notes in the preface that
the dual heritage is "a condition of anguish, because to be *Mestiza* or *Mestizo* is to dangle between being Spanish and indigenous . . . existing between
gratitude and rage. It means choosing white or brown. It means acceptance
or denial of color" (i). Limón positions a series of strong women characters
between two opposing male icons who represent the poles of Latino *mestizaje*—a Rarámuri (Tarahumara) indigenous male hero defeated by a Castilian
patriarch who, Limón argues, stands as a metaphor for the "Mestizo's white

side which denies, and even assaults, the haunting presence of his brown ancestor who dwells inside of him" (ii).

Shortly before his death in Los Angeles in 1965, Flavio Betancourt, the central patriarch of the novel, narratively reconstructs the trajectory of his life. Having risen to landed wealth in Mexico by winning property in a card game, Don Flavio continually rejects the indigenous side of his heritage and contests the efforts of his sister, wife, daughter, and granddaughter to move beyond his patriarchal and racial authority. But just as he cannot control the lesbian love that develops between his wife and his sister, so too is he powerless to prevent the desire of his daughter and granddaughter to unite with the indigenous part of their heritage. Consummating his power-consolidating marriage to Velia Carmelita by forcing unwanted sex on her, Flavio is powerless when she finds love, companionship, and sexual fulfillment with his sister. In parallel fashion, despite their daughter Isadora's acquiescing to the marriage partner her father arranges for her, she later lives in a forbidden love relation with the Rarámuri Jerónimo whom she has loved since childhood. Although Flavio has Jerónimo murdered and interns Isadora in an institution for the insane in Zapopan "where men hide disobedient women," he cannot ultimately repress the indigenous side of his *mestizaje*: his granddaughter Alondra journeys to Mexico after his death, searching for her interned mother, and ultimately finds happiness by returning to her father's Rarámuri village in Chihuahua.

In this post-Chicano-movement novel, Limón expands upon the earlier preoccupation of some Chicano writers with the recuperation of indigenous heritage. Now, avoiding stereotypes and romanticism, Limón links ancient cultural beliefs to richly developed people of past historical moments and inscribes *mestizaje* with key gender issues. On the eve of the movement in 1965 Los Angeles, the Chicana Alondra returns to Mexico to undergo an epiphanic moment of discovery of her *mestizaje* while listening to nuns chant the Canticles in a convent in Zapopan: "*I am black, but beautiful, O daughters of Jerusalem.* Alondra felt her breath catch in her throat because she had never heard such words before. Her mind raced. She was not black, but she was Rarámuri. She was copper. She was mahogany. She was cacao. She was peyote" (271). Discerning in this key moment an invitation to come home to the Rarámuri caves of Chihuahua where she enters into spiritual communion and dialogue with her mother in their ancestral site, Alondra redresses the grievances of patriarchy and racial repression in ways distinct from those engaged in during the early Chicano movement.

Cherríe Moraga also expands the constituents of Latina identity formation to include the important elements of sexual preference and control of one's own sexuality. In a poignant dramatic monologue in *Giving up the Ghost*, Corky renarrativizes on the stage the scene of her rape as a young girl. The rape, which is overcoded as the site of incest and child abuse as well, constructs the narrator's identity on several negative levels.[4] The janitor's ethnicity, signified through his slurred Spanish, makes Corky feel bad about herself because "I was Mexican too but couldn't understand him that good" (39). She feels "*tonta*," or stupid, not only because his instructions to her seem illogical now, but also because at the time she had been naive enough to follow his orders. In reifying fashion, she identifies herself as a sight, noting that she is humiliated even beyond the sexual assault itself; she fears that someone might enter the room and see her and the janitor in the compromising position that he has talked her into assuming as a part of the fictional narrative he tells her preceding the rape.

Moraga's most forceful elaboration of negative identity formation in this scene occurs in the shouted closing line, "HE MADE ME A HOLE!" (43). Signifying sexual choice and autonomy, the vaginal orifice is an opening when one willingly participates in sex; it transmutes into its opposite, the "no opening" (41), when one is raped. In the absence of an open hole, Corky's rapist makes one in her and, in the process, reduces her identity to that of a hole, as the double signification of the scene's closing line implies.

Moraga further overcodes the motif of the hole with the positive semes of lesbianism and speech. With Norma, Corky had discovered her own hole, "wet 'n' forbidden," along with Norma's, which became "wide 'n' deep like a cueva . . . when she wanted it to" (42). In contrast, with her assailant, "there was no hole / he had to make it" (43). Estranged from her own body during the rape, Corky notes, "I saw myself down there like a face with no opening . . . no features / no eyes no nose no mouth / only little lines where they shoulda been / so I dint cry" (43). Denied the openings that enable self-expression and identity — a vagina, a mouth, eyes, and a nose — she can neither sexually express herself, verbalize, cry, or signify an identity through particular facial features. Featureless, expressionless, speechless, she has been temporarily disempowered by male sexual violence, until the moment in which she recuperates her powers of speech on the stage. Through the polysemous image of the hole, Moraga shows that sexual violence configures identity along a series of negative poles:

Opening	Choice	Lesbianism	Language	Mouth
$\updownarrow$	$\updownarrow$	$\updownarrow$	$\updownarrow$	$\updownarrow$
No opening	Rape	Heterosexuality	Silence	No mouth

Negatively objectified through her ethnicity, her self-perceived stupidity, her reduction to a sight, and the polyvalent encodings of the sign "hole," Corky reveals that gender, ethnicity, and sexual preference are noncompetitive narrative components for Moraga and integral elements of a continuum.

These narratives of Cisneros, Viramontes, de Monteflores, and Moraga integrate the problematics of class, ethnicity, race, gender, the aesthetic, and, in Moraga's case, sexual preference rather than foregrounding one or another in an unsuccessful attempt at closure. The violence of their texts, then, occurs not on the level of narration and attempted ideological closure but rather intradiegetically as an eruption of a previously repressed group of social antagonisms that results in physical violence against women and other explosive attempts by both women and men to resolve issues of social justice.

Foregrounding without Exclusion

In certain narrative instances, writers foreground issues of gender after having delimited other crucial poles of the configuration of identity. The other elements are not negated, nor do they surface in the text as a kind of narrative violence, as Butler-Evans argues is the case with some black women writers. Rather, the foregrounding is sometimes appropriate for the temporal and thematic specificity of the narrative project. As I argue in chapter 3, for example, Rosario and Aurora Morales celebrate their multiple racial, ethnic, and national identities in "Ending Poem," at the same time overcoding these identities with a feminist recuperation of women's everyday life and labor; they foreground feminism as the primary link between mother and daughter without occluding the other diverse constituents of their identities.

For Julia Alvarez, the narrative reconstruction of identity involves changing relations of class, gender, and ethnicity. Herself an immigrant to the United States at age ten, Alvarez uses implicitly autobiographical first- and third-person narrators to depict the opposing positions of identity that the members of one family enter into in the move between two national realities. Their class privilege in the Dominican Republic reverses into its opposite once they are in the United States. Gender identity changes as the characters engage in a series of ruptural tactics that explode against various attempts to reassert the patriarchal order both in the new home and on return trips to the island. And ethnicity is problematized throughout the book as the characters try to adapt to life in the United States and often exist in a suspended state between two sets of cultural practices.

In "A Regular Revolution" (*García Girls*), for example, these three parameters of immigrants' changing sense of identity interact overtly. Yolanda, the implicit first-person narrator, observes that despite her father's decision to give up hope of returning to the Dominican Republic after nearly four years in the United States and his resignation to becoming "un dominican-york," the four daughters "shifted from foot to foot, waiting to go home" (107). The family's reversed class position in the United States underlies the girls' desire to return; the narrator cites inferior housing and consumer goods as the reason for the dissatisfaction. But their schoolmates' disparaging comments about the girls' ethnic background also cause unhappiness, and because of two incidents that threaten the parents' control over the girls' sexuality, the parents attempt to reestablish the class privilege that the family enjoyed in the Dominican Republic by enrolling the girls in an elite preparatory school in Boston. Gender and ethnic "trouble," to use a limited redeployment of Judith Butler's phrase, are to be combatted, the parents hope, by a reassertion of the sense of upper-class privilege in the girls' evolving sense of identity.

Again, however, the girls at first fail to assimilate because their schoolmates view them as Other, inserting the variable of ethnicity into the apparent class unity of the school. "Our privilege smacked of evil and mystery whereas theirs came in recognizable panty hose packages and candy wrappers and vacuum cleaner bags and Kleenex boxes" (108), the narrator notes, humorously signaling the commodity reification that underlies her classmates' privilege — the companies their families owned such as Hanes, Reese, Hoover, and Scott. Whereas the Anglo students at first assault the ethnic identity of the immigrant girls with denigrating terms such as "spic" and "greaseball," the attack takes the form of viewing the Latina Other as exotic and mysterious.

Strategies of rebellion against gender restrictions, engaged in together with their peers, are the successful mode of integrating with dominant U.S. culture in the initial "revolution" in this story, not class or ethnic solidarity. Forging their mother's signature to attend dance and football weekends off campus, they learn to "kiss and not get pregnant"; soon they view the traditional expressions of sexuality from the island as outmoded, preferring instead "the American teenage good life" (108).

Although class and ethnicity are factors in the development of an immigrant identity for the four sisters, Alvarez highlights the centrality of gender struggle in the "regular revolution" the sisters undertake. As discussed in chapter 5, the girls exhibit a protofeminist solidarity in the subcultural transgressions recounted in this story. Whereas the father, a beneficiary of patriarchal privilege, had engaged in rebellious strategies against the Dominican state, the four sisters direct their subcultural transgressions against the patriarchal parental authority that tries to control their sexuality. Gender struggle assumes a centrality in the forging of immigrant consciousness in Alvarez's work without enacting the narrative violence that Butler-Evans critiques.

Ethnicity, Gender, and Politics as Narrative Violence

It would, indeed, be unreasonable to expect every text by a Latina writer to harmoniously integrate competing social discourses about gender, ethnicity, class, and sexuality. Helena María Viramontes, for example, employs an Anglo name for the protagonist of her story "Birthday," but given the postmodernist experimentation of many narratives in the 1985 volume, this tag is an unstable indicator of identity. Indeed, Latinas have a variety of names. What is important for Viramontes in this story, however, is not a reductionist concern with the ethnicity of her character but rather a series of important gender issues. The presence or absence of ethnicity is not a ruptural element; this aspect of identity is not central to the story.

In contrast, Roberta Fernández leaves certain crucial gender issues unresolved in a story that on other levels importantly integrates gender, ethnicity, race, and class. The original version of "Esmeralda"[5] begins with two epigraphs that establish the primary structural opposition of the story. Lines from the romantic Mexican song *"Solamente una vez"* stand in contrast to a poem by Ntozake Shange about the frequency of violence against women in contemporary society. If the story, by employing these epigraphs, sets out to emphasize the continuum between these outwardly distinct versions of relations between men and women, it ultimately wavers in its commitment to this goal.

On one level, "Esmeralda" is a story about the demystification of romance and patriarchal oppression—the realization that the two form a continuum. The ostensible flattery that the Mondragón brothers direct to Verónica in the form of *piropos*, or compliments, parallels the local newspaperman's printed references to her as *"una esmeralda brillante,"* "[a] beautiful jewel on display" (113), as she sells tickets to the movie theater from inside a glass booth. Verónica's well-founded fears that this apparent flattery is not harmless stem from her experience of her uncle's patriarchal tirade against her some years before. His threat to "take her anytime I want" (119) is fulfilled and repeated when the Mondragón brothers rape her as she walks home from the theater one evening. Fernández shows that the uncle's patriarchal wrath results from his class hatred as well, for he is angry that Verónica is romantically involved with one of his workers.

The story also highlights certain positive narrational sites in which women can recuperate from patriarchal violence; for example, the women of Verónica's family rearticulate the figure of La Llorona as they engage in a talking cure, a positive use of personal narration to heal the psyche after trauma. But there are two important gender issues that the story leaves unresolved.

Fernández's narrative rendering of the romantic moment of Verónica's first love relationship passes uncritically over an important age disparity that embeds an inequality in the relationship. "He was from Sabinas Hidalgo, and he was only seventeen at the time" (118), Verónica tells her interlocutor, the young narrator, neglecting to mention that she herself was only twelve, barely beyond childhood. Fernández has argued that critical readings of this age inequality fail to understand Mexican cultural traditions.[6] But no matter how common the cultural practice, the power relations of gender inequality continue to obtain. In making this argument, she foregrounds the discourse of ethnicity and is unable to attain ideological closure, as Butler-Evans has argued occurs in the work of Bambara.

It might be argued that the blind spot Fernández evidences here ruptures into the text as an absence that is also a disturbing presence. Further, the story closes with a scene of the young narrator dreaming that she is like Esperanza inside the glass dome, while a "cinnamon-colored stranger" reminiscent of the seventeen-year-old worker of Verónica's first love relationship smiles and offers gifts. One is left with the sense that history has had no effect, that the young narrator, despite hearing Verónica's story and telling it to us, will continue to engage in the uncritical romantic dreams that disguise patriarchy's violent side. In effect, the story wavers between demystifying the continuum between romantic flattery and patriarchal oppression and occluding the important connection between the two.

In Sandra Cisneros' 1991 "Never Marry A Mexican," the discourse of nationalism figures importantly in the protagonist's attempts at recuperation of personal power in her love relations. This character's nationalist and sometimes essentialist utterances erupt on the pages of the text, however, creating a kind of textual violence and casting a critical light as well on the ostensible gender autonomy for which she strives in the story. While at one level the character's sense of gender and ethnicity evidenced in these utterances can be read as noncompeting narrative tropes—integrated parts of her move to empowerment—on another level their resounding untruth overcomes the easy and pleasurable recognition that affords them the veneer of truth.

The protagonist, Clemencia, learns that her mother's words of advice, "Never marry a Mexican," also signify the unwritten racist dictum shared by some white men in the United States: it is fine to take a Mexican woman as a lover but not to marry her. Clemencia's revenge involves a recuperation of her own powers of seduction. She effects gender reversals in the actantial, or functional, positions of the characters of the first narrative, in which she was seduced by her Anglo art teacher; in this second narrative, she is the prime agent and seduces her ex-lover's high-school-age son, now her own art student. The reconfigured narrative also employs a troublesome nationalist discourse as Clemencia tries to compensate for her marginalization: "That dumb bitch of a wife of yours, I said, and that's all I could manage. That stupid stupid stupid. No Mexican woman would react like that. Excuse me, honey. It cracked me up" (76). Just as we should question the uncritical narrative pleasure that occludes the power inequalities in the teacher's seduction of the student, so should the germ of truth that underlies the character's essentialist statements about Mexican identity be appropriated critically. The modes in which the character's essentialist statements about ethnicity produce narrative violence in the text should foreground as well the problematic nature of Clemencia's gender revenge. To extend Butler-Evans' model, the narrative violence in this story centers around the character's inharmonious pseudo-resolution of both the discourses of gender and ethnicity.

The title of the 1996 novel *Mangos, Bananas, and Coconuts: A Cuban Love Story* by Himilce Novas evokes the stereotypical ethnicity of the title of Daniel Reveles' *Enchiladas, Rice, and Beans* (Ballantine, 1994). Much of Novas' book seems to mechanistically push the correct buttons of multiculturalism, presenting a requisitely tropical and transgressive view of the Cuban and Cuban American Other. Exaggerated religious revivalism and sexist metaphors in which bananas, mangos, and coconuts represent various stages of women's sexual desirability are recurring tropes in the novel, along with the more transgressive themes of incest and cannibalism that carry ethnic stereotypes to extremes.

Novas frequently fails to establish the requisite distance between text and pre-text in many sections of the novel that she might intend as parody, resulting in confusion about which utterances are serious and which are parodical. A phrase such as "A pair of tennis shoes walking on water by themselves" (116) clearly invokes the biblical intertext in parodical fashion. But are we to read a description of paternal child abuse, such as the following, as satire or parody because it deploys the flippant narrative style used throughout? "And while he told his stories in his slow, hypnotic voice, his wide, rough hands caressed her throat, her rosebud breasts, her girlish arms. He would slip his fingers between her thighs and prod her petals with his thumb. He would press his hungry member against her, forcing himself only slightly, mindful of not rupturing the virginswath, letting his hot, viscous explosion run down her like a waterfall" (36). And is the description of sexual desire when Esmeralda meets Juan intended seriously or as parody? "Esmeralda felt the veins in her neck swell and her blood heat like water in a test tube under flame. She felt her knees soften and go limp, like coconuts ready to drop. She felt a large palpitating heart in her flower and a hot river of love running out from her the minute Juan put his arm across her shoulders and escorted her into the street" (95). It is unclear which of the novel's ethnic stereotypes Novas is humorously criticizing and which she is deploying as formulaic means of selling books.

Careless historical errors and spelling mistakes suggest a quick formulaic deployment of stereotypical ethnicity rather than a carefully crafted literary work. Fidel Castro is about to triumphantly enter Havana on December 31, 1959, instead of 1958, according to the novel. The twins who are born in May 1959 meet each other in the United States at age twenty-nine when, according to the book, Clinton is president. Certain rhetorical devices that play on ethnicity and gender inversion fail to be apt parallels. Explaining the practice of men keeping a *casa grande* for their wife and a *casa chica* for their mistress, Novas suggests that Juan, who pays for an apartment in Manhattan where he and Esmeralda can be together, is himself the mistress and Esmeralda's father the "cuckold husband" (106). This attempt to redeploy the ethnic cultural motif as a gender reversal fails because Juan still plays the important material role of the man in paying for the apartment and paying Esmeralda a salary to replace the job she has resigned from to spend time with him.

On one level the novel aims to overturn conventional gender distinctions by suggesting that people have both male and female selves that might become visible to them in a moment of truth looking in the mirror, as occurs for the protagonists. However, heterosexuality is privileged in the novel's choice for developing this theme rather than having the protagonists be identical instead of fraternal twins—either both female or both male. With so many taboo subjects part of the novel, why is there no explicit homosexuality? The suggestion that we are incomplete if we see ourselves only as male or female is subordinated in the novel to the discourse of formulaic ethnicity. Gender issues —even that of a father's sexual abuse of his daughter—function as the secondary pole of a competing discourse, to use Butler-Evans' concept. Protestant revivalism, out-of-body experiences, tropical fruit metaphors, cannibalism, father-daughter and brother-sister incest, parricide, and a few Spanish words and neologisms are the predominant tropes the novel deploys to foreground its ethnicity, overwhelming the attempt to address important gender issues.

Published in July 1995, Margarita Engle's *Skywriting* preceded Novas' novel by a year and introduces much more subtly certain motifs that Novas carries to an extreme. Also set in Cuba and the United States, Engle's novel focuses on the reunion of a separated brother and sister who are like twins when they finally both marry in a joint celebration after the brother is freed from a Cuban prison. Also, Engle uses the motif of exotic fruit much more subtly than Novas in describing a publishing company's attempt to market a historical Cuban chronicle by changing the work's title and picturing exotic tropical images on the cover. And where Novas attributes literal cannibalism to a Cuban refugee journeying to the United States, Engle describes a mother who at the cost of her own death, sacrifices the last drop of potable water on the raft so that her child can survive the trip.

Engle's is a novel of principle with an important message about humanity's need always to be on guard against totalitarianism and tyranny. She develops the key motifs of language, writing, and communication through both dense and transparent codes at various moments of history, suggesting that the persistence in creating contestatory written signs—even when they appear no longer to be needed—is perhaps the strongest weapon against tyranny. Like Carmen de Monteflores, Engle uses the theme of the written word to foreground homologous structures; but where Monteflores suggests a correlation between colonialism and patriarchy, Engle posits a continuum between the Spanish Inquisition and post-1959 Cuba.

Engle's characters are connected to one another, to other oppressed or potentially oppressed people, and to the past through the recovery and deployment of a variety of written signs. The Peregrín family, whose name invokes the Spanish word for pilgrim (peregrino), traces its history to Extremadurans escaping the Inquisition, one of whom leaves a buried manuscript for future generations to decipher. The handwritten, coded narrative entitled "The Chronicle of Antilia" preserves one version of history and recounts the love story of Vicente and "Sirena"—a Spaniard and Indo-American who meet during the Conquest. Written by the couple's embittered son in the villa of Trinidad, Cuba, in 1550, the crónica narrates the family's dream of a haven called "Antilia," "where no one who is being chased by attackers can be found, and no one falsely accused of treason can fail to encounter solace and peace" (154). The utopian message that the writer wishes to pass on to future generations is that "Nothing defeats love." Where brother hated brother in the sixteenth-century chronicle, brother and sister will be reunited in love in the twentieth-century continuation of the chronicle—the novel we are reading.

The ancestor's denunciatory narrative will also serve as a model of writing that future generations must themselves carry on, with variations, to defeat tyranny. In the twentieth century the contestatory writing takes the form of the deciphering and translation of the old chronicle, the construction of new chronicles, mass-cultural adaptations of the ancestor's story, letters written in code, the reappropriation or taking back of the poetry of José Martí, aerial skywriting by a character to disseminate messages against tyranny to the public, and *Skywriting*, the novel, written in the year 2033 as a continuation of the Peregrín family's chronicle. Camilo, the narrator's brother who finally escapes from Cuba after being imprisoned, continues to write dissenting messages across the sky even after the fall of Castro to urge continued vigilance about the possibility of tyranny: "sending smoke signals, forbidden jokes, poetic metaphors, parables, tales of small everyday events, which when sent across the sea, become significant, like omens or oracles, the prophecy of ordinary people speaking in tongues. ¡Skywriting! ¡La escritura aérea!" (264–65).

But like the exotic ethnicity that overpowers Novas' text, the obsessive motif of a single political truth overpowers Engle's text. Unlike Cristina Garcia, who argues for a postmodern indeterminacy with respect to political "truths" about the Cuban Revolution, Engle posits a single master narrative about the revolution that turns the novel's strong principles into obsessions. In so doing, Engle enacts a kind of narrative violence that detracts from her important point about the necessity for constant vigilance against actual or potential tyranny.

So great is the novel's obsession that the text refuses to utter the name of Fidel Castro, referring to him throughout only as "the Commander," with "his name pronounced only as a curse" (282). Along with reasonable critiques of authoritarianism, the novel moves to extremes, suggesting that an air-traffic controller deliberately misguided a plane in order to kill a political dissident, and that there is documentary proof that "sorcerers" sold human flesh on the black market and that hungry Cubans ate it without question. Unlike Garcia, who rejects clear-cut, black-and-white "truths," *Skywriting* can see no good at all in leftist movements, unidimensionally categorizing Peru's Sendero Luminoso, for example, as the "cruel and totally irrational shining path" (186).

While the novel moves ahead in time to the year 2033, after Castro's fall or death (the text vacillates between these two explanations for the end of totalitarianism on the island), its protagonists move back in time to recuperate their ancestors' historical home. After her retirement, the narrator moves to Cuba to live above her ancestors' cave and raise a few cattle and a small field of sugarcane. There she writes the novel we are reading, which, although it is published in 1995 before it is diegetically written, is an attempt to continue the protest chronicle begun by her ancestor during the Conquest of the Americas. Similarly, she and her husband attempt to rebuild the ancestral home in Cuba the way the sixteenth-century ancestors would have liked, moving back in time rather than ahead with the movement of history.

The principle of vigilance becomes an overarching paranoia by the end of the novel, reminiscent of Sherwood Anderson's concept of the grotesque in *Winesburg, Ohio*, whereby people cling to truths that originally were beautiful but become distorted as *idées fixes*. Having returned to the cave of their ancestors in Cuba, the Peregrín brother and sister are reminded by an angel that "the Commander could loom anywhere" (282); they begin to devise an indecipherable code, "just in case the people of the North . . . turn their problems over to some attractive human leader who promises homemade earthly miracles" (283). With a paranoic anarchism, they claim to be "evolving away from our rulers."

Engle's important message about guarding against tyranny and her emphasis on various modes of writing to counter authoritarian political structures are overpowered by the novel's unidimensional presentation of Cuban society since the revolution. This totalizing discourse creates the kind of narrative violence that Butler-Evans attributes to certain African American texts. Representing one perspective of several in the heterogeneous Cuban American population of the 1990s, Engle's novel stands in contrast to the postmodern openness of Cristina Garcia's *Dreaming in Cuban*.

Although I do not propose to prescribe how writers should write, or to present my readings as correct interpretations and therefore new master texts, my critique of the narrative dissonance I perceive in some texts stems from a comparative, evaluative reading of many narratives by contemporary Latinas. I have suggested that three varieties of narrative harmony and dissonance cross the spectrum of Latina narrativists and sometimes appear in contrasting form in the works of an individual writer. Certain texts of Cisneros, Viramontes, de Monteflores, and Moraga integrate issues of gender, ethnicity, social justice, and the aesthetic as elements of a continuum. A second variety of text emphasizes one or another of these issues without excluding or overpowering the others. In the third instance, however, texts "shout" or "scream," as Viramontes terms it, by emphasizing one or another issue in unidimensional terms. The result is a type of aesthetic "violence" or dissonance in the narrative project that sometimes overpowers other elements of the text.

Toward a Multivalent Narrative

While mainstream multiculturalism quickly moved to capitalize upon the populist narratives of U.S. Latinas burgeoning in the final decades of the twentieth century, this fiction to a large degree has resisted that closure. Among the heterogeneous narratives written by Chicana, Puerto Rican, Dominican American, and Cuban American women in the post-Chicano-movement period of the 1980s and 1990s are texts that both elude and succumb to mainstream closure to varying degrees. Enmeshed within the cultural space of the porous borders of postmodernity, U.S. Latina narratives transcend the facile categorization of publication by large or small presses; both mainstream and regional publication venues offer examples of commodified and contestatory feminine ethnicity. And while I have sometimes focused on what I view as the dominant tendencies of particular works toward the commodification of ethnicity or the contestatory rupture of stereotypical exoticization, no work falls completely within either category of this heuristic dichotomy.

Rather than presenting a master reading of a body of precanonical, emergent writing, I have hoped to follow through instead on various points of entry that these rich narratives themselves suggest. Such an undertaking can only touch the surface, I believe, for neither the texts nor this reader are fixed and unchanging. As I have argued, new Latina narrative defies the containment of the term I use to name it both because of the dynamic relation of texts to readers and because of the continual growth of this narrative production. A crucial sign of the vitality of this literary movement is that any study can only be partial and effectively unfinished; new novels continue to appear even as one attempts to close a critical intervention at a given moment.

Although, as I have argued, various narratives succeed to greater and lesser degrees in negotiating hegemonic and populist forms of multiculturalism, all of the works in this study bring to the fore what might be termed the "feminine space" of contemporary ethnicity. Frequently, the feminine and feminist problematics raised in these narratives remake the ethnicity elaborated in the culture of the Chicano movement and erode the artificial border between gender and ethnicity. As the Latino population of the United States continues to grow and contribute richly to this country's diversity, the narrative production of Chicanas, Nuevomexicanas, Puertoriqueñas, Cubanas, Dominicanas, and other Latina women in the United States will continue to situate the ruptural elements of feminine ethnicity in the foreground of American letters.

Introduction

1. Exceptions to this time frame are writers such as Nicholasa Mohr, Isabella Ríos (Diane López), and Berta Ornelas, who published fiction in the 1970s.

2. See, for example, Soto's story "Absence" in *Spiks*, 1970, trans. Victoria Ortiz (New York: Monthly Review Press, 1973), 49–57. See also Marta Sánchez's seminal study of Piri Thomas' *Down These Mean Streets*, in which she analyzes the displacement of racial hierarchy onto gender hierarchy in this classic Nuyorican narrative: "La Malinche at the Intersection: Race and Gender in *Down These Mean Streets*," *PMLA* 113 (1998): 117–28.

3. This does not prevent, as I discuss in chapter 1, the marketing of one minority writer with the cultural accoutrements of another. Random House used art by the same Chicana artist whose work appears on the cover of Sandra Cisneros' *Woman Hollering Creek and Other Stories* (1991) on the cover of a book by a male writer from the Philippines, F. Sionil José, *Three Filipino Women* (New York: Random House, 1993). Difference must conform to certain uniform features—here, those that have successfully marketed a writer of another ethnicity.

4. See Samia Mehrez, "The Subversive Poetics of Radical Bilingualism: Postcolonial Francophone North African Literature," in *The Bounds of Race: Perspectives on Hegemony and Resistance*, ed. Dominick La Capra (Ithaca, N.Y.: Cornell University Press, 1991), 255–77.

5. The 1990 U.S. Census showed that "Hispanic people" increased 53 percent over the 1980 figures, to 22.4 million. About half of that increase was due to immigration, but other factors in the higher count included high birth rates, citizenship granted to Latino residents, and the counting of illegal residents. These figures do not include the 9.8 million people who classified themselves as "other race," most of whom, according to the Census Bureau, are Latino; because "their cultures have established different racial categories since so many are of mixed Spanish, Indian, and black descent," they check "Other" when faced with the U.S. categories. Nonetheless, in a significant occlusion of racial difference within the Latino community, the Census Bureau persists in classifying most of these nearly 9 million people "white," apparently against their wishes. See Felicity Barringer, "Census Shows Profound Change in Racial Makeup of the Nation," *New York Times*, 11 Mar. 1991: 1+.

6. Michael Lev ("Tracking the Hispanic TV Audience," *New York Times*, 13 Dec. 1989: 17) claims that "90 per cent of U.S. Latinos/Latin Americans speak Spanish" (cited in Flores and Yúdice, 58).

7. Zentella, "Bilinguals in the Barrios: Crossing Linguistic, Racial, and Cultural Frontiers," lecture at the University of California, Santa Barbara, 10 Feb. 1995.

8. Applying Chomsky's notion of universal grammar, specialists in bilingualism such as Almeida Jacqueline Toribio argue that native bilingual speakers employ and recognize grammatically and syntactically correct bilingual utterances. For example, an English-dominant bilingual speaker using correct code-switching might choose to switch between the following segments: "The students / had seen / a foreign film," but never between the auxiliary and participle "had" and "seen." Similarly, a native bilingual speaker might switch at the following points: "Mary said / that her brother is sick," but never between the words "that" and "her" in this sentence. Toribio notes that code-switching is prohibited between a functional element (e.g., articles, demonstratives, numbers, auxiliaries, negation, and morphological endings for tense and agreement) and its complement but, in contrast, occurs freely between a lexical (nonfunctional) element and its complement; e.g., "They used to serve *comida peruana*" (lectures, University of California, Santa Barbara, 12 May 1994 and 14 Feb. 1995.) Pfaff and Chávez (1986) show that even in Chicano drama, a genre that most closely approximates natural discourse, literary variations in the natural speech patterns of code-switching occur. While "balanced bilinguals" (those proficient in both languages) engage in intra-sentential code-switching without violating the rules of grammar of either language, various locutions in Chicano drama diverge from natural patterns of code-switching. Sometimes this aesthetic code-switching has a symbolic function, the authors argue (233, 237–52).

9. See also Aparicio's "La vida es un Spanglish disparatero: Bilingualism and Nuyorican Poetry" and Cordelia Candelaria's "Code-Switching as Metaphor in Chicano Poetry" in *European Perspectives on Hispanic Literature in the United States*, ed. Geneviève Fabre (Houston: Arte Público Press, 1988), 147–60 and 91–97.

10. It is my hope that a number of Latina narrativists whose work is not discussed here—including Kathleen Alcalá, Beatriz de la Garza, Terri de la Peña, Patricia Preciado Martin, Carole Fernández, Alicia Gaspar de Alba, Beverly Silva, Laura del Fuego, Elena Castedo, Achy Obejas, Estella Portillo Trambley, Gina Valdés, Irene Beltrán Hernández, Isabella Ríos, Berta Ornelas, Sheila Ortiz-Taylor, Cecile Pineda, Tina Juarez, and Ibis Gómez-Vega—will be the focus of studies by other scholars. For important essays of some of these writers see Herrera-Sobek 1995; Horno-Delgado et al. 1989; Saldívar 1990; Rebolledo 1995; Quintana 1996; Eysturoy 1996; Lomelí 1980; and Bruce-Novoa 1995.

11. While small presses such as Arte Público and the Bilingual Press embody much of what might be termed "populist" rather than "hegemonic multiculturalism," they too experience the dialectical pressures of multiculturalism from above and below. One press, for example, asked a Latina writer to use less Spanish in her manuscript, and then changed the last line of the text to an ungrammatical English sentence without the writer's consent. Small presses need to make their cases to government

agencies for state and national grants, and more and more frequently they are negotiating with mainstream publishers to sell paperback rights after publishing hardcover editions of books. Besides participating in populist multiculturalism by publishing with one of these small presses, writers who do so are also in dialogue—both critical and complicit—with the themes and constraints of hegemonic multiculturalism.

Chapter One

1. See Michael Di Leo, "La Boom," *Mother Jones* (Oct. 1989): 15.

2. The publication of Ponce's *Calle Hoyt: Recuerdos de una juventud chicana*, trans. Mónica Ruvalcaba (New York: Anchor Books, 1995), is part of a growing trend of mainstream publishers marketing Latina writing to Spanish-speaking readers in the United States, Latin America, and Spain. Other examples include Cisneros' *La casa en Mango Street* (New York: Vintage Books, 1994), translated by the noted Mexican writer Elena Poniatowska, and *El arroyo de la Llorona y otros cuentos*, trans. Liliana Valenzuela (New York: Vintage Books, 1996); and Cristina Garcia's *Soñar en cubano*, trans. Marisol Palés Castro (New York: Ballantine Books, 1994). Latin American and Spanish publishers are also involved in such translations, including Ana Castillo's *Las cartas de Mixquiahuala*, trans. Mónica Mansour (Mexico City: Consejo Nacional para la Cultura y las Artes/Grijalbo, 1994); and Julia Alvarez's *De como las chicas García perdieron su acento*, trans. Jordi Gubern (Barcelona: Ediciones B, 1994) and *En el tiempo de las mariposas*, trans. Rolando Costa Picazo (Buenos Aires: Atlántida, 1995).

3. See "Three Sisters," *Publisher's Weekly*, 22 Apr. 1996: 24; and Doreen Carvajal, "Of Hispanic Literature and Few Opportunities: Authors Offering Lyrical Readings and Biting Opinions," *New York Times*, 4 May 1996, nat'l. ed.: 11.

4. Ray González has argued that in some instances this commodification seems to win out: "One of the dangers today is that glamorous, high-powered agents and publishers place pressure to produce on minority writers who may not be quite ready. New York wants the Chicana novel so bad it hurts" ("A Chicano *Verano*," 773).

5. Recent advances in the field of audience theory, for example, have elaborated on Stuart Hall's 1980 formulations about preferred, negotiated, and oppositional readings of mass cultural texts. See, for example, David Morley, *Family Television: Cultural Power and Domestic Leisure* (London: Comedia, 1986); Janice Radway, *Reading the Romance: Women, Patriarchy, and Popular Literature* (Chapel Hill: University of North Carolina Press, 1984); Ien Ang, *Desperately Seeking the Audience* (London: Routledge, 1991); John Fiske, "Moments of Television: Neither the Text nor the Audience," in *Remote Control: Television, Audiences, and Cultural Power*, ed. Ellen Seiter et al. (London: Routledge, 1989); Henry Jenkins, "*Star Trek* Rerun, Reread, Rewritten: Fan Writing as Textual Poaching," *Critical Studies in Mass Communication* 5.2 (1988): 85–107; Laurie Schulze, "On the Muscle," in *Fabrications: Costume and the Female Body*, ed. Jane Gaines (New York: Routledge, 1990); Jon Cruz and Justin Lewis, eds., *Reconceptu-*

alizing Audiences (Boulder, Colo.: Westview Press, 1994); and James Hay, Lawrence Grossberg, and Ellen Wartella, eds., *The Audience and Its Landscape* (Boulder, Colo.: Westview Press, 1996).

For important analysis of the limits of negotiated and oppositional readings, see Herbert Schiller, *Culture, Inc.* (New York: Oxford, 1989), esp. chap. 7; and Celeste Michelle Condit, "The Rhetorical Limits of Polysemy," *Critical Studies in Mass Communications* 6.2 (1989): 103–22.

6. See García Canclini 1982: 104; and Martín-Barbero 1989: 21.

7. See Butler-Evans, "Ethnicity, Cultural Studies, and Marxist Discourse" and "Textual Strategies and Ideology in Amy Tan's *The Joy Luck Club*."

8. Understandably, Random House used a similar painting from Nivea González for the cover of its editions of *The House on Mango Street* in both English and Spanish. More disconcerting, however, is the publisher's decision to market another of its "minority" authors, this time a male writer in the Philippines, with cover art by the same Chicana artist (see F. Sionil José, *Three Filipino Women* [New York: Random House, 1993]). Is Random House attempting to promote interethnic solidarity by this gesture? Why, then, is not art from another minority group used on Cisneros' cover? More likely and troubling explanations are that the publisher believes that the Filipino's work will not sell without this attempted connection to the already more successful Chicana text and, worse, that some in the mainstream engage in the rhetorical trope of what might be termed "minority metaphoricity," the substitutability of one minority for another in the marketing of postmodern ethnic commodities.

9. See Sonia Saldívar-Hull's well-argued analysis of this change (1990: 128–62). Among the dozens of current studies of Cisneros' fiction, too numerous to list here, the essays of Díaz (1995) and Mullen (1996) are particularly insightful. Where Díaz, for example, argues that the stories in *Woman Hollering Creek* both define and defy postmodern subjectivity, I focus instead on the modes in which the text ruptures the postmodern "aura" overlaid on it.

10. In his pathbreaking study of Dostoevsky, Bakhtin develops the concept of polyphony, wherein a character's voice is not constructed exactly like the author's, but rather "sounds, as it were, *alongside* the author's word and in a special way combines both with it and with the full and equally valid voices of the other characters" (*Problems*, 7). These multiple voices remain unmerged rather than developing in an evolving dialectical progression toward a synthesis. Cisneros has strikingly arranged "Little Miracles, Kept Promises" so that the voices of her characters remain unmerged with one another at the same time that they coexist with and remain separate from her own authorial discursive presence.

11. That is, suckling or coddling to him too much.

12. Susan Miller refers to Garcia's book as a "magical first novel" (78); invoking Gabriel García Márquez and Mario Vargas Llosa ostensibly in order to contrast their books to *Dreaming in Cuban*, she perhaps inadvertently displays the common reading formation that categorizes U.S. Latino writing as an offshoot of Latin American magical

realism and the Boom writing of the 1960s and 1970s. (The *Christian Science Monitor*, for example, includes a few brief lines on *Dreaming in Cuban* at the end of a review that primarily emphasizes English translations of contemporary Latin American fiction, even though the review visually foregrounds Garcia's novel by prominently displaying a picture of the book jacket; see Marjorie Agosín, "Mixtures of Reality and Poetry in Latin American Literature," *Christian Science Monitor*, 24 Apr. 1992: 13). Interestingly, Roz Kaveney, in the *Times Literary Supplement* complains that Garcia's "cookery-book magic realism [is] laid on thick" (19). This resistance to the facile commodification of U.S. Latino books beneath the glowing label "magical realist" perhaps stems from Britain's distinct relation to Latin America (e.g., the 1982 Malvinas/Falkland war) and the dearth of Latino immigrants in comparison to the large number of Latinos in the United States. The pressure to contain and integrate Latino culture in Britain is not as severe as in the United States.

13. Pilar studies in the Barnard College library, for example, where Garcia went to college; subsequently, in *The Agüero Sisters*, Garcia's dedication of the book is to "Pilar," the name of both her daughter and the protagonist of her previous novel.

14. Indeed, the mouth becomes blocked by more than a tintblock on the cover of the paperback edition released in March 1993. Now a quotation from the *New York Times* review of the book covers the lower half of Celia's face: "Dazzling. . . . Remarkable. . . . Garcia stands revealed as a magical new writer. . . . Fierce, visionary. . . . Completely original." In the semiotic system of the revised cover, the words of the country's principal newspaper temporarily stand in for and precede Celia's own speech as the process of multicultural commodification proceeds.

15. See, for example, "How Assimilation Rips at Cultural Roots of Four Girls," *San Diego Tribune*, 17 May 1991: C-3; and "*Garcia Girls* Transcends Tale of Family's Assimilation," *San Antonio Express-News*, 18 Aug. 1991: L-6.

16. *Asheville Citizen-Times*, 26 May 1991: n.p.

17. See, for example, Michael Agar, "Writing Left America," *Discourse Processes* 14 (1991): 261–76.

18. "Una entrevista con Julia Alvarez," *La Tarde Alegre*, 31 May 1992: 13.

19. Bakhtin defines hybridization as "a mixture of two social languages within the limits of a single utterance, an encounter, within the arena of an utterance, between two different linguistic consciousnesses, separated from one another by an epoch, by social differentiation or by some other factor" ("Discourse," 358).

20. See Seymour Chatman, *Story and Discourse: Narrative Structure in Fiction and Film* (Ithaca, N.Y.: Cornell University Press, 1978).

21. In an earlier essay, Alvarez offered another explanation. She notes that her father, at the encouragement of the CIA, became involved in a movement to overthrow Trujillo until one of the two other members of his "cell" was arrested; the threat of denunciation under torture imperiled Alvarez's father's ability to continue work to overthrow the dictator. See "An American Childhood in the Dominican Republic," *American Scholar* 56 (1987): 71–85. Historians of the period emphasize that the United

States began to be less supportive of Trujillo from 1956 onward after Trujillo's assassination of his critic Jesús de Galíndez in New York and the American co-plotter Gerald Murphy, Trujillo's attempted murder of Venezuelan president Betancourt, and the overthrow of dictators in other Latin American countries. The United States wavered about overthrowing Trujillo, however, until it could be sure that a government that would better serve its interests could be installed.

22. The narrator calls attention to the use of the pejorative term "gabacha" by emphasizing that it is the narrator's linguistic choice, not the character's: "and the three gabachas (my term, not Fe's)" (Castillo, *So Far from God*, 29). Although the primary referent of the term in this passage is the three bridesmaids whom Fe has chosen, by virtue of its use in everyday speech the term simultaneously refers to Anglos in general, including those reading the book.

23. Doreen Carvajal has documented the inadequate presence of minority personnel in major publishing houses, even as publishers rush to reach Hispanic and other minority audiences; she notes, for example, that Hispanics make up only 1.8 percent of the professional and executive workforce, according to the latest federal figures ("Minorities Have Little Say in Book Publishing," *New York Times*, 24 June 1996). See also Iván Díaz, "Lack of Latino Literary Agents Stifles Writers Breaking into Publishing World," *Hispanic Link Weekly Report*, 3 June 1996: 1+.

24. Castillo might also have more accurately noted that there is also an important tradition of *santero* wood carvers in Puerto Rico. See Yvonne Lange, *Santos: The Household Wooden Saints of Puerto Rico* (Ann Arbor, Mich.: University Microfilms International, 1975).

25. In contrast, the Los Angeles-based writer and journalist Rubén Martínez has emphasized the hybridity of U.S. Latino culture, noting that he would begin a university course on Chicano barrio culture by showing an episode of *The Brady Bunch*. His point is that many U.S. Latinos also enjoy and define themselves through their participation in mainstream U.S. culture, not only ethnic culture. A program such as *The Brady Bunch* is just as important to understanding barrio culture as, say, a *telenovela*. Martínez and other cultural theorists insist on the hybridity of the Latino cultural experience, not only its distinctness from the mainstream (conversation with author, Santa Barbara, Calif., 24 Jan. 1994).

Chapter Two

1. For a similar feminist rereading of a biblical master text from the perspective of an under-narrativized female character, see the Mexican writer Inés Arredondo's 1960 story "The Shunammite" (in *Other Fires*, ed. Alberto Manguel [New York: Clarkson N. Potter, 1986], 104–17).

2. Viramontes has told me that she did not intend the term "contra" in her story to imply that those who abducted the woman's son were linked to the Nicaraguan Sandinista government. Rather, she intended the term to refer generically to a politi-

cal group against any government. Given the American media's prevalent usage of the term "Contra" to refer to anti-Sandinistas at the time the story was published (1985), Viramontes' use of the word is overcoded to imply strongly that the Sandinistas are responsible for this woman's misfortune. Perhaps in a subsequent edition of the story, Viramontes will devise a mode to distance that term clearly from its common usage in the United States.

3. For an excellent reading of Viramontes' "The Cariboo Cafe," see Castillo, *Talking Back*, 76–95.

4. Laclau, "Populist Rupture and Discourse," 91; see also Laclau's "Metaphor and Social Antagonisms" and Chantal Mouffe's "Hegemony and New Political Subjects."

5. Lecture/reading, University of California, Santa Barbara, 24 May 1990.

6. See Howard, 402.

7. Limón bases her narrative description of the massacre of the Jesuits on eyewitness testimony. The details of the accounts in Torrens ("U.C.A."), for example, correspond to those Limón uses. For further information on the role of the Jesuits at U.C.A. in the years before and after the assassinations and the larger social problems in Salvadoran society, see Héctor Lindo-Fuentes' review of *Jesuit Education and Social Change in El Salvador* by Charles Beirne, S.J. (New York: Garland, 1998) in *America*, 16 May 1998: 27.

8. For further details of Martínez's indictment, see Juffer. See also Martínez's own description of the events in "Afterword," *Breathing Between the Lines* (Tucson: University of Arizona Press, 1997), 55–60.

9. See Bruce-Novoa, "New Mexican Chicano Poetry." See also Martínez's poems "Point Blank," "Postscript," and "War" in Herrera-Sobek and Viramontes, *Chicana (W)rites*, 42–46.

10. See Gates, *Loose Canons*, 19–20.

Chapter Three

1. See, for example, Saldívar-Hull, "Feminism on the Border."

2. Although my focus here is on Chávez's disruption of narrative individualism and the relation of "Novena Narrativas" to the *testimonio* genre, others have classified Chávez's experimental form in different terms. See Herrera-Sobek's fine analysis in her introduction to *Chicano Creativity and Criticism* and Quintana's "Chicana Discourse" (1989) and *Home Girls* (1996).

3. See Eakin, *Fictions in Autobiography*, 3, 17–19.

4. Judith Butler points to the limitations of the Sartrean account of the reversal of power because "power . . . operate[s] in that very binary frame for thinking about gender. . . . [W]hat configuration of power constructs the subject and the Other, that binary relation between 'men' and 'women' and the internal stability of those terms?" (*Gender Trouble*, 1990: x).

5. See, for example, the 1975 report of the Church Committee of the U.S. Sen-

ate, *Alleged Assassination Plots Involving Foreign Leaders*. For an account of the CIA's participation in Trujillo's assassination, see Bernard Diederich, *Trujillo: The Death of the Goat* (New York: Bodley Head, 1978).

6. I would argue that this additional research is quite vital if American readers are to move beyond a "multiculturalist" understanding of Latin American history in which stereotypes become strengthened. I am reminded, for example, of a university undergraduate student who asked me with great puzzlement, after seeing the movie *Reds*, to explain what exactly had happened in the 1917 Russian revolution. That is, given the educational gaps of most Americans—even the college educated—cultural artifacts that attempt to dramatically re-create cross sections of history run the risk of adding to ignorance rather than to an accurate understanding of past events.

In a student survey conducted in an upper-division literature class at the University of California in 1993 after students had read *How the García Girls Lost Their Accents*, only six respondents knew the name of the dictator in power in the Dominican Republic during the events in Alvarez's book; thirty-seven students were unable to answer this question. Several students named Fidel Castro as the dictator in power at the time, and some answered that the setting was Puerto Rico or Cuba. One student who named the country as Puerto Rico wrote, "I believe that there was an overthrow of a government by a tyrant. I think the family had to leave because Carlos and his brothers were plotting a counter-movement against the tyrant's military rule. . . . I forgot the dictator's name." Another, who was able to name the country but not the dictator, wrote, "I didn't really learn anything about the political events that caused the Garcia family to come to the U.S. I know there was a dictator overthrown and Carlos Garcia had connections in the government that caused him to leave, but I don't have any clue about the [political] circumstances."

7. See Gleijeses, *Dominican Crisis*, 24; and Wiarda, *Dominican Republic*, 41, 45.

8. Gleijeses notes: "Outside of the American government only three men had direct knowledge of the role played by the United States [in Trujillo's assassination]: the leader of the conspiracy, Juan Tomás Díaz, and two men who served as intermediaries with the Americans: the Dominican 'Plutarco Acevedo' and Wallace Berry ('Wimpy'), an American citizen who was a close friend of one of the plotters" (*Dominican Crisis*, 304).

9. Alvarez alludes to the seven-month presidency of Juan Bosch in 1963 without naming him, the civil war that ensued, the U.S. intervention in the political process, and the eventual landing of U.S. marines on the island. While she gives schematic general details of the political turmoil in these months, most readers again must refer to other histories of the period for specific information. In contrast, she specifically mentions Adlai Stevenson in the story, prioritizing, to a certain degree, events in the United States, which is the setting of the story and the characters' new home.

10. See, for example, Morales' *The Rag Doll Plagues* (Houston, Tex.: Arte Público, 1992), Garcia's *Dreaming in Cuban*, Viramontes' "The Cariboo Cafe" (in *Moths*), Martínez's *Mother Tongue*, Limón's *In Search of Bernabé* and *Song of the Hummingbird*,

Arias' *After the Bombs*, trans. Asa Zatz (Willimantic, Conn.: Curbstone Press, 1990) and Martínez's *The Other Side: Fault Line, Guerrilla Saints, and the True Heart of Rock 'n Roll* (London: Verso, 1992).

11. See, for example, Joanne Omang, "For This They Died?" *Los Angeles Times Book Review*, 26 Feb. 1995: 8; González Echevarría, "Sisters in Death"; Ilan Stavans, "*Las Mariposas*: Review of *In the Time of the Butterflies* by Julia Alvarez," *The Nation*, 7 Nov. 1994: 552+; and Ava Roth, "Sisters in Revolution," *Ms.* (Sept.–Oct. 1994): 79–80; and "Three Sisters," *Publisher's Weekly*, 22 Apr. 1996: 24.

12. For further information on the Mirabal sisters, readers might read some of the sources Alvarez herself used, such as Ramón Alberto Ferreras, *Las Mirabal* (Santo Domingo, Dominican Republic: Media Isla III, 1976), or William Galvan, *Minerva Mirabal: Historia de una heroina* (Santo Domingo, Dominican Republic: Universidad Autónoma de Santo Domingo, 1982).

Chapter Four

1. See also the essays in *An Enduring Flame: Studies on Latino Popular Religiosity*, ed. Anthony M. Stevens-Arroyo and Ana María Díaz-Stevens (New York: Bildner Center for Western Hemisphere Studies, 1994).

2. And like Fernández's other stories in the volume, "Filomena" is an "intaglio," representing both the imprinting of past cultural traditions on the narrator Nenita and, because of its particular emphasis on visuality, an engraving on stone or a relief image that visually records a moment in history.

3. A proleptic, unexplained allusion to Alejandro as one of the people whom Filomena and the narrator would honor in the *ofrenda* they begin to construct as the story opens subtly warns readers about Filomena's third tragedy, not yet recounted in the story. Readers who notice the unexplained name proceed with the rest of the story with a sense of foreboding.

4. In Cisneros' 1990 story "Divine Providence," for example, she suggests that popular belief systems are perhaps more powerful than traditional Christian religious figures. At least in the young Alma's perception, the predictions of the mother-in-law and neighbor seem unlikely to be overturned "regardless of how many candles are lit, or promises made, or supplications to Saint Anthony recited, Ave María, Padre Nuestro, world without end, amen" (78).

5. In "Tepeyac," the address of the grandfather's house, "La Fortuna, number 12," corresponds to the Mexico City address of Cisneros' grandfather (see "Ghosts and Voices: Writing from Obsession," 69). Cisneros also uses her maternal grandmother's surname, Anguiano, for fictional characters in the book (see note 18 below).

6. Lydia Cabrera quotes an elderly Cuban woman's response when asked how she could worship Christian and African gods together: "God is the same but with a different necklace" ("Religious Syncretism in Cuba," 86). Although some contemporary thinkers problematize the concept of syncretism, Otto Maduro points to the

syncretic aspects of all religions, including Roman Catholicism, and urges people to understand these mixtures in positive terms ("U.S. Latinos and Religion").

7. See González-Wippler, *Santería, the Religion*, 61–62, and Fray Angélico Chávez, "Saints Names in New Mexico Geography," *El Palacio* 56:11 (1949): 333. Father Steele gives the title of the Catholic Virgin as "Nuestra Señora de las Candelarias" (Our Lady of the Candlesticks) (*Santos and Saints*, 148); see also Ean Begg, *The Cult of the Black Virgin* (London: Arkana, 1985), 253, for a discussion of the origin and history of the statue and cult of the Virgen de la Candelaria in the Canary Islands.

8. It is likely that the variations in the spellings of the *orishas'* names on the holy card result from the oral rather than written culture surrounding *santería*.

9. It is not problematic that Felicia has previously in the novel been associated with the *orisha* Oshún because, as González-Wippler explains, it is believed that because Obatalá owns all heads, he can be received by any person even if he or she has another ruling *orisha* (*Santería*, 38). Earlier in the novel, Felicia has awakened unaware of who or where she is. She discovers in a shoulder bag, along with a tube of orange lipstick, a soiled prayer card for La Virgen de la Caridad del Cobre (fig. 4.9). As the patron saint of Cuba, this virgin is syncretized with the *orisha* Oshún and is so popular that every year on September 8, her feast, a High Mass is celebrated in St. Patrick's cathedral in New York City, attended by many Cuban-American *santeros* who wear yellow in Oshún's honor.

10. Ortiz Cofer has noted that despite the influence of machismo, Puerto Rico is "really a secret matriarchy" and women are the spiritual guardians of the household. "Men may go out and have mistresses or be rowdy, but when they enter the home, it's like entering church. They obey their wives' wishes" ("An Interview," 88).

11. Ortiz Cofer bases this narrative on the Virgin of Montserrate, a Black Virgin who appeared in colonial times near Cofer's hometown, Hormigueros. Baptized in La Iglesia de Montserrate, as were her father and grandfather, Cofer notes that the Virgin's legend permeated her childhood ("Puerto Rican Literature," 46).

12. González-Wippler notes that "all santeros are spiritists (*espiritistas*), but not all spiritists are santeros" (*Santería*, 274). She also points out that in recent years some of the elements of Santería and *espiritismo* have fused.

13. See the 1992 and 1994 interviews with Ortiz Cofer by Ocasio.

14. Some changes in these negative attitudes are occurring, for example, in the recent development of Catholic ministries of body massage (see Pamela Schaeffer, "Massage: An Expanding Healing Ministry," *National Catholic Reporter*, 19 Jan. 1996: 22–23).

15. See Morales, "A Chicana Stereotypes Her Own People"; Morales expressed his reaction to the indelicate scene in *Hoyt Street* in a conversation with me on 9 July 1994. While I understand the concerns of this important Chicano literary critic and creative writer, I offer another reading of the texts here, mindful that multiple interpretations from various reading positions will continue to flourish.

16. For an important discussion of the concept of the male surveyor, see John Berger, *Ways of Seeing* (London: Penguin, 1972).

17. Chávez notes that many Catholics in New Mexico pray novenas during the days preceding the feast of the Virgin of Guadalupe on December 12 ("Our Lady of Guadalupe"). This ritual is also observed in Santa Fe in honor of La Conquistadora, "Our Lady of the Conquest."

18. The book's dedication suggests that "Anguiano" is the surname of Cisneros' maternal grandmother, a surname that Cisneros also gives to the surrogate sister figure, Lucy, in the first story; "Anguiano Religious Articles . . ." also alludes to San Fernando Cathedral in San Antonio, the city where Cisneros now lives; as we have seen, "La Fortuna, number 12" corresponds to the Mexico City address of Cisneros' grandfather.

19. For important studies of some of these alternative religious practices, see Espinosa, *Saints in the Valleys*; Steele, *Santos and Saints*; Mills, *People of the Saints*; Egan, *Milagros*; Oktavec, *Answered Prayers*; García-Rivera, *St. Martin de Porres*; Gavin, *Traditional Art of Spanish New Mexico*; Brenner, "Painted Miracles" and *Idols Behind Altars*, esp. chap. 7; Durand and Massey, *Miracles on the Border*; Giffords, *Mexican Folk Retablos*; González, *Cultura(s)*; Garduño Pulido et al., *Milagros en la frontera*; and Sánchez Lara, *Los retablos populares*. See also McCracken, "Toward a Comparative Text Grammar."

20. I draw here on the work of Argentine cultural critic Nestor García Canclini, who has argued that there exists a "multi-temporal heterogeneity" and hybridization of Latin American culture ("Memory and Innovation," 428). Because modernization has never completely succeeded in replacing the traditional and ancient, contemporary cultural practices continue to deploy the signifiers of past eras in syncretic combination with the new.

21. Because of the devotion of some of his parishioners to the Black Christ of Esquipulas, especially immigrants from Guatemala, Father Virgilio Elizondo obtained a large crucifix of the Black Christ from Guatemala for display in San Fernando Cathedral in San Antonio when he served as rector. Similar devotion to the Black Christ is practiced in other U.S. cities with Central American immigrants, including Washington, D.C.

22. See Glenna M. Stearman Park and Larry McIntire, "Jail House Rag," in *Folk Art in Texas*, ed. Francis and Edward Abernathy (Dallas, Tex.: Southern Methodist University Press, 1985), 167–71.

23. Lecture, Mount Holyoke College, South Hadley, Mass., 23 Apr. 1991.

24. See also Ruth Dodson, "Don Pedrito Jaramillo: The Curandero of Los Olmos," in *The Healer of Los Olmos and Other Mexican Lore*, ed. Wilson M. Hudson (Austin: Texas Folklore Society, 1951; Dallas: Southern Methodist University Press, 1966, 9–70).

25. See Steele, *Santos and Saints*, 90. See also Mills' description of what he terms

the "personalization" of saints and religious figures (*People of the Saints*, 58–59). He describes one account, for example, of the carrying of a figure of the Holy Child to drought-stricken fields; when a flood ensued, the figure of the Virgin was taken to the site to show her the damage her son had done. As José Espinosa notes,

> The saints are not only rewarded but reprimanded. Fresh candles, new clothing or *ex votos* are supplied when the saints are invoked or thanked, but many are the poor *santos* who have spent lonely hours or days in the darkness of a chest, a storeroom, or a closet, or wrapped in a blanket, or turned toward the wall for failure to listen to the pleas of a devotee who felt that he deserved better treatment. In the cases of St. Joseph and St. Anthony, and even the Virgin Mother, a cruel punishment was resorted to when desperate measures seemed to be the only way out of an impasse, namely, the removal of the Christ Child from their arms. (85)

26. See Steele, *Santos and Saints*, 58–60; *Holy Week in Tomé: A New Mexico Passion Play* (Santa Fe, N.Mex.: Sunstone Press, 1976); and Jaramillo, *Shadows of the Past*, 61, 70.

27. Lecture, Mount Holyoke College, South Hadley, Mass., 23 Apr. 1991.

28. One such *retablo* reads:

> I give infinite thanks to the Holiest virgin of San Juan de los Lagos for allowing me to return alive to my family's side after a terrible event that occurred during my return to town. I was coming from the United States of America when, just after crossing the border in Chihuahua, I was assaulted on the train by thieves who wanted to take my life and rob me of the money and all that I carried. But they didn't accomplish their goal thanks to the Holiest Virgin. When the bandit struck me with a dagger, an impulse made me defend myself with such force that I broke a glass window with my back and fell backwards outside, landing on the ground so hard that I thought for sure I would lose my life. And if this was not enough, the van that picked me up to bring me to the hospital turned over. This happened on November 20, 1943 at 7:00 in the evening. Antonio Alcaraz, Zacapu, Michoacán. 2-2-49." (Durand and Massey, *Miracles on the Border*, 192)

Chapter Five

1. For a contemporary mass-cultural version of this alternative ritual practice, see the monthly feature "Cartas a la bruja" in *Cosmopolitan en español* in which readers request instructions for rituals to remedy their sexual and emotional problems. See also McCracken, *Decoding Women's Magazines: From* Mademoiselle *to* Ms. (New York: St. Martin's, 1993), 254–55.

2. See also Angela McRobbie's *Feminism and Youth Culture: From "Jackie" to "Just*

Seventeen" (Boston: Unwin Hyman, 1991) for a collection of her essays on girls' subculture.

3. See Brown, "Novelist"; and *Kirkus Reviews*, 15 June 1989. Positive reviews of *The Wedding* include those in *Hispania* 73 (1990): 1005–07; *Western American Literature* 25.3 (1989): 262; and *The American Book Review* (Boulder, Colo.: English Dept. Publications Center, University of Colorado, n.d.).

4. For example, the main character, Blanca, was held back in the third grade for being a slow reader, forced to repeat seventh grade because she started the school year late, after the picking season, and made to feel so stupid by the teachers that she had no desire to continue school beyond eighth grade.

5. Ponce, lecture, University of California, Santa Barbara, 23 Oct. 1992.

6. In her 1993 autobiography, *Hoyt Street*, Ponce affirms her contact with *pachuco* subculture as she was growing up in Pacoima, and the transgressive role such subcultural language and behavior played. She describes scenes in church in which girls engaged in vulgar gestures and called each other derogatory slang terms such as "babosa" (slobbery) and "hocicona" (big snout) while the priest sang "Dominus vobiscum." Ponce notes: "By the late 1940s my friends and I had picked up pachuco jargon; we loved to use forbidden words like cabrón, simón, órale. During [the Litany of the Saints], providing no adults were nearby, we would respond with "Orale, pro nobis" (167). It might be argued that Ponce is affirming her expert familiarity with *pachuco* language in this passage, if not her native speaking ability of the subcultural dialect.

7. *Hoyt Street* corroborates the existence of Lucy: "One of the best pinchers [in church] was Lucy, Nancy's older sister. Lucy was rumored to be a pachuca who hung around with zoot suiters (which was the worst thing a girl could do). Lucy was pretty, with olive skin and small, dark eyes that rarely smiled. I found it hard to believe that such a pretty girl could be a zoot suiter who wore a knife stuck in her pompadour and another stuck inside her socks" (166).

8. In a 1986 essay, Chávez points to the progressive political struggles that have reappropriated the Virgin of Guadalupe figure, among them the labor union and Civil Rights movements. Arguing that "the political and social justice dimensions of the story [of Guadalupe] are crucial to many people throughout the Americas" (58–59), Chávez emphasizes the influence of this religious figure on artists, writers, prison inmates who practice tattoo and handkerchief art, the *pachucos* of the 1940s and 1950s, lowriders, and even on the votive candles sold in supermarkets and small markets throughout the Southwest. Many Catholics in New Mexico, she notes, pray novenas (nine-day prayer cycles) during the days preceding the feast of the Virgen of Guadalupe on December 12, a religious practice that her narrative play reappropriates.

9. Some have objected that such portrayals of lesbians as homeless or prison inmates are not representative and therefore inaccurately show lesbian experience. Neither Chávez nor Castillo claims that her lesbian character represents all lesbians, however. Further, some argue that lesbianism should not be foregrounded as transgressive for this view adopts the heterosexism of the dominant culture. I would

argue, in contrast, that attempts to deny the transgressive character of lesbianism at this historical moment run aground in the material constraints of everyday, mainstream reality in which the culture of homophobia predominates in both overt and subtle forms.

10. See Michel Butor's *La Modification* (Paris: Editions de Minuit, 1957), in which second-person narration is employed exclusively throughout the novel, and Carlos Fuentes' *La muerte de Artemio Cruz* (Mexico City: Fondo de Cultura Económica, 1962), which uses this technique in approximately one-third of the novel's subsections.

Chapter Six

1. For an important analysis of the contemporary problems of identity politics, see Daphne Patai, "The Struggle for Feminist Purity Threatens the Goals of Feminism," *Chronicle of Higher Education*, 5 Feb. 1992.

2. *Fresh Air*, National Public Radio, 23 Apr. 1991.

3. The quotations in English that I reproduce here are intercalated in the text with Seña Alba's words in *jíbaro*:

> "Me dijo que pa' curalme me tenía que ponel lah manoh encima, que el podel del Dioh pasaba pol suh manoh. Yo ehtaba bien nelviosa pero creía que si él podía cural a mí mai me podía cural a mí. Bueno, pueh me quitó la ropa y me empezó a tocal y a rezal al mihmo tiempo, y dehpuéh me dijo que se tenía que acohtal sobre mí pa' que to' el podel de Dioh pasara de él a mí. . . . Eso fué lo que hizo . . . y allí mihmo me ultrajó. . . .
>
> "Empezé a grital y él me cubrió la boca . . . me dolió mucho. Me dehtrozó. Cuando telminó me limpió la sangre con un pañuelo y se arrodilló a rezal . . . y me dijo que me arrodillara que yo tenía que rezal pol me peca'o. Que lo que habíamoh hecho era un peca'o y solo le podíamoh hablal a Dioh d'eso y rezal. Y que Dioh me iba a peldonal si rezaba mucho y no le hablaba a naide d'eso." (de Monteflores, *Cantando Bajito*, 187)

4. See Herrera-Sobek, "The Politics of Rape," for an important analysis of this scene.

5. Fernández kindly allowed me to use a copy of the page proofs of this story in a course I taught in spring 1990. Because of a printing error, however, when the book appeared in July 1990, a quotation from Lorna Dee Cervantes mistakenly preceded "Esmeralda," while the two correct epigraphs, which are crucial to decoding the story, appeared with the story "Zulema."

6. Roberta Fernández, lecture and public reading, University of California, Santa Barbara, 24 May 1990.

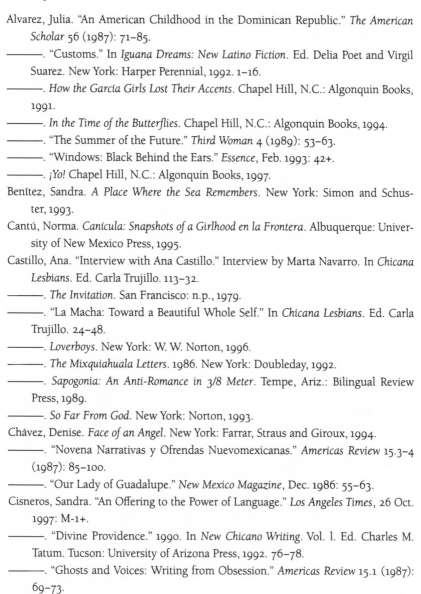

Primary Texts

Alvarez, Julia. "An American Childhood in the Dominican Republic." *The American Scholar* 56 (1987): 71–85.

———. "Customs." In *Iguana Dreams: New Latino Fiction*. Ed. Delia Poet and Virgil Suarez. New York: Harper Perennial, 1992. 1–16.

———. *How the García Girls Lost Their Accents*. Chapel Hill, N.C.: Algonquin Books, 1991.

———. *In the Time of the Butterflies*. Chapel Hill, N.C.: Algonquin Books, 1994.

———. "The Summer of the Future." *Third Woman* 4 (1989): 53–63.

———. "Windows: Black Behind the Ears." *Essence*, Feb. 1993: 42+.

———. *¡Yo!* Chapel Hill, N.C.: Algonquin Books, 1997.

Benítez, Sandra. *A Place Where the Sea Remembers*. New York: Simon and Schuster, 1993.

Cantú, Norma. *Canícula: Snapshots of a Girlhood en la Frontera*. Albuquerque: University of New Mexico Press, 1995.

Castillo, Ana. "Interview with Ana Castillo." Interview by Marta Navarro. In *Chicana Lesbians*. Ed. Carla Trujillo. 113–32.

———. *The Invitation*. San Francisco: n.p., 1979.

———. "La Macha: Toward a Beautiful Whole Self." In *Chicana Lesbians*. Ed. Carla Trujillo. 24–48.

———. *Loverboys*. New York: W. W. Norton, 1996.

———. *The Mixquiahuala Letters*. 1986. New York: Doubleday, 1992.

———. *Sapogonia: An Anti-Romance in 3/8 Meter*. Tempe, Ariz.: Bilingual Review Press, 1989.

———. *So Far From God*. New York: Norton, 1993.

Chávez, Denise. *Face of an Angel*. New York: Farrar, Straus and Giroux, 1994.

———. "Novena Narrativas y Ofrendas Nuevomexicanas." *Americas Review* 15.3–4 (1987): 85–100.

———. "Our Lady of Guadalupe." *New Mexico Magazine*, Dec. 1986: 55–63.

Cisneros, Sandra. "An Offering to the Power of Language." *Los Angeles Times*, 26 Oct. 1997: M-1+.

———. "Divine Providence." 1990. In *New Chicano Writing*. Vol. 1. Ed. Charles M. Tatum. Tucson: University of Arizona Press, 1992. 76–78.

———. "Ghosts and Voices: Writing from Obsession." *Americas Review* 15.1 (1987): 69–73.

———. "Guadalupe the Sex Goddess: Unearthing the Racy Past of Mexico's Most Famous Virgin." *Ms.*, July–Aug. 1996: 43–46.

———. *The House on Mango Street*. 1984. Houston, Tex.: Arte Público, 1985.

———. "Mexico's Day of the Dead: ¡Vivan los muertos!" *Elle*, Nov. 1991: 194+.

———. "Only Daughter." *Glamour*, Nov. 1990: 256+.

———. "The Tejano Soul of San Antonio." *The Sophisticated Traveler; New York Times Magazine*, pt. 2, *New York Times*, 17 May 1992: 24+.

———. "Woman Hollering Creek." *Los Angeles Times Magazine*, 1 July 1990: 14+.

———. *Woman Hollering Creek and Other Stories*. New York: Random House, 1991.

Corpi, Lucha. "Los Cristos del Alma." In *Palabra Nueva: Cuentos Chicanos*. Ed. Ricardo Aguilar, Armando Armengol, and Oscar U. Somoza. El Paso: Texas Western Press, 1984. 3–12.

———. *Delia's Song*. Houston, Tex.: Arte Público, 1988.

———. *Eulogy for a Brown Angel: A Mystery Novel*. Houston, Tex.: Arte Público, 1992.

de Monteflores, Carmen. *Cantando Bajito: Singing Softly*. San Francisco: Spinsters/Aunt Lute, 1989.

Engle, Margarita. *Skywriting*. New York: Bantam Books, 1995.

Fernández, Mickey. "Grace." *West Wind Review*. Ashland: Southern Oregon State, 1989. 121–34.

Fernández, Roberta. *Intaglio: A Novel in Six Stories*. Houston, Tex.: Arte Público, 1990.

Garcia, Cristina. *The Agüero Sisters*. New York: Knopf, 1997.

———. " '. . . And There Is Only My Imagination Where Our History Should Be': An Interview with Cristina Garcia." Interview by Iraida H. López. *Michigan Quarterly Review* 33 (1994): 605–17.

———. *Dreaming in Cuban*. New York: Knopf, 1992.

Limón, Graciela. *The Day of the Moon*. Houston, Tex.: Arte Público, in press.

———. *In Search of Bernabé*. Houston, Tex.: Arte Público, 1993.

———. *María de Belén: The Autobiography of an Indian Woman: A Novel*. New York: Vantage Press, 1990.

———. *The Memories of Ana Calderón*. Houston, Tex.: Arte Público, 1994.

———. *Song of the Hummingbird*. Houston, Tex.: Arte Público, 1996.

López-Medina, Sylvia. *Cantora*. Albuquerque: University of New Mexico Press, 1992.

Martínez, Demetria. *Mother Tongue*. Tempe, Ariz.: Bilingual Press, 1994.

———. "What a Moment, When the 'Voiceless' Speak!" *National Catholic Reporter*, 5 Apr. 1996: 16.

Mohr, Nicholasa. *In Nueva York*. 1977. Houston, Tex.: Arte Público, 1986.

———. *Rituals of Survival: A Woman's Portfolio*. Houston, Tex.: Arte Público Press, 1985.

Mora, Pat. "Hands." 1982. In *Infinite Divisions: An Anthology of Chicana Literature*. Ed. Tey Diana Rebolledo and Eliana S. Rivero. Tucson: University of Arizona Press, 1993. 222–26.

Moraga, Cherríe. *Giving Up the Ghost*. Los Angeles: West End Press, 1986.

Morales, Aurora Levins, and Rosario Morales. *Getting Home Alive*. Ithaca, N.Y.: Firebrand Press, 1986.

Novas, Himilce. *Mangos, Bananas, and Coconuts: A Cuban Love Story*. Houston, Tex.:
Arte Público, 1996.

Ortiz Cofer, Judith. "The Art of Not Forgetting: An Interview with Judith Ortiz Cofer."
Interview by Marilyn Kallet. *Prairie Schooner* 68.4 (1994): 68–75.

———. "The Infinite Variety of the Puerto Rican Reality: An Interview with Judith
Ortiz Cofer." Interview by Rafael Ocasio. *Callaloo* 17.3 (1994): 730–43.

———. "An Interview with Judith Ortiz Cofer." Interview by Rafael Ocasio. *Americas
Review* 22.3–4 (1994): 84–90.

———. *The Latin Deli: Prose and Poetry*. Athens: University of Georgia Press, 1993.

———. *The Line of the Sun*. Athens: University of Georgia Press, 1989.

———. "A MELUS Interview: Judith Ortiz Cofer." Interview by Edna Acosta-Belén.
MELUS 18.3 (1993): 83–97.

———. "Puerto Rican Literature in Georgia? An Interview with Judith Ortiz Cofer."
Interview by Rafael Ocasio. *Kenyon Review* 14.4 (1992): 43–50.

———. *Silent Dancing: A Partial Remembrance of a Puerto Rican Childhood*. Houston,
Tex.: Arte Público, 1990.

Ponce, Mary Helen. *Hoyt Street: An Autobiography*. Albuquerque: University of New
Mexico Press, 1993.

———. *The Wedding*. Houston, Tex.: Arte Público, 1989.

Villanueva, Alma Luz. *The Ultraviolet Sky*. Tempe, Ariz.: Bilingual Press, 1988.

Viramontes, Helena María. "An Interview with Helena María Viramontes." Interview
by Nancy Christoph. *Baneke* 3 (1995): 10–11.

———. "The Jumping Bean." In *Chicana (W)rites on Word and Film*. Ed. María Herrera-
Sobek and Viramontes. Berkeley, Calif.: Third Woman Press, 1995. 101–12.

———. *The Moths and Other Stories*. Houston, Tex.: Arte Público Press, 1985.

———. *Under the Feet of Jesus*. New York: Dutton, 1995.

Secondary Sources

Aparicio, Frances R. "On Sub-versive Signifiers: U.S. Latina/o Writers Tropicalize
English." *American Literature* 66.4 (1994): 795–801.

Bakhtin, Mikhail M. "Discourse in the Novel." In *The Dialogic Imagination: Four Essays
by M.M. Bakhtin*. Ed. Michael Holquist. Trans. Caryl Emerson and Holquist.
Austin: University of Texas Press, 1981. 259–422.

———. *Problems of Dostoevsky's Poetics*. Ed. and trans. Caryl Emerson. Minneapolis:
University of Minnesota Press, 1984.

———. *Rabelais and His World*. Trans. Helene Iswolsky. Cambridge: Massachusetts
Institute of Technology, 1968.

Barthes, Roland. *Camera Lucida: Reflections on Photography*. Trans. Richard Howard.
New York: Hill and Wang, 1981.

Beauvoir, Simone de. *The Second Sex*. Trans. and ed. H. M. Parshley. New York: Knopf, 1953.

Berryman, Phillip. "Ignacio Ellacuría: An Appreciation." *America*, 7 July 1990: 12–15.

Brenner, Anita. *Idols Behind Altars*. New York: Biblo and Tannen, 1967.

———. "Painted Miracles." *Arts* 15 (Jan. 1929): 11–18.

Brown, Eloisa Bergere. "Novelist Smudges Satirical Portrait of Pachuco Existence." *Albuquerque Journal*, 15 Aug. 1989: n.p.

Bruce-Novoa, Juan. "New Mexican Chicano Poetry: The Contemporary Tradition." In *Pasó por Aquí: Critical Essays on the New Mexican Literary Tradition, 1542–1988*. Ed. Erlinda Gonzales-Berry. Albuquerque: University of New Mexico Press, 1989. 267–96.

———. "Ritual in Judith Ortiz Cofer's *The Line of the Sun*." *Confluencia* 8.1 (1992): 61–69.

———. "Sheila Ortiz Taylor's *Faultline*: A Third Woman Utopia." In Herrera-Sobek and Viramontes, *Chicana (W)Rites*. 225–43.

Butler, Judith. *Gender Trouble: Feminism and the Subversion of Identity*. New York: Routledge, 1990.

Butler-Evans, Elliott. "Ethnicity, Cultural Studies, and Marxist Discourse." Paper presented at conference on "Chicano Cultural Studies: New Critical Directions," University of California, Santa Barbara, 26 May 1990.

———. *Race, Gender, and Desire: Narrative Strategies in the Fiction of Toni Cade Bambara, Toni Morrison, and Alice Walker*. Philadelphia: Temple University Press, 1989.

———. "Textual Strategies and Ideology in Amy Tan's *The Joy Luck Club*." Paper presented at the Modern Language Association Convention, Dec. 1989.

Cabrera, Lydia. "Religious Syncretism in Cuba." *Journal of Caribbean Studies* 10.1–2 (1994–95): 84–94.

Calderón, Hector, and José David Saldívar, eds. *Criticism in the Borderlands: Studies in Chicano Literature, Culture, and Ideology*. Durham, N.C.: Duke University Press, 1991.

Castillo, Debra. *Talking Back: Toward a Latin American Feminist Literary Criticism*. Ithaca, N.Y.: Cornell University Press, 1992.

Chabram-Dernersesian, Angie. "I Throw Punches for My Race, but I Don't Want to Be a Man: Writing Us—Chica-nos (Girl, Us)/Chicanas—into the Movement Script." In *Cultural Studies*. Ed. Lawrence Grossberg, Cary Nelson, and Paula A. Treichler. New York: Routledge, 1992. 81–95.

Chatman, Seymour. *Story and Discourse: Narrative Structure in Fiction and Film*. Ithaca, N.Y.: Cornell University Press, 1980.

Clarke, John. "The Skinheads and the Magical Recovery of Community." In *Resistance Through Rituals: Youth Subcultures in Post-War Britain*. Ed. Stuart Hall and Tony Jefferson. London: Harper Collins Academic, 1976. 99–102.

Clarke, John, Stuart Hall, Tony Jefferson, and Brian Roberts. "Subcultures, Cultures,

and Class: A Theoretical Overview." In *Resistance Through Rituals*. Ed. Stuart Hall
and Tony Jefferson. London: Harper Collins Academic, 1976. 9–74.

Clary, Mike. "Florida's Caribbean Immigrants Are Putting Their Faith in Santería." *Los
Angeles Times*, 9 Aug. 1995: A5.

Cummings, Laura. "Chucos, Cholos, and Chusma: Stigma and Pachuco Identity."
Paper presented at conference on "Chicano Cultural Studies: New Critical Directions," University of California, Santa Barbara, 26 May 1990.

de Certeau, Michel. *The Practice of Everyday Life*. Trans. Steven Rendall. Berkeley:
University of California Press, 1984.

del Castillo, Richard Griswold, Teresa McKenna, and Yvonne Yarbro-Bejarano, eds.
Chicano Art: Resistance and Affirmation, 1965–1985. Los Angeles: Wight Art Gal-
lery, University of California, Los Angeles, 1991.

Díaz, Gwendolyn. "Postmodern Pop: The Construction of Context in the Fiction of
Sandra Cisneros." In *Actes du VI congrès européen sur les cultures d'Amérique Latine
aux États-Unis: Confrontations et métissages*. Ed. Elyette Benjamin-Labarthe et al.
Bordeaux: Maison des Pays Ibériques, 1995. 133–40.

Durand, Jorge, and Douglas S. Massey. *Miracles on the Border: Retablos of Mexican Migrants to the United States*. Tucson: University of Arizona Press, 1995.

Eagleton, Terry. *The Ideology of the Aesthetic*. London: Basil Blackwell, 1990.

Eakin, Paul John. *Fictions in Autobiography: Studies in the Art of Self-Invention*. Princeton, N.J.: Princeton University Press, 1985.

Egan, Martha. *Milagros: Votive Offerings from the Americas*. Santa Fe: Museum of New
Mexico Press, 1991.

Eisenstein, Sergei. *Film Form: Essays in Film Theory*. Ed. and trans. Jay Leyda. New
York: Harcourt, Brace and World, 1949.

Espín, Orlando O. "Popular Catholicism among Latinos." In *Hispanic Catholic Culture
in the U.S.* Ed. Jay P. Dolan and Allan Figueroa Deck. Notre Dame, Ind.: University of Notre Dame, 1994. 308–59.

Espinosa, José E. *Saints in the Valleys: Christian Sacred Images in the History, Life,
and Folk Art of Spanish New Mexico*. Albuquerque: University of New Mexico
Press, 1960.

Eysturoy, Annie O. *Daughters of Self-Creation: The Contemporary Chicana Novel*. Albuquerque: University of New Mexico Press, 1996.

Flores, Juan, and George Yúdice. "Living Borders/Buscando America: Languages of
Latino Self-Formation." *Social Text* 24 (1990): 57–84.

Flores-Peña, Ysamur. "The Garments of Religious Worship." In *Santería Garments and
Altars: Speaking Without a Voice*, by Flores-Peña and Roberta J. Evanchuk. Jack-
son: University of Mississippi Press, 1994. 13–26.

Franco, Jean. *Plotting Women: Gender and Representation in Mexico*. New York: Columbia University Press, 1988.

García Canclini, Nestor. "Memory and Innovation in the Theory of Art." *South Atlantic
Quarterly* 92.3 (1993): 423–43.

———. *Las culturas populares en el capitalismo*. Mexico City: Nueva Imagen, 1982.

García-Rivera, Alex. *St. Martin de Porres: The "Little Stories" and the "Semiotics of Culture."* Maryknoll, N.Y.: Orbis Books, 1995.

Garduño-Pulido, Blanca, Carolina Sada, and María Eugenia López Saldaña, eds. *Milagros en la frontera: Los Mojados de la Virgen de San Juan dan gracias por su favor*. México, D.F.: Consejo Nacional para la Cultura y las Artes y el Instituto Nacional de Bellas Artes, 1990.

Garza Quiros, Fernando. *El niño Fidencio: Un personaje desconocido*. Monterrey, México: Editorial Alfonso Reyes, 1970.

Gates Jr., Henry Louis. *Loose Canons: Notes on the Culture Wars*. New York: Oxford, 1992.

Gavin, Robin Farwell. *The Traditional Art of Spanish New Mexico*. Santa Fe: Museum of New Mexico Press, 1994.

Giffords, Gloria K. *Mexican Folk Retablos: Masterpieces on Tin*. Tucson: University of Arizona Press, 1974.

Gleijeses, Piero. *The Dominican Crisis: The 1965 Constitutionalist Revolt and American Intervention*. Trans. Lawrence Lipson. Baltimore, Md.: Johns Hopkins University Press, 1978.

González, Jorge A. *Cultura(s)*. Colima, México: Universidad de Colima, 1986.

González, Ray. "A Chicano *Verano*." *The Nation*, 7 June 1993: 772–74.

González Echevarría, Roberto. "Sisters in Death." *New York Times Book Review*, 18 Dec. 1994: 28.

González-Wippler, Migene. *Santería, the Religion: A Legacy of Faith, Rites, and Magic*. New York: Harmony Books, 1989.

Gramsci, Antonio. *Selections from the Prison Notebooks*. Ed. and trans. Quintin Hoare and Geoffrey Nowell Smith. New York: International Publishers, 1971.

Greimas, A.-J. "Reflections on Actantial Models." In *Narratology: An Introduction*. Ed. Susan Onega and José Angel García Landa. New York: Longman Publishing, 1996. 76–89.

Greimas, A.-J., and J. Courtés. *Semiotics and Language: An Analytical Dictionary*. Trans. Larry Crist et al. Bloomington: Indiana University Press, 1982.

Gutiérrez, Gustavo. *Gustavo Gutiérrez: Essential Writings*. Ed. James B. Nickoloff. Maryknoll, N.Y.: Orbis Books, 1996.

———. *A Theology of Liberation: History, Politics, and Salvation*. Ed. and trans. Sister Caridad Inda and John Eagleson. 1973, 1988. Maryknoll, N.Y.: Orbis Books, 1994.

Gutiérrez-Jones, Carl. "When the World Dissolves: The Magical in Morales' *The Brick People*." Paper presented at the Modern Language Association Convention, San Francisco, Dec. 1991.

Hall, Stuart. "Encoding/Decoding." In *Culture, Media, Language: Working Papers in Cultural Studies, 1972–79*. Ed. Stuart Hall, Dorothy Hobson, Andrew Lowe, and Paul Willis. London: Hutchinson, 1980. 128–38.

———. "The Rediscovery of 'Ideology': Return of the Repressed in Media Studies."

In *Culture, Society, and the Media*. Ed. Michael Gurevitch, Tony Bennett, James Curran, and Janet Woollacott. London: Routledge, 1982. 56–90.

Hayslett, Francesca. "Latina Writers." *Elle* (Aug. 1991): 106–8.

Hebdige, Dick. *Hiding in the Light: Of Images and Things*. London: Routledge, 1988.

Herrera-Sobek, María. Introduction to *Chicana Creativity and Criticism*. Ed. Herrera-Sobek and Viramontes. 9–39.

———. "The Politics of Rape: Sexual Transgression in Chicana Fiction." In *Chicana Creativity and Criticism*. Ed. Herrera-Sobek and Viramontes. 171–81.

Herrera-Sobek, María, and Helena María Viramontes, eds. *Chicana Creativity and Criticism: Charting New Frontiers in American Literature*. Houston, Tex.: Arte Público, 1988.

———. *Chicana (W)Rites on Word and Film*. Berkeley, Calif.: Third Woman Press, 1995.

Horno-Delgado, Asunción, Eliana Ortega, Nina M. Scott, and Nancy Saporta Sternbach, eds. *Breaking Boundaries: Latina Writings and Critical Readings*. Amherst: University of Massachusetts Press, 1989.

Howard, Richard A. "One Year Later." *America*, 24 Nov. 1990: 401–2.

Hudson, Wilson M., ed. *The Healer of Los Olmos and Other Mexican Lore*. 1951. Dallas, Tex.: Southern Methodist University Press, 1966.

Hutcheon, Linda. *The Politics of Postmodernism*. New York: Routledge, 1989.

Iwata, Edward. "Hot Properties: More Asian Americans Suddenly Are Winning Mainstream Literary Acclaim." *Los Angeles Times*, 11 Sept. 1989, sec. 5: 1+.

Jaramillo, Cleofas. *Shadows of the Past*. Santa Fe, N.Mex.: Ancient City Press, 1972.

Juffer, Jane. "An Ominous Indictment." *Columbia Journalism Review* 27.1 (May–June 1988): 4+.

Kakutani, Michiko. "The Dreams and Yearnings of a Family of Exiles." Review of *Dreaming in Cuban* by Cristina Garcia. *New York Times*, 25 Feb. 1992: C-17.

Kaveney, Roz. "Revolution in the Family." Review of *Dreaming in Cuban* by Cristina Garcia. *Times Literary Supplement*, 25 Dec. 1992: 19.

Kay, Elizabeth. *Chimayó Valley Traditions*. Santa Fe, N.Mex.: Ancient City Press, 1987.

Kingsolver, Barbara. "Desert Heat." Review of *So Far From God*, by Ana Castillo. *Los Angeles Times Book Review*, 16 May 1993: 1+.

Laclau, Ernesto. "Metaphor and Social Antagonisms." In *Marxism and the Interpretation of Culture*. Ed. Cary Nelson and Lawrence Grossberg. Urbana: University of Illinois, 1988. 249–57.

———. "Populist Rupture and Discourse." *Screen Education* 34 (1981): 87–93.

LaDuke, Betty. "Yolanda Lopez: Breaking Chicana Stereotypes." *Feminist Studies* 20.1 (1994): 117–30.

Lazaroff, Leon. "Greasy Kid Stuff." *Mexico Journal*, 7 Aug. 1989: 27–28.

Leal, Luis. "Sandra Cisneros: From Mango Street to Tepeyac." In *No Longer Voiceless*. San Diego: Marín Publications, 1995. 127–34.

Lomelí, Francisco. "Isabella Ríos and the Chicano Psychic Novel." In *Minority Voices: An Interdisciplinary Journal of Literature and the Arts* 4.1 (1980): 49–61.

Madrigal, Alix. "Crossed Allegiances of a Cuban American." In "Review," *San Francisco Chronicle*, 11 Apr. 1993: 4.

Maduro, Otto. "U.S. Latinos and Religion: An Interview with Otto Maduro." Interview by James Torrens. *America*, 14 Aug. 1993: 16+.

Marin, Louis. "The Autobiographical Interruption: About Stendhal's *Life of Henry Brulard*." *MLN* 93.4 (1978): 597–617.

Martín-Barbero, Jesús. "Repossessing Culture: The Quest of Popular Movements in Latin America." *Media Development* 2 (1989): 21–24.

Márquez, Roberto. "Island Heritage." Review of *The Line of the Sun*, by Judith Ortiz Cofer. *New York Times Book Review*, 24 Sept. 1989: 46.

McCracken, Ellen. "Community-Oriented Introspection and the Demystification of Patriarchal Violence." In *Breaking Boundaries*. Ed. Horno-Delgado et al. Amherst: University of Massachusetts Press, 1989. 62–71.

———. "Latina Narrative and the Politics of Signification: Articulation, Antagonism, and Populist Rupture." *Crítica* 2.2 (1990): 202–7.

———. "Toward a Comparative Text Grammar of Visual and Verbal Semiosis: Material Religious Culture and Chicana Fiction." In *Semiotics Around the World: Synthesis in Diversity*. Ed. Irmengard Rauch and Gerald F. Carr. New York: Mouton de Gruyter, 1997. 717–20.

McLemore, David. "A Meeting Place with God." *San Jose Mercury News*, 20 Apr. 1996: E-1+.

McRobbie, Angela. "Settling Accounts with Subcultures." *Screen Education* 34 (1980): 37–49.

Mena, Jennifer. "Women on the Verge . . . Four Brash Latina Writers Transform the Literary Landscape." *Hispanic* (Nov. 1995), www.hisp.com/women.html.

Miller, Susan. "Caught Between Two Cultures." *Newsweek*, 20 Apr. 1992: 78–79.

Mills, George. *The People of the Saints*. Colorado Springs: Taylor Museum, 1967.

Mitchell, W. J. T. *Picture Theory: Essays on Verbal and Visual Representation*. Chicago: University of Chicago Press, 1994.

Morales, Alejandro. "A Chicana Stereotypes Her Own People." Review of *The Wedding* by Mary Helen Ponce. *Los Angeles Times Book Review*, 19 Nov. 1989: 10.

Mouffe, Chantal. "Hegemony and New Political Subjects: Toward a New Concept of Democracy." In *Marxism and the Interpretation of Culture*. Ed. Cary Nelson and Lawrence Grossberg. Urbana: University of Illinois, 1988. 89–104.

Mullen, Harryette. "Into the Briar Patch: Afro-American Fiction in the Next Decade." Paper presented at the Center for Literary and Cultural Studies, Harvard University, 1990.

———. " 'A Silence Between Us Like a Language': The Untranslatability of Experience in Sandra Cisneros's *Woman Hollering Creek*." *MELUS* 21.2 (1996): 3–20.

Oktavec, Eileen. *Answered Prayers: Miracles and Milagros along the Border*. Tucson: University of Arizona Press, 1995.

Ostling, Richard N. "Shedding Blood in Sacred Bowls." *Time*, 19 Oct. 1992: 60.

Palmié, Stephan. "Afro-Cuban Religion in Exile: Santería in South Florida." *Journal of Caribbean Studies* 5.3 (1986): 171–79.

Pfaff, Carol W., and Laura Chávez. "Spanish/English Code-Switching: Literary Reflections of Natural Discourse." In *Missions in Conflict: Essays on U.S.-Mexican Relations and Chicano Culture*. Ed. Renate von Bardeleben, Dietrich Briesemeister, and Juan Bruce-Novoa. Tubingen: Gunter Narr Verlag Tubingen, 1986. 229–54.

Porter, Dennis. *The Pursuit of Crime: Art and Ideology in Detective Fiction*. New Haven, Conn.: Yale University Press, 1981.

Prescott, Peter S. "Seven for Summer." Review of *Woman Hollering Crrek and Other Stories* by Sandra Cisneros. *Newsweek*, 3 June 1991: 60+.

Pulido, Rachel. "Sandra Cisneros." *Mirabella*, Apr. 1991: 46.

Quintana, Alvina E. "Chicana Discourse: Negations and Mediations." Ph.D. diss. University of California, Santa Cruz, 1989.

———. *Home Girls: Chicana Literary Voices*. Philadelphia: Temple University Press, 1996.

Rebolledo, Tey Diana. *Women Singing in the Snow: A Cultural Analysis of Chicana Literature*. Tucson: University of Arizona Press, 1995.

Richard, Nelly. "Cultural Peripheries: Latin America and Postmodernist De-centering." *Boundary* 2 20.3 (1993): 156–61.

Rivero, Eliana. "From Immigrants to Ethnics: Cuban Women Writers in the U.S." In *Breaking Boundaries*. Ed. Horno-Delgado et al. 189–200.

Romano, Octavio. "Don Pedrito Jaramillo: The Emergence of a Mexican-American Folk Saint." Ph.D. diss. University of California, Berkeley, 1964.

Romero, Archbishop Oscar. *Voice of the Voiceless: The Four Pastoral Letters and Other Statements*. Trans. Michael J. Walsh. Maryknoll, N.Y.: Orbis Books, 1985.

Said, Edward. *Orientalism*. 1978. New York: Vintage, 1979.

Saldívar, Ramón. *Chicano Narrative: The Dialectics of Difference*. Madison: University of Wisconsin Press, 1990.

Saldívar-Hull, Sonia. "Feminism on the Border: From Gender Politics to Geopolitics." Ph.D. diss. University of Texas at Austin, 1990.

———. "Feminism on the Border: From Gender Politics to Geopolitics." In *Criticism in the Borderlands: Studies in Chicano Literature, Culture, and Ideology*. Ed. Héctor Calderón and José David Saldívar. Durham, N.C.: Duke University Press, 1991. 203–20.

Sánchez Lara, Rosa María. *Los retablos populares: Exvotos pintados*. Mexico City: UNAM, Instituto de Investigaciones Estéticas, 1990.

Stallybrass, Peter, and Allon White. *The Politics and Poetics of Transgression*. Ithaca, N.Y.: Cornell University Press, 1986.

Steele, Thomas J. *Santos and Saints: Essays and Handbook*. Albuquerque, N.Mex.: Calvin Horn, 1974.

Todorov, Tzvetan. *Mikhail Bakhtin: The Dialogical Principle*. Trans. Wlad Godzich. Minneapolis: University of Minnesota Press, 1984.

Torrens, James S. "U.C.A.—The Witnesses Talk." *America*, 24 Nov. 1990: 394–400.

Trujillo, Carla, ed. *Chicana Lesbians: The Girls Our Mothers Warned Us About*. Berkeley, Calif.: Third Woman Press, 1991.

Turner, Faythe, ed. *Puerto Rican Writers at Home in the USA*. Seattle, Wash.: Open Hand Publishing Company, 1991.

Turner, Kay F. " 'Because of This Photography': The Making of a Mexican Folk Saint." In *Niño Fidencio: A Heart Thrown Open*. Ed. Dore Gardner and Kay F. Turner. Santa Fe: Museum of New Mexico Press, 1992. 120–34.

———. "The Cultural Semiotics of Religious Icons: La Virgen de San Juan de los Lagos." *Semiotica* 47 (1983): 317–61.

———. "Mexican American Home Altars: Towards Their Interpretation." *Aztlán* 13.1–2 (1982): 309–17.

———. "Mexican American Women's Home Altars: The Art of Relationship." Ph.D. diss. University of Texas at Austin, 1990.

Vásquez, Mary S. Review of *The Wedding*, by Mary Helen Ponce. *Hispania* 73 (1990): 1005–7.

Voloshinov, V. N. *Marxism and the Philosophy of Language*. Trans. Ladislav Matejka and I. R. Titunik. Cambridge, Mass.: Harvard University Press, 1986.

Weiss, Amelia. "Fantasy Island." Review of *Dreaming in Cuban*, by Cristina Garcia. *Time*, 23 Mar. 1992: 67.

Wiarda, Howard. *The Dominican Republic: Nation in Transition*. New York: Praeger, 1969.

Williams, Raymond. *Marxism and Literature*. New York: Oxford University Press, 1977.

Zimmerman, Marc. *U.S. Latino Literature: An Essay and Annotated Bibliography*. Chicago: MARCH/Abrazo Press, 1992.

Numbers in italics refer to the illustrations

extrasensory experience, 90–91
ex-votos, 19–21, 96, 129, 132, 135; in San Fernando Cathedral, 21, *131*

feminism: in Chávez, 169; in Cisneros, 17, 20, 133, 135, 137, 140, 147, 172, 180; in Garcia, 26; in *Getting Home Alive,* 68, 192; in Limón, 44; politics of, 24; as rupture, 39; and subculture theory, 152; varieties of, 16–17, 66; and the Virgin of Guadalupe, 103, 139–42, 172–73
Fernández, Mickey, "Grace," 46–48
Fernández, Roberta, *Intaglio,* 56–58, 71, 94–95, 97–101, 216n. 5
food, 25, 49, 69, 92
Francis of Assisi, Saint, 97, 112
Franco, Jean, 64

Garcia, Cristina, 84, 107, 116–17, 156, 199, 200, 207n. 13; *Dreaming in Cuban,* 11, 22–26, 74, 111–17, 156–57, 168
García Canclini, Nestor, 13, 144, 213n. 20
Gates, Henry Louis, Jr., 12, 64, 209n. 10
gender, 4, 8, 117, 178, 184, 189, 192, 196; "trouble," 6, 39, 193–94
Gómez-Vega, Ibis, 5
González, Nivea, painting by, 17, *18*
Gramsci, Antonio, 41, 154
Greimas, A.J. (actants), 181, 196
grotesque, the, 121

Haiti, 81, 109–10
Hall, Stuart, 41–42, 64, 205n. 5
Hebdige, Dick, 137, 153, 158, 161
hegemonic bloc, 41, 47, 154
Herrera-Sobek, María, 204n. 10, 209n. 2, 216n. 4
heterology, 14, 39
"hiding in the light," 137, 153, 161, 171–72

history: of Central America, 62; of the Dominican Republic, 30, 74, 80–86, 210n. 9; role of, 9, 73–93; of U.S. Latinos, 4
Holy Week, 38, 122
homosexuality, 117, 137, 171–72, 197
Hutcheon, Linda, 15–16, 24, 74, 75
hybridity (hyridization), 29, 101, 102–3, 127, 128–49, 151, 170, 213n. 20; definition of, 207n. 19

identity: in Alvarez, 28, 108, 192; in *Cantora,* 70–71; in Cisneros, 19, 196; construction of, 179; ethnic, 31, 182; fluidity of, 5, 28; in *Getting Home Alive,* 68–69; and individualism, 9, 65–80, 93; of Latinos/Latinas, 65, 84; negative formation of, 191; politics, 216n. 1; and subculture, 151
ideological state apparatuses, 76
ideology, 13, 41, 155, 189; as "common sense," 154
immigrants, 3; Central American, 62, 63, 213n. 21; Cuban, 23–26; Dominican, 158, 192–93; Haitian, 81, 109–10; Latina, 28; Mexican, 92, 182; Puerto Rican, 67, 68, 79; Salvadoran, 105
individualism, 65–66, 72, 77, 152–53, 178; disruption of, 66, 67–73, 153–54
interpellation, 181, 187
intertexts, 19, 29; visual, 20, 130, 137, 139, 149

jamaicas, 6, 124
Jaramillo, Don Pedrito, 142, 145
jíbaros, 187, 188, 216n. 3
Jude, Saint, 20
justice, social. *See* social justice

Laclau, Ernesto, 5, 13, 14, 42, 52–53, 55–56, 62, 153
La Conquistadora, 134, 213n. 17
La Llorona, 17, 195

Novas, Himilce, *Mangos, Bananas, and Coconuts,* 196–97

novena, the, 96, 122, 127–28, 169, 213n. 17

Novoa, Juan Bruce, 117, 209n. 9

Nuestra Señora: de la Candelaria, 109, 212n. 7; de la Caridad del Cobre, 112, 114, 212n. 9; de los Dolores, 132

ofrendas, 96–101

oral tradition, 3

Orientalism, 5–6

Ortiz Cofer, Judith, 107; *The Line of the Sun,* 75–76, 91, 117–120; *Silent Dancing,* 74, 75, 91, 93, 118–19

Other, the: definition of, 50–51; as exotic, 5, 13, 14, 27, 108, 193; identity politics and, 6, 19, 179,; popular religiosity and, 101; repositioning of, 9, 50–55, 63, 64, 94; surveillance by or of, 79, 154; and transgression, 80, 122, 196; U.S. Latinos as, 35, 36

Our Lady of Salud, 118, 119

overdetermination, 78, 180, 186

pachuco/a, the, 9, 152, 160–69, 174, 215n. 6

parody, 25, 38, 136–37, 161, 162, 164, 166–69, 196–97

patriarchy: and authority, 46–47, 70; and the Catholic Church, 169, 173, 178; and colonialism, 187–89, 198; and control of sexuality, 83; escape from, 17; and the Latino Renaissance, 152, 179; and power, 31, 38, 185; and privilege, 22, 193; transgression against, 153–58, 159–60; and violence, 26, 37, 44–45, 180, 181, 195

penance, 103, 124

perruque, la, 41, 55

pilgrimage, 99, 144, 170, 175; figurative, 101

political unconscious (textual repression), 28, 37, 117

politics of signification, 9, 41–64, 157, 170, 173

polyphony, 19, 206nn. 10, 23

polysemy, 17, 24, 205–6n. 5

Ponce, Mary Helen, 149, 215n. 6; *Hoyt Street,* 74, 91–93, 121–27; *The Wedding,* 121, 160–69

Poniatowska, Elena, 25, 205n. 2

popular religiosity, 3, 19–22, 38, 41, 45, 67, 72–73, 95–149, 183

postmodern ethnic commodity, the, 4, 6, 8, 10–39, 149, 201, 205n. 4; definition of, 12; and Sandra Cisneros, 17, 21; *Dreaming in Cuban* as, 24, 26; *So Far from God* as, 32

postmodern ethnicity, feminine space of, 8

postmodernism, 15–16, 17, 19, 22

poverty, symbols of, 19

pregnancy, 167, 176; abortion, 176–78; miscarriage, 49, 168–69, 176–77

priests, 58–60, 87–88, 124, 188–89; massacre of Jesuits in El Salvador, 59–60, 209n. 7; women's role as, 98–101

processions (religious): Good Friday, 145; May, 121, 124–25

prolepsis, 71–73

promesa (manda), 106, 109, 118, 122, 124, 129, 147–48

protofeminism, 125, 159–60, 193

publishers: mainstream, 5, 7, 8, 11–15, 21–22, 34, 200, 203n. 3, 206n. 8, 208n. 23; regional and small, 8, 12, 204n. 11, 216n. 5

Puerto Rico (Puerto Ricans), 3, 79, 117–20, 176

Quintana, Alvina, 170

race, 79, 118, 179, 186; and self-hatred, 90–91, 187
racism, 90–91, 181
rape, 25, 36, 70, 181, 188–89, 191–92, 194
readers, 14, 15, 81, 86, 129, 178. *See also* audiences
Recuerdo de Tepeyac (Mexican backdrop), 101–2, *102*
reification, 12, 15, 78, 108, 180–81, 191, 193
religion, 9, 85–86, 92, 95–149; official, 95–96, 98, 101, 105, 106, 117, 119, 120, 124, 127, 128, 129, 137, 149
religious culture, material, 97–103, 105–49
repressive state apparatus, 180–81
retablos, 97, 99, 120, *132, 133,* 143, 145, 146–47, 214n. 28
Richard, Nelly, 13
rites of passage, 84–85, 167, 180, 183
ritual, 3, 15, 99–101, 157, 214n. 1
Rivera, Tomás, . . . *Y no se lo tragó la tierra,* 4, 71
romance, 36, 76–78; politics of, 25, 78–80, 194–95
Romano, Octavio, 142
rupture, 22, 24, 39, 152–53, 192, 195

Said, Edward, 6
Saldívar, Ramón, 65
Saldívar-Hull, Sonia, 206n. 9
San Antonio de Padua, 118–19, 133–34, *136, 172*
Sanctuary movement, 63, 105
San Fernando Cathedral (San Antonio, Tex.), 21, 129–31, 145, 146, 147, 213nn. 18, 21
San Lázaro, 19
San Martín de Porres, 147, *148,* 213n. 19
San Sebastián, 115, 147–48
Santa Bárbara, 112, *113,* 114, 119

Santa Librada (Librata), 137, *139,* 143
Santería, 26, 107, 108–38
Santo Niño de Atocha, El, 97, *96,* 105, 123, 126, 129, 131–32, 145
santos (bultos), 105, 106, 108, 109, 110, 130–31, 134, *134,* 213n. 25
self-referentiality, 23, 62, 78, 139, 174
Seven African Powers, *111,* 111–12, 137, 143
sexual assault, 24, 36
signifiers: arbitrary nature of 157; contradictory, 63–64; in domestic space, 47; empty, 184; inaccuracy of, 108; indexical, 63; floating, 169; metonymic, 67, 145–46, 181; misreading of, 72; polysemous, 72, 73, 191–92; rearticulation of, 42, 64; religious, 73, 106, 110, 128, 170; resignification of, 185; vestimentary, 46, 47, 63, 116, 162; visual, 124
simulacrum, 73, 75, 76–77, 78, 88–91
skeleton musicians, 98, *99*
skull, sugar, 97, *98*
social antagonism, discourse of, 13–14, 22, 39, 192
social change, 3–4, 8, 41–42, 151–52
social justice, 95, 105–7, 147, 149, 180, 182
Soto, Pedro Juan, *Spiks,* 4, 203n. 2
spiritism, 117–20, 212n. 12
Steele, Thomas J., 212n. 7, 213nn. 19, 25, 214n. 26
subculture, 9, 46, 55, 158–78, 193; definition of, 151; feminist critique of 152, 158, 161
surveyor, 79; male, 124–25
syncretism, 9, 107, 108, 109, 111, 138–39, 143, 211n. 6

Teresa, Saint, 125
testimonio (testimony), 19–20, 23, 59, 61, 66, 69, 70, 84, 87, 89, 104

Toribio, Almeida Jacqueline, 204n. 8

transgression, 9, 30, 31, 121–22, 151–78; feminist, 20; linguistic, 124, 129, 133–34; political, 31; sexual, 9–10, 32, 46, 117–18, 137; subcultural, 193

translations (Spanish-language), 7, 12, 205n. 2

tree-of-life candleholder, 97, 97

tropicalism, 27

tropicalized language, 34, 68–69

"trouble," 6, 28–32, 39, 193–94

Trujillo, Rafael, 30, 31, 80–86, 93, 109, 207n. 21

Turner, Kay F., 123, 128, 143

unfinalizability, 22, 23, 24, 169

Vatican Council II, 106, 124, 126, 127

Villanueva, Alma Luz, 152; *The Ultraviolet Sky*, 66, 153, 154

Viramontes, Helena María, 49–50, 51–52, 58, 59, 104; "Birthday," 177; The Cariboo Cafe," 51–52, 58; "The Jumping Bean," 184–86; "The Long Reconciliation," 177–78; *The Moths and Other Stories*, 184; *Under the Feet of Jesus*, 180, 182–84

Virgen de la Caridad del Cobre. *See* Nuestra Señora de la Caridad del Cobre

Virgen de San Juan de los Lagos, La, 98, 100, 124, 135–37

Virgin of Guadalupe, 123, 140; in Cisneros, 101–3, 129, 139–42, 147 176; devotion to, 19–21, 97, 99, 105, 123; and El Niño Fidencio, 143, 144; and feminism, 103, 139–42, 172–73; and penitence, 44, 45; political reappropriation of, 170, 215n. 8; reconfiguration of, 96

vision, 9, 121–27, 128, 149

visual imagery, 85, 129, 161

voice, 9, 19, 28–29, 32–34, 43, 45, 70, 121, 127–28, 146–48

Voloshinov, V.N., 41, 64; theory of "reported speech," 163–64, 166

voodoo, 27, 109–10

Yoruban religious traditions, 108–9, 111–17, 119–20

Zentella, Ana Celia, 6

ABOUT THE AUTHOR

Ellen McCracken received a Ph.D. in Comparative Literature from the University of California, San Diego, and from 1977 to 1992 was a professor in the Department of Comparative Literature at the University of Massachusetts, Amherst. Since fall 1992 she has been a professor in the Department of Spanish and Portuguese at the University of California, Santa Barbara, and was the director of the Program in Latin American and Iberian Studies from 1993 to 1995. She is the author of *Decoding Women's Magazines: From* Mademoiselle *to* Ms. (London: Macmillan and New York: St. Martin's, 1993) and has published scholarly articles on contemporary Latin American literature, literature and the mass media, U.S. Latina literature, mass culture, cultural studies, and the semiotics of popular religiosity.

McCracken is currently writing a book on the life and work of Fray Angélico Chávez, one of the major figures of twentieth-century New Mexico letters; editing a volume of scholarly articles on Chávez's cultural production to be published by the University of New Mexico Press; and completing a study of U.S. Latino material religious culture.